ADVERTISING
Career Directory

4th Edition

ADVERTISING
Career Directory

The Career Directory Series

Edited by Ronald W. Fry

The Career Press
62 Beverly Rd.
PO Box 34
Hawthorne, NJ 07507
1-800-CAREER-1
FAX: 201-427-2037

"The Different Perceptions Of Employers And Students" by Ralph M. Gaedeke and Dennis H. Tootelian, California State University, Sacramento, appeared in *Marketing News,* copyright 1989 by the American Marketing Association and is reprinted with their permission.

The Career Directory Series

Advertising Career Directory, Fourth Edition

Paperback ISBN 0-934829-59-4, $19.95

Copies of this Directory may be ordered by mail or phone directly from the publisher. To order by mail, please include price as noted above, $2.50 handling per order, plus $1.00 for each book ordered. (New Jersey residents please add 6% sales tax.) Send to:

The Career Press Inc.
62 Beverly Rd., PO Box 34,
Hawthorne, NJ 07507

Or call Toll-Free 1-800-CAREER-1 to order using your VISA or Mastercard or for further information on all books published or distributed by The Career Press.

Table of Contents

ADVERTISING
Career Directory

Section One: Agency Areas Of Specialization

Section Two: Other Areas Of Opportunity

Section Three: The Advertising Scene Outside New York

Section Four: The Job Search Process

Section Five: Job Opportunities Databanks

Section Six: Appendices & Index

Foreword

Getting The Most Out
Of Your Directory

Thank you for purchasing this volume. We have worked long and hard to produce a book that is both as credible and up-to-date as possible. I'm sure you will let us know if we have succeeded!

This *Advertising Career Directory,* now in its fourth edition, was specifically created to help *you* break out of the pack hunting for a job in any area of the agency business. It won't just tell you how to get a first job at an agency—this *Directory* is a compendium of *all* the resources you'll need to make the *series* of decisions necessary to get that first job...or to give you a better understanding of the business so you can move on from your first job.

And it's written by the *pros*—the top people in advertising today—articles and advice written specifically for this volume and directed specifically to *you.* (For those of you interested in working in advertising, marketing or sales, but on the *corporate* side, the third edition of our *Marketing & Sales Directory* is now available. For those of you leaning more to public relations—what many call "free advertising"—the fourth edition of our *Public Relations Career Directory* has also just been published.

Anyway, to return to those of you interested in working for an ad agency. We've attempted to organize this *Directory* in such a way that reading it is a logical, step-by-step, educational progression.

The articles in the first part of this volume offer an overview of the industry, as well as a look at some specialized areas of advertising, a geogrpahical tour of agencies in major cities nationwide, and detailed discussions of the major areas of job specialization.

After studying these chapters, you should be well on your way to deciding exactly *what* you want to do—the following chapters will help you figure out *how* to go about getting your first chance to *do* it, including a detailed Job Search Process that will take you through evaluating yourself and potential employers, preparing resumes and cover letters, the interview process, and, finally, sifting the job offers.

Our exclusive *Job Opportunities Databank* then lists hundreds of agencies throughout the United States and, for the first time, Canada, including information on training programs, key contacts, even actual and expected entry-level job openings. This information is exclusive to this *Directory*, gathered through our own surveys of these agencies.

Finally, two appendices—(A) advertising trade organizations and (B) trade publications. More important information to make sure you get exactly the right first job in advertising.

When we began this project in 1985, students we queried indicated an intense need for a *guide to resources*—articles and advice on every aspect of the agency business by the pros out there doing the work, listings of major agencies (with then-unavailable information like who to talk to, potential openings, educational requirements, specific titles, etc.), the trade organizations to contact, the trade magazines to read, etc.

The overwhelmingly positive reaction to the first three editions of this volume proved that we had achieved our initial goal: To produce the most comprehensive, all-inclusive guide to the advertising industry for entry-level people ever published.

We feel confident that with this fourth edition we have succeeded in the more difficult goal we set for ourselves this time: to make the best book on getting into advertising even better.

Most of all, we hope it helps *you* get exactly the job you want in this exciting business.

Good luck!

1

Quo Vadis, World?

Norman Vale, Director-General
International Advertising Association

Quo vadis, indeed. Where in the world the world is going is a question the international business community has always concerned itself with, but never more so than right now. Global dynamics are shifting dramatically as walls tumble, borders open, dictators "retire." Combine those truly incredible and unexpected events with the impending unification of the European Common Market and the increasing impact of the Pacific Rim countries, and you have a business climate that is fascinating, to say the least.

The dramatic changes in international commerce will have direct and substantial effects on international advertising. Here's a brief look at how international advertising evolved, where it's headed, and what you can do to prepare yourself for participation in what promises to be an exciting, challenging, and rewarding field.

The Marketplace Takes Shape

To better understand what's ahead, a look at how business responded to political and economic changes in the past is helpful.

1950s: Post War Recovery

As the world got back on its feet following World War II, European and Asian countries had to start virtually from scratch to rebuild their infrastructure destroyed by the war and, consequently, lived through a long period of deprivation. In the United States, rather than rebuild what *had been*, we were fortunate enough to be able to build upon what we still *had*. Our post-war boom fueled the U.S. economy and made the U.S. an important consumer market.

1960s: U.S. International Expansion

With such a head start, U.S. companies found openings in which to establish new markets and profit opportunities in the free world. At about the same time, the "brand revolution" began, as corporations began to extend their marketing opportunities by placing importance on individual brand-name products over corporate names. This was the beginning of U.S.-based companies' successful foray into the international arena.

1970s: Focus Shifts to Foreign Companies

The free world became more common, commercial brain power was no longer a U.S. monopoly, businesses matured, and, for the most part, technology began a decade of egalitarianism. Large foreign-based corporations looked outside their countries and saw niche opportunities, wholesale benefits, and openings where competition yielded profitable investments. The non-U.S. marketers began their international move, and their advertising agencies began to follow.

1980s: Enter Globalization

Contrary to what scientists were saying about the universe expanding, the world got smaller. Thanks in part to the accessibility of worldwide media, international borders in the free world became insignificant, as major corporations crossed from one country to another with products and services that met the world's increasingly homogeneous needs and wants. "Global" replaced international, transnational or multinational as the word to describe how corporations should approach their worldwide business.

1990s: Centers of Economic Clout

There are three critical centers of influence that will take us through the next decade:

- *North America,* as a result of the 1989 trade agreement between the U.S. and Canada;
- The *European Community*'s 12 member countries that form the Common Market and, as of January 1, 1993, will become the largest consumer market in the world;
- *Japan and Korea,* through a combination of industrial output and strong financial reserves to support increased products and services and overseas developments.

Developments In Advertising

Let's look at developments that took place in the advertising business during these same decades:

1950s: Export Advertising

U.S. companies created advertising in this country and sent it abroad without too much consideration of its final destination. The international or global mindset was not fully evolved, and neither were most companies international capabilities.

1960s: International Overtures

Marketers began to perceive commonalities in overseas markets that created possibilities for international advertising—which, at that time, meant buying space in papers or magazines that reached consumers in two or more countries.

1970s: Multinational Takes Off

U.S. and foreign-based companies were operating in so many markets around the world that the techniques of common strategy and execution became more cost efficient and, therefore, more attractive. Multinational advertising—advertising in 4-5 countries or more—hit its stride in this decade.

1980s: The Era of Globalization

Megatrends author John Naisbitt and Harvard Business School Professor Ted Levitt began the decade championing the concept that the successful corporation could do and sell the same things in the same way everywhere it operated. The advent of satellites allowed advertisers to think about reaching consumers all over the world at the same time with the same message. In 1985, "Live Aid," for example, simultaneously reached an estimated 1.5 billion people in more than 100 countries. Events such as World Cup Soccer regularly achieve almost the same global reach.

The Growth Of Advertising

The following chart illustrates the scope and growth of advertising volumes in the United States and the balance of the free world. It also graphically demonstrates why global opportunities may be in your future:

Worldwide Advertising Trends

(in billions of U. S. dollars)

(Year)	1960	1970	1980	1990	2000
Worldwide Ad Expenditures	18	36	110	313	780
Non-U. S. Ad Expenditures	6	16	55	163	460
U. S. Ad Expenditures	12	20	55	150	320

As you can see, in the '60s and '70s, advertising outside the United States was developing its own momentum, but still did not come close to the level of advertising dollars invested in the U.S. During the '80s, all media expenditures approached the fifty-fifty mark.

What Will The '90s Bring?

For the '90s, we can expect international advertising expenditures to surpass U.S. volume. Reasons for this include:

- *New media* available, following full satellite deployment.

- *New markets,* such as China and its one billion people.

- *Increased confidence* in doing business away from home countries, achieved through four decades of experience.

- *Rapid technological improvements,* including continuing growth of computer interfacing, electronic mail (which will make it easier to do what we do), and high-definition TV (which will make what we do more attractive to consumers).

- *Strengthened gross national products* in so many countries.

- The *elimination of trade barriers* within the European community, come January 1, 1993.

- A *competition-driven increase in production* from Western Europe and the Pacific Rim, as those countries continue to generate products and services that will be supported by advertising and promotion funds.

- The *recent events in Eastern Europe.* All of us who have dedicated our lives to international business applaud the changes as we attempt to understand how they will affect our economic, political, commercial, and financial strategies. Following the initial chaos, we should expect order and opportunity to arise, creating a far better commercial climate for people considering an international future.

Preliminary forecasts indicate that worldwide expenditures will be nearing one *trillion* dollars by the year 2000. And of that, close to 60 percent will be invested outside the U.S.

So should you consider an international career in advertising? Quo vadis...world!

Creating *Your* International Career

It's clear that the opportunities for well-trained advertising professionals on both the agency and client sides will increase during the next ten years. There are several substantive reasons for choosing to "go international."

- Inevitably, the world will be one large market. The best-prepared people for management positions will have a combination of U.S. and international experience.

- The relatively small scale of operations for agencies outside the U.S. necessarily increases your exposure to all facets of the business. Working within a small management group provides an accelerated advancement track; the chance to be involved in the decision-making process comes more quickly in comparison to a parallel course in the U.S.

- The challenge of working and living in a foreign culture is professionally and personally enriching.

How To Get Ready

Should you decide to invest yourself in the global advertising arena, here are six important steps that you can take to prepare yourself for a career in a foreign country:

1. Acquire solid agency experience in either a large U.S. agency or its counterpart in another country, and plan to stay there for 3 to 5 years—less time may not sufficiently prepare you for that next international step.

2. Attempt to work your way into a multinational account, particularly if it's a feeder operation. Many positions are available within agencies where products and services are similarly introduced and available in foreign markets.

3. Make your management aware of your interest, be diligent in your pursuit, and find an appropriate mentor within your organization.

4. Be open-minded and flexible about the country assignment offered. There is a world beyond London and Paris; besides, the talent pool in both England and France is sufficiently large. You may find similar challenges and satisfaction along with greater opportunity for advancement in other countries.

5. Don't view a career in international advertising as a free ticket to travel. It's hard work, and any other perception will not be appreciated by prospective employers.

6. Above all, have patience, patience, and even more patience.

Witnessing world developments in the coming decade will be fascinating. The prospect of participating in them is even more so. Good luck to those of you who choose a career path that leads you to the international arena.

NORMAN VALE has spent 25 years in agency management, lived and worked in three countries, and was a senior officer for Grey International—a $3.2 billion global advertising and communication agency—for 16 years. Early this year, he was named the first director-general of the International Advertising Association.

Mr. Vale has been an occasional lecturer on international advertising and marketing at St. John's University, Wharton, NYU Graduate School of Business, World Trade Institute and at seminars and congresses in the U.S. and Europe. While those have been delivered principally in English, he also speaks Spanish, some Portuguese, and German. He was the chairman of the 4A's International Committee and is a World Board Director of the IAA.

2

Advertising From Both Sides Of The Brain

Ronald Scharbo, President and Chairman
Burton-Campbell, Inc.

As you venture into the agency business, let me issue a daring challenge: *How you think* may be just as important to the enjoyment and success of your first job as *what you know*.

It's an intriguing phenomenon that, as we get well into our advertising careers, most of us fall into one of two categories: the left-brain types or the right-brain types.

But which type are you?

Left-brainers are the disciplined, logical thinkers...the number crunchers. If you are a left brain type, you will likely shine in account service, research or media. Right-brainers—the creative visionaries—usually star as copywriters and art directors.

The amazing thing about the agency business is that these two very different types must somehow come together to produce one successful campaign.

If both sides *don't* come together, agencies are dominated by one or the other...and the resulting ads quickly show which side won out. Left-brain agencies turn out ads that are smart, but dull—strategy statements in print. It's advertising likely to go unnoticed.

On the other hand, right-brain agencies turn out ads that are arresting to look at, but don't seem to really say anything. You probably recall seeing what you thought was a great commercial...but been unable to remember what was advertised even a few hours later.

The Fears That Set The Two Sides At Odds

In other words, if either side is given complete control, it will probably produce advertising that neither side wants. Nevertheless, each type may well vie for complete control.

Left-Brainers Fear The Creative Thought Process

Left-brainers usually write the creative strategy and the creative work plans—the "blueprints" of advertising. As account people, they often have most of the votes on the creative review boards and can veto anything they don't understand. They also control the research that brings in the most powerful voting bloc of all—the consumer test groups, who can usually be counted on to vote against anything that's "too far out."

Why do many left-brainers try to seize so much control that they end up strangling the work? Because they're scared, and because the right-brainers—the creative people—let them.

Left-brainers are scared because they fear the creative thought process, one that is totally alien to their own "logical" pattern. They steer for the safe middle ground and avoid risks. After all, if a print ad or TV spot bombs, it's the left-brained account executive who has to take the heat from the irate client. So they adhere strictly to the numbers and avoid being different....and, in the process, avoid the freshness and excitement that's essential for superior advertising.

Right-Brainers Fear Their Creativity Will Be Stifled

Right-brainers, on the other hand, may shoot strictly for awards and not seemingly not care about results. They want something pretty for their portfolios. Something exciting and new. Unfortunately, it might not sell anything.

Why do they do this? Because they, too, are scared.

The right-brainers are afraid that their best ideas will be stifled by those unimaginative, left-brained bean-counters. So the right-brained copywriters and art directors vow to die before allowing the unsuspecting account executives to even *think* of changing a comma, let alone a word or picture.

Good Agencies Forge A Consensus

Though I've painted such a seemingly bleak picture, there *is* light at the end of the tunnel—in fact, the same light at the end of *both* tunnels. There don't *have* to be battles between the two sides...and in the good agencies, there aren't.

Let me strike a blow for future harmony and give you some tips on how to work with the "other side" by recognizing and managing an important process that takes place at any good agency.

For starters, every professional in every agency should agree that there's really only one common purpose: to create effective advertising. And that to *be* effective, advertising must stand out. Break through the clutter. Have impact.

Clients *like* impact. It's cost-efficient. It does the job with fewer magazine insertions or TV rating points. But to get impact you have to be different, and that involves risk. Risk demands going beyond reference sources, case studies and the hard data—into that no man's land where being wrong can be very expensive. Clients hate risk, especially if it may cost them a lot of money if they (and their agency) are wrong.

Here is where the left- and right-brainers oftentimes come into head-to-head conflict. But it's also the same point at which, working together, they can rise above the ordinary and arrive at the real goal: *advertising that works.*

Finding The Good Agencies

How do you find an agency where the left-brain and right-brain people are willing to work together to create the best possible campaigns? Here are ten characteristics to look for:

1. A Healthy Mix Of Good People And The Right Attitude

Bad account people can cancel out good creative people, and vice versa. The best agencies have account executives who possess the same excitement and passion for the product as the creative people. Try to find out how the AEs are involved in the creative product.

2. Management's Commitment To Always Doing Better Work

The agencies most likely to grow and prosper are those that get everyone asking, "Is this my best?" all the way down the line.

3. The Courage To Take Risks...

...and the ability to go easy if one fails. We all know that if you fear the consequence of failure, you won't try. Certainly in an agency, if your ideas are always met with, "You must be crazy. The client will never buy that!" you will stop trying and shoot for the easy sell. So look for management's permission to take risks.

4. A Planning Process Open To Both Sides...

...and open to overhaul when necessary. An agency's research and planning process should tell both the account people and the creative side about the product, its best buying prospects, what's important to them, and how the competition is communicating to those same potential buyers. Then it should stop.

The best research tells you only *what* to say, not *how* to say it. Its goal should be to isolate the one most important message—not to generate a laundry list of 27 product benefits you could never state in one ad anyway.

5. Limited Decision Authority

In our agency, only two of us can say "no." The account people cannot kill work—they can only critique it. And the creative side is expected to listen and respond appropriately. We want both an active dialogue and a protected environment for new ideas.

6. Involvement Of The Creative People In The Research Mechanism

Yes, research can help you. But only if you avoid the pitfalls.

Consider qualitative research in its most common form—focus groups. Nothing is more harmful than a misdirected focus group. They should be used to probe or explore, but never as a means of ranking or "approving" different campaign executions. And the right-brained creative people should be encouraged to attend and learn first-hand what makes the prospect—that potential buyer his or her ad is supposed to be reaching—really tick.

In quantitative research, agencies can go overboard sampling people so they have the security of big numbers on their side. Such research may be unnecessary in the face of already-good judgment and strong rationale. But some clients don't like good judgement and rationale—they want the raw data to back up every decision. The challenge here is to win without sacrificing the product. And the solution is to keep creative people directly involved in the interpretation of the results.

But above all, remember that a lot of what really works on the air and in print got there without testing.

7. AEs Who Are Teammates, Not Adversaries

A healthy agency will bring its good AEs in at the rough concept stage and see what they think—for input, *not* for approval. This gives everyone a shared sense of authorship and helps the AE sell harder later.

8. The Desire And Ability To Sell Their Work, Not Just Show It

Virtually every advertising pro I know has been in a presentation where someone holds up a layout and says, "So, this is the ad...what do you think?"

For starters, the agency must be excited about its work, or no one else will be. Work must be presented with enthusiasm and conviction to gain a client's confidence, because—remember—risk is scary.

So look for an agency that uses aids and props to communicate its ideas. That shows actual photographs to demonstrate the intended style. Plays music to set the mood. All of these things help to sell—and mean the agency's committed to selling.

Finally, a good agency will press hard when it truly believes that it is right. While it's not necessary to fall on your sword over everything, you should defend your work from unnecessary changes and expect your colleagues to do the same.

9. Client Involvement—Before, During And After The Fact

No matter what ad execution an agency hopes to do, it can't be done unless the client supports the effort. Most clients are left-brain types, just like account people, so they have trouble relating to the intangible. The agency has to sell them.

So look for an agency that creates the magic. The fact is that some clients willingly give you the freedom to do just that. After all, they hired their agency to do something they know they *can't* do. And be aware of those who try too hard to manage the process and prevent "problems with the client"—and end up strangling the work.

10. Appreciation Of The People Who Make Things Happen

Management should know who the champions are, not just in creative, but throughout the entire agency.

Ask how they acknowledge good work—in person, in memos, in public, etc. And make sure there are financially fair salaries and perks. A nice touch is a spot bonus given for performance "above and beyond."

You are the young talents of tomorrow's agencies. If you absorb your educational training, if you can learn to work well with those other brain-types, and, ultimately, if you can just flat-out do the job, the best agencies will continue to praise and promote you accordingly—with no complaints from anyone.

Good Luck!

RONALD SCHARBO has served as president and chairman of the Atlanta agency, Burton-Campbell, Inc., since 1975. He was previously executive vice president/director of account service at Atlanta's McDonald & Little and has held a number of other agency positions.

A graduate of Duquesne University, he is chairman of the Atlanta Council of the American Association of Advertising Agencies and active in many other professional and civic organizations.

3

How To Make Sure You Never Become Disillusioned With Advertising

John V. Chervokas, Executive VP/Chief Creative Officer
Sudler & Hennessey

With your eye-popping spec portfolio, your obvious passion for the business, and your wily use of the advice you're receiving in this book, some day soon you may find yourself hired, actually *hired*, by an advertising agency. Now what?

As a *copy trainee*, what will you find yourself doing from 9 to 5? Reading strategies...and tagging along. Clipping competitive ads...and tagging along. Writing body copy for a trade ad...and tagging along.

If you are hired as a *junior art director*, you won't be asked to tag along that much. No, but you will be riveted to the drawing board, sketching variations of your boss's lay-out or specing type for slides for a new business presentation or redesigning the agency's Company Policy handbook.

Eventually you'll drift into the more glamorous crannies of agency creative life, but early on, it will be very easy for you to get your bushy tail down. True, disillusionment with the ad biz is more stereotypically associated with the veterans. We hear of the account man who packs it in for an apple orchard in Vermont or the creative biggie who chucks it all to run a little hotel in Anguilla. Still, disillusionment can also start early on in one's career.

But it also can be avoided both early—and later. And always.

How?

By making a concerted effort, whatever else you are working on, to also be creating advertising for a *pro bono* account. That's free advertising. For a cause. Or a charity. Or a better world.

No matter if you are loaded down with work on a hair spray, a dry beer, or an airline, offering your talent and time for an awareness campaign for a debilitating illness, for a fund-raising effort for the needy, or for a campaign to build a new wing on your local hospital will keep your creative passions stoked—and, more importantly, your book fresh.

You see, pro bono advertising almost *always* results in advertising you're tickled to slip into your portfolio. That's certainly *not* always true with your paying accounts.

And there's another reason to constantly be doing pro bono advertising. You, and those around you, both in the business and in your home life, will get a better understanding of just how powerful, how *good* this thing called advertising can really be. Pro bono advertising, more than any deep treatise on the economic importance of advertising, justifies the business—and, coincidentally, your involvement with it.

How can you become disillusioned with a career that can actually save lives?

JOHN CHERVOKAS's latest pro bono campaign is for the National Hospice Organization, for whom he has developed the theme, "a special kind of caring...a loving way of dying."

Section 1

Agency Areas
Of Specialization

4

Great Is Better Than Good

Sander A. Flaum, President and Chief Executive Officer
Robert A. Becker, Inc.

The attributes of a "good" account manager in a "good" advertising agency are well documented. A typical job description might read as follows: strong communication skills, both verbal and written; a better-than-average work ethic; personable, well-groomed, and ambitious; a better-than-average IQ.

And if being "average" and working in an "average" agency is where you see yourself, this article is *not* for you.

However, if you are among the minority of individuals who want to leave the realm of mediocrity and strive to be a truly *great* account manager, then I have some advice for you. After 25 years in the industry (eighteen on the client side and seven in the agency business), I think I've learned something about "what makes great!"—that is, those special attributes that enable the "cream" to rise to the top. Consider these ideas and separate yourself from those who would settle to be just "good."

Sit In Your Client's Chair

All of you who enrolled in undergraduate or graduate advertising or marketing programs should realize just how little they have prepared you for the reality of the advertising world. Frankly, your college major isn't in the least important! What *is* significant is your ability to sell...all the time—externally to your client and internally to your management and creative people.

You must be able to communicate effectively via well-written presentations and exciting face-to-face interactions. If public speaking isn't your "cup of tea" and you struggled to pull "C's" on writing assignments, advertising probably is not your niche.

The consensus in this industry is that the needs of the client would be best served if anyone wanting to be an account executive first had to spend several years as a product manager. We have always held the view that the needs of a product manager can be understood best by an account person who has already sat in that chair.

If a product isn't making quota, who cares whether the background of the magazine ad is blue or green? The manager of that product needs a person on the other side of the desk with an understanding of distribution, pricing, packaging, and, of course, marketing and sales strategy.

Working for a client company gives you the opportunity to work with a variety of account people and adopt the characteristics and methods of the exceptional ones. Of course, becoming a corporate product manager—at least for a package goods company—means an MBA degree in many cases.

A positive attitude, a desire to accept coaching (from any level), and a compulsion for detail and follow-up can compensate somewhat for a deficiency in the skills mentioned above.

Become Conspicuously Proactive

This term is so difficult to define, yet so pointedly essential to the making of the *great* account executive. We train our young people to literally shower their clients, on a continuing basis, with fresh ideas to enhance brand performance. We encourage them to think big, think "out-of-the-box" on their brands, think competitively. To become *proactive*, an account executive must be convinced that the brand competitive to his is taking bread and butter off his table. In other words, we want "hungry" account people.

The concept of proactivity evolved from the notion that if the client is paying a fair hourly rate for marketing counsel and creative thinking, we'd better have account people who stay a half step ahead of their clients. Product managers need another marketing head—an experienced, strategic brain—on the other side of the desk to consult with before "decision time."

Be A "Great" Manager

One of the qualifications of the "great" agency person is his or her ability to lead people, to manage and motivate them. While I've read the great books on effective management and have taken the full complement of management courses during my MBA and post-MBA studies at Columbia University's Arden House, I'm still inclined to believe that great managers are born, not made.

Great managers have that charismatic style of getting the big things done faster and better. They are leaders who know inherently how to get the best out of people—at their agency as well as the client company. They have a presence, a respect, a credibility, an obvious posture that makes people want to follow and listen and do. They radiate a silent benign power that everyone wants to be close to. John Kennedy had it; Iaccoca has it; Donald Trump has it; Jessie Jackson has it. Do you?

Great managers are focused people. They have the rare ability to ignore (for the moment) priorities #2 to #5 when priority #1 has to be accomplished...now! They can instantly focus all their energies—creative and active—on the one big task at hand. Other things that are in need of attention but can be put off for a day or a week or a month are put into less critical priority slots and handled only when they need to be.

It takes great mental discipline to stay on that one big project until it's successfully completed. Moving off a "high pressure" project to finish some other task is always tempting. Great managers fight off the temptation and stay with the top priority job until it is done.

Settle For Nothing Less Than Excellence

Great account people are compulsive people. They have an obsession to do each successive task better than the previous one. They strive for excellence. Our theme at Becker is: "If it's not excellent, don't show it!"

The uniquely qualified account executive will not settle for an ad, commercial spot, promotional plan, media proposal, etc., unless it's the *best* it can be. Ernie Lewis, manager of professional advertising at Procter & Gamble, advised agency people recently: "Do it right the first time."

Mr. Lewis' point is well taken. There's *always* time, it seems, to *re*do the storyboard. But there's *never* enough time to get it done properly the *first* time. Our people are instructed never to bring material to the client until they are totally satisfied with the effort.

Great account people will call the client—despite an approaching deadline—and bravely request additional time to "get it right" before bringing it to them. The agency person who really cares about the interests of the client and about his or her brand will argue for more time to bring art, copy, or design to the point of satisfaction—at least from the account person's perspective.

Learn The Business Of Our Business

Most account people hesitate talking about fee reconciliation, billing, or post-30 day invoices with their clients. They see themselves as the clients' marketing and advertising consultants and maintain that a discussion of billing would impinge on the sacred "client-agency relationship." Nonsense!

Marketing managers discuss quotas, budgets, billing, the full spectrum of financial matters every day. They pay hourly fees to lawyers, plumbers, electricians, and painters every day. So why would anyone think it wrong for a brand manager to review billing with his agency representative?

The *great* account person considers himself a business manager. He is providing a unique service to his client for which he expects to earn a fair hourly rate and a 20% profit (what any moderately successful business should be able to achieve).

The *exceptional* account executive wants to and should be paid for the dedicated hours his agency team spends on the brand. He is fiscally responsible and responsive to his client—doing hard-bill estimates, revised estimates (when necessary), and on-time billing, with documentation for out-of-pocket expenses.

Thus, a good financial background and understanding of agency finances are a must for the talented, growth-motivated agency account executive.

So *That's* What Great Is!

Now let's rewrite that job description we started with to reflect the desperate need in this industry for truly *great* account managers: They must possess excellent communications skills, a proactive attitude, leadership, managerial and motivational skills, a drive for excellence, and a solid background in agency finances.

If you are one of those rare individuals who already possesses three out of five of these qualities and is motivated to acquire the remaining two, then you are well on your way to becoming a *great* account manager.

SANDER A FLAUM joined Robert A. Becker, Advertising Inc. in August 1988. He previously served as executive vice president and director of marketing at Klemtner Advertising.

Prior to entering the advertising business, Sander worked for seventeen years as a senior marketing director with Lederle Laboratories, a division of American Cyanamid Company. During his tenure with this major pharmaceutical manufacturer, he served on the task force to take the ethical vitamin line over-the-counter. He also served as task force chairman to launch the Lederle Generic Products Division. As product group director, Sander was responsible for the introductions of most of the important Lederle ethical and biological products from 1974 through 1982. As an advertising account supervisor, he helped launch Calan SR and Lozol.

Sander is also a member of the editorial advisory board of *Pharmaceutical Executive* and an adjunct professor of marketing at the graduate school of business at Fairleigh Dickinson University. He is the author of four published articles and was a featured speaker at two international marketing symposia—Paris in 1982 and Lugano in 1988. He holds a BA from Ohio State University, an MBA (magna cum laude) from Fairleigh Dickinson University, and attended Columbia University's graduate school of business program in advanced marketing studies.

5

Measuring Up To
A Career In Media

Frank P. McDonald, President
R. J. Palmer, Inc.

There are three things that we're going to talk about in this chapter: what the Media department does, why working in Media is such an interesting career, and, most important, how to secure an entry-level job in this area. As we discuss these three questions, we will also delineate the interests and aptitudes shared by most media people and suggest how these traits may contribute to career advancement.

Let's begin by refuting two commonly held misconceptions about media people.

Myth #1: A media person is a numbers person working in relative isolation —providing answers only when asked, then retreating into the shadows until called upon again.

Though the media person is familiar with the numbers involving the "pull" of the different media and the cost for space or time, his or her job is a totally-integrated part of the advertising and marketing process.

Myth #2: Media buying is strictly a dollars and cents business.

If this were true, those media with the lowest costs would corner all the business. Sometimes the *opposite* is true. The "money aspect" is only one element (along with media strategy and synergy) in the complex marketing mix the Media function must construct.

What's Different About The Media Function?

Media is different from any other function within the agency. The media person's contribution is more tangible, more apparent, than that of his or her colleagues. If you prefer to be a specialist rather than a generalist, find it stimulating to talk to clients about their business, and feel comfortable being regarded as an expert whose viewpoint is largely unquestioned, Media may be the right place for you.

What are media people like? They come from a variety of educational backgrounds: economics, mathematics, psychology, to name just a few. Their experience is more diversified, their perspective less fixed, than those in other areas of the agency. Media persons become collectors of disparate pieces of information. They must be familiar with all aspects of the individual accounts assigned to them and have an intimate understanding of the media used as advertising vehicles for those accounts. The media person must have both an *internal* (the different departments of the agency) and an *external* (from agency to clients) focus.

A media person working in either planning or buying can be confident when discussing the effectiveness of media with producers, writers and editors. Inevitably, these discussions will focus on how a particular medium can work best for an advertiser.

A media person's recommendations on how to improve a medium's delivery—make it more audience effective—will receive a fair hearing. These suggestions can range from graphic elements, such as photography or design, to shifts in television programming, even subjects for a mini-series.

The media person, naturally, has to be able to make different media work together to deliver an advertising message with memorable frequency and impact, a process called *media synergy*. Creation of a synergistic environment—correlating the client's message and the media environment—can make the difference between effective communication and no communication at all. The key part of this communication, of course, is contained in the message elements—art or copy. But other factors, such as the right medium, the appropriate vehicle (newspaper, magazine, TV program, etc.) within that medium, and the positioning within that environment, can improve performance. Marketing selections like these are the responsibility of the Media department.

What Media Departments Do

Media departments are responsible for two principal functions—planning and buying.

Media Planning

Media planners must possess broad knowledge of all areas of media, a basic understanding of the entire marketing process, and a detailed awareness of each client's marketing position (especially where they stand vis-a-vis competitors). The planner, working with the client and members of the agency account group, plays a key role in formulating the overall marketing and advertising strategies for each client.

The planning process starts with the establishment of media objectives and strategies, proceeds through research to validate the recommended plans and culminates in the construction of a fully-orchestrated media plan.

Once the client approves the plan, the planner places the order for all print media buys, negotiating with magazines, newspapers and out-of-home media for the best prices and positioning.

The planner is responsible for issuing purchase requests to national and local broadcast buyers, including the amount of advertising *("weight levels")* and timing requirements of the broadcast portions of the media plan.

Though there are exceptions to this, the planner often is responsible for keeping track of budgetary expenditures. The planner regulates expenditures, checking bills to ensure charges are legitimate and that the media budget is not exceeded.

After the buy, the planner files the "post-buy analysis"—a report that includes data ranging from documentation that the advertising actually ran to estimates of audience size.

Media Buying

The second major job responsibility within an agency Media department is that of *media buyer*, who purchases time or space, the basic advertising commodities. Most of this activity is now concentrated in the purchase of the electronic media—radio/TV/cable—so at some agencies, the term media buyer has been changed to *broadcast buyer*.

The media buyer, like the media planner, works within an area of constant change. The number of commercial messages continues to increase. The time units for these messages come in ever-differing sizes. The buyer has to know the market, the potential for clutter or saturation, and the time units that will work best for his client.

The buyer has to know whether the market condition is *soft*—so he can bide his time—or *hard*—a condition that might persuade him to buy now. A wise buyer negotiates for the long term, realizing that extracting the last pound of flesh may not be the wisest course when a medium is slipping and its pricing structure soft. He or she will, of course, seek the best price/value relationship but may not try to squeeze out the last penny, fearing a backlash in future negotiations. After all, what goes around comes around—the seller will remember such hardnose policies when the market turns around and *he* is in a position of strength.

The buyer's judgment of these factors determines the tactical strategy for the ensuing campaign. Other factors such as advertiser positioning (placement on a particular program) or sponsor identifications become at least as important as those of cost.

Like his or her planning counterpart, the media buyer must possess a general familiarity with all media in order to excel in practicing this specific discipline. The buyer must be especially sensitive to the marketplace conditions (prices) for each medium he or she appraises as a purchase possibility. Media costs are substantial, and the buyer has to be versed in all the elements to do the best for his or her client.

The influence of supply and demand on price is a key factor in obtaining the optimum cost/value ratio for dollars invested. When negotiating the media buy, the buyer isolates the appropriate audience for the advertiser's product. Such demographic parameters as age, sex, income, are vital considerations. Ratings of the particular broadcast vehicle are forecast, and the resulting purchase equation aims to obtain the lowest price for the best positioning within the selected program. Often, the buyer presses for performance or rating guarantees that insure his client against underdelivery, with provisions for additional commercial announcements or a cash rebate if a station or network doesn't achieve standards agreed upon in advance.

Buyers must be particularly sensitive to programming opportunities. This means the buyer must have specific knowledge concerning current competitive data on both a local and national level—what programs are being cancelled, shifted or added to a schedule. An alert buyer can apply this information to link the advertising message to the program on a buy-to-buy basis, resulting in a more pertinent, and perhaps more effective delivery of an advertising message.

The basic purchase ingredient of any media buy is not "the audience," but "your client's audience." In order to find this specific ingredient, the buyer must establish key guidelines.

The media forecast must be accurate. Negotiated price, no matter how favorable, becomes largely academic, and essentially inefficient, if the medium performs below anticipated audience levels. While overestimating performance is a major problem, it is also a serious concern if performance appreciably exceeds estimated levels. In that case, funds that might have been directed to some other activities remain tied up purchasing media weight beyond levels that were necessary.

Media Department Responsibilities

The primary responsibility of an agency's Media department is to place the clients' advertising messages in the most effective and efficient manner.

Before any advertising can be placed, the media person should know answers to the following questions:

- Who are the client's competitors?
- When and where is the product or service used?
- Which audience(s) does the client want to reach?
- Who purchases the product or uses the service?
- Where do these prospects live?
- What are their interests?
- What publications do they read?
- What TV shows do they watch?
- What is the best combination of media to reach them—television and magazines, radio and billboards, etc.?

The agency's goal is to put together the most efficient package within the media budget, one that takes into consideration the answers to all of these questions. The media specialist must rely on his or her own knowledge of available media resources to put together such a plan.

Using Available Research Tools

The **Simmons Market Research Bureau (SMRB)** and **Mediamark Research Inc. (MRI)**—the two major suppliers of syndicated research—measure the demographics of magazine readers and supply secondary data on radio, newspapers and television and information on product usage and consumption. Using a national projectable sample of 20,000 adults, they extract detailed demographic, media and marketing information. All of the data is coded and can be cross tabulated to suit a subscriber's needs.

Nielsen, Arbitron and the newly-minted, British-based measuring service, **AGB**, produce a wealth of statistics about broadcast media and their audiences, providing a valuable resource for planners. *Standard Rate and Data Service (SRDS)* volumes supply information about print and broadcast media, including advertising prices and unit availability.

Some recently developed systems with specialized approaches to identifying target audiences and their preferences include **PRIZM** and **Cluster Plus** (geodemographic systems) and **VALS** (Values and Lifestyles), a system which generates psychographic portraits of the targeted groups.

Essentially, these research tools provide the answers to the questions posed earlier. Once the media specialist can construct a demographic "snapshot" of the target audience and figure out how it can be reached, various media can be selected and combined to reach as much of that audience as efficiently as possible.

There is no such thing as a 100 per cent "right" media plan. Some approaches work; others don't. Research can only serve as a guideline for what is essentially a commonsense process. The media planner must be familiar with the reach and cost efficiency of a broad range of media in order to implement a plan appropriate to each client's needs. While the available research tools are helpful, the work of the media planner is still more art than science.

Media's Relation To Other Agency Departments

Media department staffers use the capabilities of the other agency departments to their advantage; such interaction makes the media specialist's job easier. However, budgetary and technological restraints continue to apply—the most dramatic way of communicating a client's sales message might not be economically sensible or technically feasible. Media must deal on a daily basis with three other key agency departments:

Research Department

Media looks to Research for analyses of demographic data and for specially-conducted research. *Focus groups*—carefully-moderated discussions with consumers about a client's product or product category—are one form of such customized research. Media specialists must familiarize themselves with the techniques used to gather the data—the shortcomings as well as advantages of each—so they can make cogent recommendations to the client.

Creative Department

Media advises *copywriters* and *art directors* of new creative opportunities, such as new print space unit sizes, changes in electronic media, or new advertising vehicles. Not only are media specialists constantly attuned to these developments, but they gauge the impact of these changes on the current media plan. The media specialist's recommendation often goes beyond conventional media to such underestimated "sleepers" as in-flight magazines, transit advertisements, direct mail or handbills, and a wide variety of offbeat and unorthodox alternative advertising vehicles, such as sandwich boards, T-shirts, balloons and skywriting, that *can* sometimes make a measurable difference.

Account Management Department

Account management serves as the "eyes and ears" of the client within the agency. *Account supervisors* are responsible for coordinating the entire advertising effort and providing background to the other departments on such matters as the client's marketing plans and the creative strategies that will be used to implement them.

Media is responsible for ascertaining that the advertising recommended *can* be implemented and determining available options. For example, skywriting may be a great way to reach large numbers of people with a simple message. But if it's actually to be part of a client's media plan, then the Media Department must research detailed weather forecasts for the proposed area at the time of the campaign. If the message gets blown across the sky in a blur, the media budget will have been ineffectively used, and no one will care how good the idea looked on paper.

The Background Of An Ideal Media Person

A media person should have good mathematical and analytical skills, though with the increasing use of computers to compile media plans and store data, there is less manual "number crunching" than before. Aspiring media specialists should develop the ability to listen carefully and act on what they have learned. Media is concerned with constantly varying strategies, many different personalities and ever-changing advertising media opportunities. What might be an effective media plan today may have to be totally reworked tomorrow.

Several academic disciplines provide a good background for a career in Media, including mathematics, psychology and marketing. But since so much of the work is highly specialized, on-the-job training is necessary no matter how diversified the candidate's educational background.

It is essential to have the ability to work with great attention to detail on projects that may never come to fruition...and not be discouraged. The media person's work can be intense and tedious. The client can switch marketing strategies. Unanticipated fluctuations are bound to occur in the marketplace, forcing the media plan to be recalled and reworked...again. The media staffer accepts these conditions as part of the Job. Change is a way of life for media specialists, so people who can adapt quickly to new sets of circumstances are often successful.

The ability to negotiate is another important job requirement. Media buyers spend a lot of time working to get the best price for their clients. In order to negotiate effectively, intimate knowledge of the various advertising options is imperative. The media buyer needs to be constantly aware of supply and demand. Both the client and his competitors will be trying to buy advertising time or space in the furthest-reaching, least-expensive media. Demand for effective media, as determined by research, has a significant effect on price.

Media specialists preview upcoming network television schedules and predict which series will succeed, which will fail. While research can provide indications on each program's expected audience demographics, trying to anticipate which new shows are going to be successful and, therefore, a good use of the client's media budget, is still a tricky business. In developing a media plan or completing a negotiation, judgment and intuition are as important as statistical data.

Early on in their careers, media people often assume large amounts of responsibility. When a media planner makes a recommendation, or a buyer executes that plan, a lot of the client's money is involved. It is not unusual for junior media people to be involved in the making of multi-million dollar media decisions. They must be able to fulfill their responsibilities from the outset of their careers.

Making The Most Of Your Job Interview

You must be well prepared *before* you set foot inside any advertising agency. Thoroughly research *your* target agency. Be familiar with the accounts. Look up these accounts' competitors and find out what *their* advertising agencies are doing. Media rests on the principle of competition—picking effective and efficient advertising vehicles that make your client's advertising work harder at less expense than that of his competitors. It follows that any conversation about what the agency is doing must include an analysis of the competition. How much each client is spending is not usually public knowledge, but a study of the advertising will give you an "amateur's" opinion of its effectiveness.

Before the interview, take some time to really look at the advertising you see on television, in magazines and newspapers, and hear on the radio. The goal of the interview is not to critique this advertising, but to be able to discuss it in general terms, especially in terms of the way it relates to media. A rudimentary knowledge of Nielsen ratings and other demographic techniques would help this discussion.

Agency media people are not professional interviewers, so if the discussion lags, be the sustainer—don't rely on the interviewer to keep the conversation going. Don't be afraid to be wrong. The interviewer may know a fact that disproves your point, but your opinion will provide the beginnings of a meaningful conversation about media. That's what you are there for!

One way to take charge of the interview and show sincere interest in media is to pick several topics and be able to address them in an informed and intelligent manner. These topics may be general—the relative merits of television vs. print advertising—or more specific—split :30 commercials (two 15-second sales messages for two different products in a single, 30-second "pod").

There are few rigid career paths in Media people grow into their positions. So demonstrate a curiosity about the buying process and the specific projects the agency's Media department are working on right from the start.

Once You've Landed A Media Job

After you've landed your first job, can you advance? The answer is "yes"—and in almost any direction. Whether in the planning or buying areas, the ability to make decisions lies at the heart of Media. Though the plan is presented to the client as the agency's recommendation, each member of the Media department must pull a considerable amount of weight in developing and executing that plan.

There are formal training programs available in Media (see the listings in the *Job Opportunities Databank* later in this volume), but the real training is on the job. How fast you move up has much to do with your own ability. As a rule of thumb, however, expect to be a trainee for six months to a year after you are hired. After two years in the field, expect to be promoted to media planner. Standards differ widely from agency to agency, so these guidelines are certainly not written in stone.

Whatever agency you choose, whatever their training program, you'll find a career in Media to be exciting, stimulating and rewarding. That's what it is for the thousands of media professionals whose footsteps you'll be tracing.

FRANK P. MCDONALD was elected a senior vice president and named executive media director of N W Ayer in 1987, when the nation's oldest advertising agency merged with Cunningham & Walsh. He joined C&W in 1963 as a media buyer. He progressed through the Media Department and was made a vice president/associate media director in 1967. He also served as director of TV programming. He was promoted to director of media services in 1971 and elected a senior vice president in 1972, and in February, 1974, elected to the board of directors. He left N. W. Ayer soon after the merger to accept his current position.

Before joining C&W, Mr. McDonald was responsible for the media planning and buying of all media on the Bristol Myers account at Doherty, Clifford, Steers & Shenfield, Inc. He began his advertising career at Dancer-Fitzgerald-Sample, after receiving his BA degree in 1960 from St. John's University. He is an active member of a number of industry trade associations, especially the various 4A's councils and committees involved with media.

6

Getting Started As A Copywriter

Ron Bacsa, Creative Art Supervisor & Kaye Brinker, Copywriter
Bozell

Advertising is often defined as the business of persuading the public to buy what your client wants to sell. But before you have a chance to persuade *any*body to buy *any*thing, you have to get into the business. And that means persuading someone to take a chance on *you*.

If you want to be a copywriter, that's not always easy.

Good grades won't do it. Neither will a good school, a good resume, or a "knock-'em-dead" interview. There is only *one* way to get a job as a copywriter. And that's by building a portfolio—a presentation of your work.

The Portfolio—Your Calling Card

Every semester 20 to 30 students enroll in our course in building a portfolio. Some of them are right out of college, others have been working for years. Some majored in communications, others majored in anything from computer science to philosophy. Some have always wanted to write, others are still testing the waters. But no matter how diverse their backgrounds, ages, and abilities, they all know what counts in getting a job as a copywriter is a portfolio.

Like a salesperson with a sample case, you have to demonstrate what you have to sell. Only in this instance, your sample case is called your portfolio (or, more simply and usually, "your book") and what you have to sell are your ideas—your ability to think strategically and creatively. In fact, being a good thinker is as important as being a good writer.

If you took any advertising courses in college, you may have already started creating ads to put in your portfolio. If you didn't, you should consider taking a course now. Not only will it provide you with professional insights into your work, but it will give you the opportunity to find out if copywriting is what you really want to do.

There are no shortcuts to putting a book together. It will take time. It may take money. But in the end, it will be the most important investment in your career that you can make.

What's In A Book

Your portfolio has to demonstrate your ability to think strategically, as well as your creativity. Therefore, it should contain three or four campaigns, not just a lot of unrelated ads. A campaign is a continuation of an idea through a series of ads. Your book should also contain a couple of outstanding single ads. And, if you have an excellent TV storyboard, you may want to include that also.

And What's *Not*

Since a book is only as strong as your weakest ad, what you *leave out* is sometimes as important as what you *keep in*. You should begin by omitting anything unrelated to advertising—like essays for the college newspaper. Also omit anything that's cute but does not sell a product. In fact, one good rule to follow is: When in doubt, leave it out.

Creating Ads For Your Portfolio

One of the rules of advertising is that there *are* no rules...no absolute way to do things. There are, however, certain generalizations. And generally the first step in creating an ad is devising a strategy, which simply means asking yourself, "What is the problem?" and "What are the best ways to solve it?"

Looking back at the history of advertising, you would find that in the 1950s, problem solving was often dependent on a Unique Selling Proposition (USP). For example, if you were selling a fountain pen that had a silver tip, you might tell the public that this new pen with a silver tip lets you "write smoother."

The 1960s were known as the "Image Era." One example of this approach was created by David Ogilvy for Hathaway shirts. He used a man wearing a black eye patch in each Hathaway ad.

The 1970s were known as the "Positioning Era." Schaeffer Beer positioned itself as "the one beer to have when you're having more than one." This was clever because 20% of the people consumed 80% of the product.

The 1980s utilized all these approaches.

What happens in the 1990s will be up to you.

In almost every ad, you will see a logo or sponsor signature which identifies who is doing the advertising. This frequently appears in the bottom right hand corner of the page with a phrase, called the *tag line*, that sums up how the sponsor wants the audience to perceive its product or company. Since tag lines are built from strategic thinking, creating your tag line first will sometimes help you create your ad.

From Strategy To Execution

After you've devised a strategy, you have to find a way to execute it. This is what turns a concept or strategy into an ad. This is your opportunity to demonstrate how creative you can be.

Explore every possibility from emotionalism (hitting people where the heart is) to humor to demonstration (showing the product in use) to comparisons. It seems that ads that compare "this" to "that" consistently win awards. An example of this is a campaign created for *Rolling Stone* magazine that was voted one of the top ten of the 80s. It was a trade campaign directed to the advertising industry to get them to consider *Rolling Stone* as a media purchase for their clients.

Each ad was a spread—two facing pages of the magazine. On the left-hand page was the word "Perception." On the right, "Reality."

To get across the message that most advertisers probably misperceived who really read *Rolling Stone*, for instance, the picture on the left ("Perception") showed a "hippie" from the 1960s; the right-hand page ("Reality") was a picture of a "yuppie" from the 80s. *Rolling Stone* created an entire campaign by using just these two words and changing the pictures to communicate particular messages about the magazine that they wanted the advertising community to know.

Most important of all, if you have news to tell, tell it. And tell it in the headline. No matter how good a writer you are, most readers don't get past the headline. Your headline must be as intriguing as you can make it. Some writers depend on rhymes, others like alliteration, puns, word twists, or quotations.

Open your mind to every idea. Look at magazines, Award Annuals at art director clubs, and television. Go to movies, museums, and concerts. Listen to the radio.

Then, when you think you have a great execution, ask yourself: "Is the work on strategy? Does the selling message come through? Is it executed with flair or brilliance or humor or drama? Does it reward the viewer for watching, the listener for listening, the reader for reading?" These are the questions we are asked about the ads we do at Bozell. If you can answer yes to all the above, chances are you've created a good ad.

Getting Your Portfolio Seen

Since it often takes six months to a year to find a job, make sure you've invested enough time in putting together your book. But once you're satisfied that you have a good book, it's time to get it seen.

Use every approach you can think of to get your book seen. Make a list of any personal contacts you have. Try employment agencies. Although they tend to specialize in middle or senior people, they just might have that job for a junior that you're looking for.

Finally, bring your book to agencies on your own. This means doing a little homework first. Find out who the creative person is that screens books at an agency, then send him or her a resume. This should be followed by a phone call. Most likely, you'll be asked to drop off you book; you have to be willing to do this to get it seen. After all this, if the creative director likes your book and there's an opening, you may be asked to go in for an interview. This is how it works at a large agency. At smaller agencies you may get an interview before someone looks at your book, or at the same time. The only way to become experienced at interviews is to go on them. So go on an many as you can. Each time you will be a little more comfortable.

The Indirect Way To Get Started In Copywriting

Not everyone who has a good book gets hired as a junior copywriter. There are not enough jobs to go around. But there are other ways to enter the Creative department. And we think that just about any way you can get a foot in the door is a good way to get started.

These days, both men and women can get jobs as secretaries (sometimes called *creative assistants)* in the Creative department. It's not a bad way to get started, since it will give you a chance to find out how an agency works *and* a way to get your work seen by people in a position to help you. Agencies like to hire people they know. So as you become known on the inside for doing a good job at whatever you've been hired to do, you'll also have a better chance of getting hired for an available position than someone from the outside. There are other entry-level positions you might want to explore, but make sure that whatever they are, you'll be dealing with the Creative department.

Now What?

If you like to write and like working with people, chances are you'll succeed.

If you're willing to work hard, chances are you'll get ahead.

And if you're willing to take risks, to do what hasn't been done before, there's no limit to how far you can go. Or how fast you can get there.

Prior to joining Bozell as creative art supervisor on the Chrysler account, **RON BACSA** was with Ally & Gargano and Doyle, Dane Bernbach. He is a graduate of New York City Community College and an active member of the New York Art Director's Club.

Except for a brief stint at The Marschalk Company, **KAYE BRINKER** has spent her entire advertising career as a copywriter at Bozell (formerly Bozell, Jacobs, Kenyon & Eckhardt). She is currently working on the Merrill Lynch account. She received her BA degree from the College of New Rochelle and MS from Long Island University.

Ron Bacsa and Kaye Brinker have received many advertising awards. They are also instructors at the School of Visual Arts in New York City.

7

What Your School *Won't* Teach You

Walter Kaprielian, Chairman & Creative Director
Kaprielian/O'Leary Advertising

There isn't a school in the world that can properly prepare you to enter the art directing business. The educational system is not structured to project what really happens in the field.

You'll be mad at *your* school when you find that out. But it's not *their* fault—the business just moves too fast for them to keep up with it.

In school, you're conditioned to work as an individual entity. You earn grades as an individual. You become dependent on your own skills and not the skills of others. You graduate, and one day and one dollar later, you step from being a student to being a professional. From that day on, you start to work with others...and for others...and you'll do better work because of it.

Out Of School...Into The Real World

But first, you've got to find a job.

No one goes through that process without a truckload of fears and questions. Mostly about themselves, their portfolio, and this strange industry that has been projected as being so tough, unforgiving, and competitive.

The portfolio has been the center of your life for the past year, and it leaves your hands with nightmares of getting lost or stolen, and, with its loss, your career going down the drain.

The real truth is that entry-level people are no big investment for the hiring party. A great deal of effort is *not* spent in finding a beginner, and, in fact, the task of finding *you* may very well be relegated to an art secretary or assistant.

Why? You're just not that important...yet! Everyone is searching for a diamond in the rough, but not everyone has the ability to recognize one...so what do they look for?

Agencies Are Not Panting To Hire You

First, they really *don't* want to see you. Most would rather have you send your book. Why? So they don't have to spend time talking to someone they might not consider. It's awkward for all concerned. It's also quite disconcerting *for you* to watch someone flip through the pages of your book and glance for three minutes at your seven hundred hours of work. Is that cruel or unfair? Strange as it may seem, you *can* tell a lot about someone without lingering over each page.

But They'll Look At Your Portfolio

What did they see while they "flipped" through your book?

They saw if you were neat or if you were a slob. If hired you *will* touch other people's work. If you don't respect yours, how will you handle *theirs*?

They saw if you had good hands. Do you letter better than you can draw...or vice versa? Do you have any extraordinary skills? They saw if you have a good set of eyes (how are things placed on the page?) and your sense of color, design, taste.

They saw if you have a sense of order. Can you edit?

They saw if you have a good head. Are there ideas behind what you have? Do you think out problems, or are your solutions ordinary and expected? Is there a modicum of unusual thinking in the book?

No one expects a genius, but a glimmer of hope that you *might* be one is nice. You'll probably be judged on the balance between your manual skills and your mental ones. It will be weighted a bit more towards manual. Why? Because the reason most agencies hire a beginner is because they *need* manual help—paste-ups, comp lettering, mechanicals, cutting mats, flaps, anything that saves a higher-priced person's time.

You May Even Get An Interview

If you get called in because your portfolio has stirred some interest, what does the interviewer look for? First of all, he's *not* looking for a person who's late for their interview. Be on time, be presentably dressed, and be pleasant. Most of the people in the business are pretty nice. They know you're on the verge of a nervous breakdown and wouldn't like it if you weren't. Show me a cool, relaxed, under-control, entry-level interviewee, and I'll show you a person who'll probably get canned for long lunch hours and goofing off.

Everyone has memories of their first interviews. You'd be surprised at how tolerant and understanding people are of your dilemma. Hopefully, your nervousness will project some of your enthusiasm and eagerness. Remember, all men are *not* created equal; if they were, there would be no need for portfolios and interviews.

Interviews are important even if you *don't* get chosen. The more places you go, the more of a "feel" you'll get for the kind of places there are to work in. Some places project a pulse of what working there would really be like. Seeing the environment and the kind of work done is important. Hard as it might be to believe right now, there are places at which you may choose *not* to work. Be observant. Don't be afraid to trust your instincts.

If you get sent from person to person and place to place, don't get discouraged. It might be a compliment—no one sends a loser to one of his friends.

Should you go to a studio or an ad agency? Who knows? Most of us would have taken the first job that was offered. I know *I* would have.

In every other form of education, you have to pay for post-graduate work. In our field, you get paid for it. If you get your first job in a studio and decide it's not for you, terrific! What better time to change course? The same holds true if your first job is an advertising one.

Are You Prepared For This Career?

Does the level of your education matter? Ours is not an industry of MBAs or PhDs. If anyone asks you what school you went to, it's for conversation. If anyone asks you what kind of degree you have, it's even more conversation. This is not to put down higher levels of education. If your heart and head wants it, by all means do it. You probably won't later on. It's just that it's not a prerequisite for consideration.

You Got A Job! Now What?

You just got a job. Oh, my God, what do you do *now*? You do what you would do on any job. You open your eyes wider, your ears get bigger, and your sense of smell get sharper. Drink in what's going on. If someone doesn't introduce you around, introduce yourself. Find the people who are doing the good work. Throw away your wristwatch—it's not a 9-to-5 world anymore.

Try to understand what responsibilities will be considered yours, and then do them better and more thoroughly than anyone has done them before, no matter *how* unimportant they may seem.

If someone else is overloaded, offer to help. If someone is exceptionally talented, watch how they work. There isn't a book written that will teach you better.

Know who your boss is. Service him or her well. Try to understand the problems he or she faces and how they are solved.

Will you advance? Can you move ahead? The first step in getting a promotion is doing what you were hired to do very well. Would *you* promote anyone incapable of doing what you had hired them to do in the first place?

Always be worth more than you're being paid...it keeps you in the drivers seat.

Are there jobs that are below you in status? Sure! Do them! You'd be surprised at how your cooperation can work for you. It allows you to ask for things from others...and your company.

Stop complaining. It's a bore. Everyone knows what's wrong. If you can joke about it, fine. No one needs someone else to depress them. Remember, other people recommend you for promotion. People who you've made feel and look good.

When a disaster looms, try not to panic. Confidence breeds confidence. You'd be surprised at how few people have any.

Always keep an eye out for what's new. Come up with it before anyone else does.

Stay young. It has nothing to do with chronological age. It has to do with attitude.

When one solution will do, do three. When three are needed, do seven.

If everyone is giving photographic answers, take a look at artwork.

If everyone is approaching things seriously, consider a cartoon.

Be thought of as someone who takes a fresh approach to things. The first step to fame is being noticed.

Is It Already Time To Move On?

How long should you stay in one place? I don't know if that is as important as figuring out how long to stay at one *job*. A rut is dangerous. You should watch out for it at any stage in your career.

I worked at BBD&O for eleven years. I stayed because my jobs kept changing ...upward. I started as a photostat clerk and left as a group head (with one or two people that I used to order photostats for as part of my group). I left because I got offered twice my salary and didn't know how to refuse it.

I worked at Ketchum Advertising in New York for eighteen years. I came in as an art supervisor and left as president. I didn't have the same position for more than two years. Each change was an upward one. I didn't change agencies, I changed jobs. If the jobs didn't change, I'm sure I would have changed agencies. There really is no single, perfect answer to the question of staying or moving on. The only thing I would say is that a resume with a whole series of six-month positions does tend to indicate a certain amount of instability on your part.

It Can Be A Wonderful World

You are not entering a "union" business. Growth in position, income, and job security is very much related to individual value and performance. You *can* lose your job tomorrow, through no real fault of your own. On the other hand, you can double your salary tomorrow, too.

I mentioned before that now—as you're preparing to graduate and find your first agency job—is a time that is filled with fear and questions. Don't be afraid—enjoy every minute of it. You're on the threshold of a life that will not be boring or dull. You really wouldn't want to work 9-to-5 in a supermarket, would you?

Whether you find your first job in an agency or a studio, a small company or a large corporation, the *way* you work, the enthusiasm with which you perform, and your interest in what you do will play a great role in your success. Go for it. Get rich and famous!

Prior to becoming a partner in his own company, **WALTER KAPRIELIAN** was president and CEO of Ketchum Advertising, New York. His career also includes stays at BBD&O and Grey Advertising.

President of The Art Directors Club Scholarship Fund, and past-president/chairman of the Advisory Board of The Art Directors Club, Mr. Kaprielian is the holder of over 100 awards for creative excellence from numerous industry organizations and competitions.

A member of the American Institute of Graphic Arts and The National Academy of Television Arts & Sciences, he also serves on the Advisory Board of New York City Technical College, and has been an instructor at The School of Visual Arts.

8

How To Prepare Your Portfolio

Shinichiro Tora, Art Director, *Popular Photography*
Promotion Art Director, *American Photo, Popular Photography*
Diamandis Communications, Inc.

Art students who have just finished art or design school and have started looking for their first jobs must be prepared to show interviewers a portfolio book that expresses their talents and skills. Assembling your first professional portfolio should be considered your initial, tentative step into the professional world of design.

Why is the portfolio so important? Because it presents your talents and skills in a visual form that requires no further explanation. Employers are always looking for creative talents who will help their businesses. While viewing a portfolio, the employer can objectively weigh each young's artist's potential to perform productively. The portfolio is the *only* way you can prove your artistic talents. It's your sales kit. As such, a neat, well-organized portfolio, showing off your talent and professional skills, is the best way for any artist to promote yourself to potential employers and land that important first job.

Before putting your portfolio together, you must first know something about the business side of the creative world and the types of positions available. Commercial, creative art and design is a large and varied field. Professionals may work in advertising agencies, publishing companies, printing companies, design and photo studios, package design studios, architectural design offices, construction companies, and almost any other industry. Jobs may be found in many different departments—Art, Promotion Art, Creative Arts, Planning Design, Editorial Art, to name a few. As a designer, you can specialize in numerous areas—fashion, graphics, editorial, industrial, architecture, and many more.

Given all these choices, the first step may be the hardest—selecting the particular industry or area in which you want to work. Otherwise, you'll be unable to set up a portfolio which will demonstrate the abilities and skills you possess that are necessary to get an entry-level position in *that* particular field.

The portfolio should, therefore, be carefully focused to highlight *only* the kind of work endemic to either the industry or specific job you're pursuing. Even if you are multi-talented—skilled in a number of disciplines and styles—you can't show off everything in a single portfolio.

And you shouldn't try. I've sometimes interviewed persons who have shown me such "unfocused" portfolios. I find them confusing. A person who does a little bit of this and a little bit of that fails to perfect any specific artistic skills. Such portfolios don't provide sufficient samples in my specific areas of interest. So if you have a variety of talents, create a separate portfolio for each major category—illustration, photography or design.

Putting Together An Illustration Portfolio

If you are looking for a job as a staff illustrator in an Art department or contemplating freelance illustration, this kind of portfolio is what you need.

First, select your best original drawings, reproduction prints, or proofs (if you have them), about 20 to 30 in all. (That's, I think, the best size for a portfolio presentation.) If your paintings are unusually large (bigger than 30" x 40"), you should make smaller, photographic copies. Otherwise, you probably won't even be able to *carry* your portfolio, and, if you *do* manage to drag it along, interviewers won't have enough room in their offices to spread it out and go through it. You might consider making photographs of *any* canvas paintings, even the small ones. Canvas is just too bulky to fit comfortably in your presentation case.

The photographic copies you intend to use in your portfolio must be faithful, good-quality reproductions. Use black & white film for black & white drawings, color prints or transparencies for color materials. If you plan to make 35mm slides, use slide protector vinyl sheets. They're available at any photographic or art supply store and hold 20 slides each.

Unfortunately, slide projectors are sometimes unavailable and viewing 35mm slides on a light table is an injustice—They're really too small to view the details. I prefer using 8 x 10 or even 11 x 14 color prints or, if you must use slides, 4 x 5 color transparencies for reproducing illustrations. (But, unless they're too large or are 3-D or computer-graphic illustrations, I personally would really rather see the original illustrations, rather than photos.)

You should mount each drawing, printed proof, or photo print on white or black illustration board of uniform size. This will give the portfolio a neat appearance. The preferred size is a maximum of 24 x 18. If you have many small illustrations, you may group more than one on a single board. If your drawing was made on illustration board, don't mount it again, but do try to maintain a uniformity of board size.

When mounting an illustration, leave at least two inches of space all around it. This will protect the painting from fingerprints. You can also put your credit in this border area. In order to protect the painting fully, lay a clear acetate sheet over each board.

The credit for each painting—your name, address, telephone number, and, preferably, the title of the illustration—should always appear *somewhere* on every illustration. If you want to use a rubber stamp, that's all right (though I prefer the title with each in the border area). Paintings may be held for a rather long time and could easily become mixed up with other artists' work, so such identification is mandatory.

Putting Together A Photographic Portfolio

The student of photography who is probably aiming to become a professional commercial photographer, art photographer, or photojournalist, needs to create a different portfolio.

There are two ways to break into the professional photography ranks. One is to start as an assistant to an established photographer or in a commercial photo studio. Either job will teach you the special techniques and skills you need to know to sell your work directly to magazines, ad agencies, or stock photo houses.

The second way is to avoid such an apprenticeship and become a professional freelance photographer immediately. I don't recommend it. You need not only quite a bit of talent, but several lucky breaks to even have a chance.

Whether you choose commercial or art photography, you must develop a solid foundation of photographic skills. Shoot, shoot, and *keep* shooting. Practice as much as you can. Photographs can be of a single subject, a series, or any other variation, but they must be sharp, clear images. Then select the best shots from each series or group for your portfolio.

Today, most professionals shoot color, which most advertisers and publications prefer. But black & white prints are still used and a selection of black & white photos should be included in your photographic portfolio. Prints or transparencies are acceptable.

Advertising agencies, generally speaking, tend to prefer large-size (4 x 5 or even 8 x 10) color transparencies; fashion photographers usually use 2 1/4 x 2 1/4 film. Magazines are generally flexible as to format. Stock photo houses prefer 35mm slides.

There are two ways to present a 35mm color portfolio. One is simply to utilize the slide protector sheets mentioned earlier. The other is to organize your slides in a carousel tray (ready for projection) of anywhere from 80 to 140 slides.

A maximum of ten sheets or one carousel tray is probably sufficient for any presentation. If you lean towards the tray method, however, make sure you arrange to have a slide projector available when you make an interview appointment.

To display large-size transparencies, cut black matte board to uniform size. Use 8 1/2 x 11 boards for 4 x 5 film, 11 x 14 for 2 1/4 x 2 1/4 or 8 x 10 transparencies or films. "Gang up" twelve of the 2 1/4 shots per board. Use one board for each 4 x 5 or 8 x 10.

To prepare a 2 1/4 presentation board, draw four rules on the back of the board, 1 1/2 inches from each edge. Draw three boxes horizontally, four vertically, each separated by half-inch spaces. Now cut out these box windows. You can then make as many such matte boards as you need.

Put each 2 1/4 transparency in a plastic sleeve and tape each photograph to the back of the matte board so the image shows through the windows you've created. In a similar manner, cut out a single window in the center of the board to mount 4 x 5 or 8 x 10 transparencies. It's also better to mount prints rather than just leaving them loose. Mounting will protect them from fingerprints and other damage and display each photograph in an attractive way.

As previously discussed, make sure each slide or print is fully identified with your name, address and telephone number, especially if you are sending your work to a stock photo agency. Since they handle millions of photos a year, one unnamed slide can very easily get lost in the shuffle. Use 20 to 30 mounted shots in one portfolio case.

Putting Together A Design Portfolio

If you're looking for a job in advertising, editorial, or graphic design at an ad agency, magazine publisher, design studio, or similar media arts firm, you will need to put together a design portfolio. There are two types, depending on where you want to work and the specific kind of design with which you want to be involved—an *advertising design portfolio* and an *editorial design portfolio.* They are distinctly different categories and not at all interchangeable. A portfolio designed for advertising should not be used if you are applying for a publishing job, and vice versa.

An advertising design portfolio should contain concepts for as many of the following as possible: newspaper and/or magazine ads (single ads or entire campaigns for consumer, business, or trade publications), annual reports, booklets or brochures, sales kits, direct mail pieces, record jackets, packages, calendars, letterheads, point-of-purchase materials, corporate identity programs, a sample TV story board, and posters. In other words, sample ads for all the various media and myriad collateral pieces an agency utilizes in its attempt to sell its clients' products or services.

An editorial design portfolio should concentrate on editorial page and layout designs, cover design, book design, and some typographic designs that would be used for presentations.

If at all possible, I would recommend you "customize" each portfolio before the inter-view with the specific art director you're scheduled to see.

To prepare either type of portfolio, start by collecting as many interesting magazines—new and old—as possible. These will provide you with the raw materials necessary to create your own sample ads or editorial designs. Using these ads and stories as a base, recreate various designs *your* way. At this stage, work freely and don't worry about size and space limitations. Once the concept design is worked out, sketch out each of your ideas and, finally, pick the best ones. Using general magazine sizing and layout formats, turn your sketches into finished mechanicals.

(If you are working on editorial designs, you must furnish keyed layout sheets for the text column format (2, 3, or 4, generally) you are using. This is an important element in editorial design and should, therefore, be carefully prepared and certainly not omitted.)

Now find the photographs or illustrations that fit your designs, either from the magazines you've culled or your own selection of original illustrations or photographs. Advertising agencies especially like to see such original artwork in a design, rather than pictures from cut-up magazines. Set actual headlines by using press type, which is available in a wide variety of typefaces and sizes at most art supply stores. Text can be neatly cut out from your magazine pile. (If you can't find a text section that's long enough for a particular design, just cut out what you have, photocopy it and add the two together.)

If you have some experience in darkroom techniques, you can try 3M color key processing for color lettering on clear acetate, tacking it over the photographic print or illustration. You can also create drop-out lettering on a black background by first using press type on clear acetate and then making a direct print on photo enlargement paper. This can also be colored with magic markers. These and other creative techniques will make your overall presentation far more attractive.

Your paste-up should be neat and clean. Remove all excess cement. Trim the finished work to magazine size and mount it on uniform-sized white or black boards. For two-page spreads (whether for advertising or editorial), mount them on a single board, just as they would appear in the magazine. Ten to twenty designs are probably sufficient for a solid presentation.

Finally, with portfolio in hand, you start making the rounds, looking for an appointment with the right art director. Good luck!

In addition to his responsibilities as art director at *Popular Photography* and promotion art director for *Popular Photography* and *American Photo*, Diamandis Communications, Inc. (formerly CBS Magazines), **SHINICHIRO TORA** is an active member of the Society of Publication Designers, the Society of Illustrators and the Art Directors Club. Since 1974, he has coordinated annual shows in Japan for the latter two organizations. He has chaired numerous association and professional committees and served on the board of directors of the Art Directors Club from 1986-1988. He has received a variety of awards for art direction, illustration, and design annually since 1973, including the 1974 Gold and 1977 Silver Awards from the Society of Publication Designers; the 1980 and 1986 Gold, 1982 and 1986 (two) Silver and 1981 & 1985 Distinctive Merit Awards from the Art Directors Club; and the 1984 Silver and 1986 Gold Awards from the Society of Illustrators.

9

The Producer Vs. Everyone

**Carole Cohan, Sr. VP/Director of Broadcast Operations
McCann-Erickson New York**

Studying film and advertising in college is fine. However, once you leave the Ivy Halls, you will find that theory and textbook experience won't get you your first job.

A producer is a different animal. If you want to grow up to be a commercial producer, then get ready to work, work, work.

What A Producer Actually Does

The producer at the agency does many things, but most of all, he or she must be a great mediator, an expert at compromise.

The producer is the third person in the writer/art director creative team. It is this team that works together to finally produce a commercial that will eventually be broadcast.

The top line of what a producer does is interpreting the storyboard (a flat piece of artwork that approximates each shot), so that the concept is transformed into a breathing, living thing. But that simple-sounding task involves a multitude of other decisions and responsibilities.

The producer:

- Works with the Business department to get an in-house price for the client.

- Recommends and calls in directors' reels.

- Competitively bids the commercial.

- Draws up the estimate.

- Starts the casting process.

- Makes sure that the art director and writer are meeting with the director and that there are open lines of creative communication.

- Coordinates all creative and logistical aspects of the job.

- Arranges all pre-production meetings.
- Draws up a production schedule.
- Makes sure everything is approved before the shoot.
- Runs the actual shoot.
- Edits the commercial with the art director and writer.
- Does all the paperwork for talent payments, etc. necessary to close out the job.

Getting In And Moving Up

Some of the necessary qualities you need or that I look for are:

- Positive attitude;
- Willingness to listen;
- Basic understanding of film and videotape;
- Initiative (self starter);
- Love of what you are doing; and, most importantly
- Do you live at home?

The latter is important because starting salaries for assistant producers are around $17,000—$20,000. Since most agencies that have an assistant program are in large cities, this salary doesn't leave much room for anything but transportation and lunch.

The Necessity Of College

I feel you must graduate from college. Believe it or not, remnants from our philosophy, English and history courses are constantly rising up and fusing with what we are doing today. A well-rounded, good, solid education is most important.

Film courses are a must—you'll learn the technical aspects of the field you are going into and start to build a vocabulary of film terms.

If you are lucky enough to have a school that teaches techniques in videotape, this is another must. Almost all commercials are shot on film today, but completed on videotape.

I would also try to take a basic drama course, which will help you when you start to deal with talent—you must understand what a performer does and how to get a good performance from an actor.

To summarize, important courses to take are:

- Film theory
- Videotape
- Drama
- English: Romantic Poets etc.
- History; American, International
- Philosophy
- A good Writing course
- Public Speaking

Entry-Level Titles

Getting the necessary educational background is the easy part; landing your first agency job the difficult one, no matter how extensive your preparation. Most agencies today do not have assistants on staff. If you are lucky enough to get an interview with someone, sell yourself and get in...anyway and anyplace you can. The entry-level position at most agencies is *assistant producer* or *production assistant*.

While at the agency as an assistant, make sure you are always available. The assistant who disappears on a project or doesn't stay late and aggressively demonstrate his or her talents, capacity for work, and hunger for success at every possible opportunity tends to be cut from the group. You will probably put in at least two to three years as an assistant before you are promoted to producer.

CAROLE COHAN joined McCann-Erickson as director of broadcast production in 1986. In this position, she is the senior executive responsible for producing television and radio commercials for more than 20 McCann New York clients, including ATT, Black & Decker, Coca-Cola, Gillette, Lever, Mennen, Miles Labs, Nestle, RJR Nabisco and Sony. More than 60 people in the production and broadcast operations department report to her.

Prior to her present position, Carole was executive vice president/director of broadcast production at Saatchi & Saatchi Compton, where she was also a member of the board of directors. She worked at Grey Advertising as vice president/production group head from 1974 to 1983.

She was vice president/executive producer at McCann from 1967 to 1974 and began her career in 1965 at Sammy Davis, Jr. Enterprises, where she became vice president/associate producer. Carole holds a B. S. from Emerson College, lives in New York City and has one daughter.

10

"The Making Of TV 101-60"

Thomas I. Ford, Executive VP/Director Audio Visual Communications
CNH Associates, Inc.

VIDEO	AUDIO
AE bursts into Copywriter's office	AE: *"Listen Charlie, Ajax Widget Company wants a TV commercial right away. Got any ideas?"*
Copywriter looks up at the ceiling, sucking his teeth...then lunges for his PC and begins rattling the keys.	CW: *"Ajax Widget, eh? Sure Man, I got one that'll knock their socks off, know what I mean? Look, we open with this gorgeous chick on Waikiki Beach, okay? And then..."*

Now this is a script that will never play in any ad agency worth its 15% commission. Because a TV commercial does not spring—*Eureka!*—full blown from an isolated inspiration wambling about in a writer's fertile brain...like Athena from the head of Zeus when Vulcan beaned him with his hammer. For in every well-planned marketing effort, there is a clearly-defined, logical development from perceived need to focused advertising vehicle.

And you—the agency television producer charged with translating a well-calculated concept into an effective motion picture communication product that hits and motivates its consumer targets—must be ever alert to maintain the integrity of the marketing logic, the research enlightenment, the creative crafting that has led to the implementation effort now in your hands.

How does an agency arrive at a good commercial concept and the proper execution that will appeal to the right consumers and boost the product's sales to the desired degree? What are the foundation elements of a professionally-developed TV commercial that must be understood and realized with an abiding awareness and care throughout the production process?

Let's look at it this way: Like a living thing, a TV commercial is conceived, gestated, delivered. It has both father and mother—its father is a *marketing plan*; its mother, a *creative concept*—

who "conceive" it when a client and its ad agency agree they're compatible with a product, a need, and a budget.

First And Basic—The Marketing Plan

Let's say Client ABC has a widget to sell. Ad Agency XYZ is selected to handle the advertising. To begin, they draw up a marketing plan. It's basic to advertising for any product or service.

Positioning Is Key

A key element in the marketing plan is the positioning of that particular widget brand in the global widget marketplace. For proper positioning of a product is critically important for effective marketing and a successful advertising campaign. Each TV commercial wil! draw the breath of life from this aspect of its product.

Perhaps our widget is number one, biggest and best in all the world. If so, then its advertising must support that concept. Maybe it's number two, working harder, giving more to meet—and eventually beat—the competition. In that case, marketing efforts in all media must hue to *that* position. And so on down the line, all the way to the last widget in the category which has nowhere to go but up!

Research To The Rescue

To help establish this and other necessary considerations, research is probably required. Because we must communicate information about our product in ways and through media that are appealing and meaningful, we need a profile of our target consumers: Who they are. Their needs and interests. Their age group. Their educational level.

Additionally, research will help us pinpoint what consumers want in a widget: The benefits they expect. The drawbacks they find. The advantages they look for. It helps us understand consumers' perception of our widget versus other widgets on the shelf. And this helps us in our positioning decision.

This research effort will probably take the form of *focus group* interviews—small assemblies of average consumers who, under the guidance of a research leader, are encouraged to discuss our product. The discussion is recorded. And the research data is compiled and analyzed.

Incorporating all this data, the marketing plan is now devised. It describes how we position our widget among other widgets. It recognizes the share of market we have now. It projects the share we want to reach in the future. It recognizes obstacles to be faced *vis a vis* our competition. It establishes the benefits and the promise we'll communicate to our target consumer. It indicates the best means for reaching her or him. It budgets the monies needed to accomplish this.

The Critically Important Creative Concept

With the marketing plan approved, a creative concept is the next requirement. It will establish our creative strategy, our approach to communicating our promise, the benefits we offer to our target consumer. Most importantly, it will establish the theme of our advertising campaign—our key phrase or slogan.

Visualizing The Concept

We must first determine the best possible execution for our creative concept—in our case, a 60-second television commercial. There are a great many possible ways to go about this. There is the news approach: "Now! New from Widgetek...!" Simple and direct.

Others become more convoluted:

Slice-of-life: "What's a mother to do?"

Slice of death: "Why doesn't *our* widget do what *their* widget does, Jackson?"

Sentiment: "Reach out and touch...!"

Comedy: "Where's the beef...?"

Fantasy: "I dreamed I was..."

Nostalgia: "Just like Mom's..."

Musical: "I wanna buy the world a..."

The list goes on.

Further, it must be decided whether our execution will use live action or animation, electronic graphics, quick-cutting MTV effects. All these aspects have to be carefully considered before writer and art director blend words and pictures for a final concept. And the producer must maintain an abiding awareness of background considerations in the progress of production.

Brainstorming—Initiating The Creative Process

Okay—marketing plan and creative concept are client-approved and ready. Now begins creation of the 60-second TV commercial. Writer and art director generally work as a team, scripting and storyboarding ideas. Chances are, they'll call in their producer to discuss practicalities, suggestions, and, of course, budget considerations.

There will likely be two or three storyboards with different treatments of the basic concept. They'll be presented to the client, and he'll select the one he prefers. (The client will want to know, at least in ballpark numbers, what each is going to cost and you'll have to provide a rough estimate for each.)

The First Production Task—Estimating

If you're familiar with production costs—crew rates, equipment and studio rentals, location fees, talent fees and use payments—and can estimate the number of shooting days required, how many hours for editing time, electronic effects, voiceover and music recording hours, you do it yourself. If not, you call a reliable production house, an editing facility, a talent payment unit, and/or a music studio, explain the tentative nature of the situation to them, and ask for rough cost estimates.

As you do this, you're careful to select studios that can handle the production if it gets a green light. You add a 10% contingency fee to cover extras after the figures are all added up. You'll know it's better to come in on the high side—and later announce you can save costs—than to come in low and have to deliver the bad news that costs will be greater than expected.

If your agency doesn't have it already, you'll get a set of AIPC film or videotape production estimate forms and fill them out. That way, you won't find you've left something out later on—like wardrobe, special props, artwork, animals, transportation, messengers, meals, or one of the zillion other things that have to be included.

Many agencies require bidding production houses to submit these forms as a matter of course. But you know it's a good idea to keep your own, as well. You will find the AIPC phone number in your production reference manual if you don't have it in your head.

Test Commercials—"Disposable Production"

There's another step that may have to be taken before you get your final go ahead to produce a TV commercial: testing. Client and account executive may decide they want to test a couple of the executions submitted. That means shooting the commercials using artwork on an animation stand rather than real sets and live actors.

To do this, you get in touch with a couple of production companies that specialize in test commercials (sometimes called *animatics*). You'll discuss the storyboards and request bids. You may simply shoot the storyboard itself, or your art director may execute a series of larger renderings.

Then you'll record voice-over talent for dialogue or the announcer track. You'll call a talent agency or casting service, audition your cast on audio tape, select stock music from a supplier with a good library, and get Account and Creative Group approval.

You arrange recording studio time—probably a couple of hours—to record voice-overs and edit selected takes to make the completed voice track. You mix voice, music and sound effects—if any—for the final master track.

You do all this "to picture"—that is, watching the visual tape on a studio monitor as you record. This way cast and announcer achieve accurate sync with each scene or action as it appears. So you save additional editing time to lock up voice and picture later.

You screen the finished tape for agency and client approvals. You order copies and deliver them to the local TV stations or the research organization involved.

Testing may be done either on air with next day telephone polling or in focus group interviews at supermarket sites or conference centers. In a few weeks, data will be delivered describing consumer recall, comments and overall communication effectiveness for each test commercial.

TV 101-60—Getting The Green Light

Finally, after all these important preliminary considerations, TV 101-60 gets the green light. Now your real work begins.

The Production Budget—The Bidding Process

Step number one is obtaining bids and selecting the production house to handle your job. You get cost estimates from three suitable companies. Their track records, directors, cinematographer, videographers, and creative capabilities must be right for the kind of production TV 101-60 requires. You get sample tapes from studios that you, the writer and art director would like to consider. You may screen through a number of sample reels before selecting three you'd like to have submit bids for your commercial.

In order to "compare apples to apples," you write up a description of all the requirements presented by the commercial—sets, locations, props, wardrobe, special effects, artwork, concept, approach, visual style, shooting techniques. These "specs" will ensure that each production house is bidding on the same information in every aspect.

Eye On The Doughnut...Pass It On!

You may call a meeting with all three production house representatives to discuss TV 101-60's specs at a single collective meeting. This, again, ensures that each has the same understanding of your commercial's needs and aspects. Or you may choose to meet separately with each individual "rep." In any case, here, too, you make doubly sure everyone is targeting the key objectives established in the marketing plan and creative concept.

For TV 101-60 is carefully aimed to communicate specific points of information—including benefits and promises—to your target consumers. It is designed to elicit a desired attitude, a particular reaction of heart or intellect toward your widget. All your production people must understand who TV 101-60 is talking to and what your "ideal consumer" must recall after it's been viewed. You make sure irrelevant production ideas do not carry it off on a tangent that will miss your designated target.

Planning Is All: Pre-Production

After your production house bids are in, you compare figures and capabilities, consult with your writer and art director, and select the one that best suits your commercial's creative needs and your client's budget.

With that done, you contact a good editing/completion facility—one that has a good editor and the necessary electronic effects capabilities to meet the requirements of TV 101-60. You consult with them about the number of editing hours, graphics and electronic effects hours you'll need to edit and complete the commercial. If it's been decided to shoot on film, you figure in film (negative)-to-tape transfer costs.

You'll probably want to do your work on videotape because tape gives you more flexibility with special effects, transition flips and wipes, and graphics. However, you'll do your finished master on one inch videotape, whether you shoot on film, 3/4 inch or Professional Beta, because it gives you the best replicating quality for your quantity air tapes. Of course, you can also shoot your original footage on one inch videotape. That gives you optimum quality, but it's also considerably more expensive.

You'll save money by putting your commercial together in rough form first, without electronic effects or titles. It's called "off-line" editing and the hourly costs are relatively cheap. You'll have your camera tapes transferred to 3/4-inch or 1/2-inch VHS tape with visible time code. Then you save expensive "on-line" studio time editing the master by simply conforming it to the off-line rough-cut using the visible time code numbers to find your edit points quickly. If you spent a lot of time searching for selected takes in an on-line edit suite, you'd find yourself needlessly eating up your completion budget.

You've figured into your completion budget the costs for the master itself, a duplicate master, and all videotape stock costs. You know there will be problems if these are left out of the estimate after working out all the various hourly requirements.

You check your talent payment people and add your talent costs—session fees and wardrobe payments. Talent is paid extra for any wardrobe they provide. You get an estimate for on-air use payments even if you don't figure them into your production budget. When your agency doesn't have the expertise to estimate union—SAG or AFTRA—costs, you use an independent talent payment company to make the calculations and handle payments.

Those Very Important Odds And Ends

Special artwork for product and package labels with simplified graphics generally will be needed. Some labeling has too much clutter to be effective on the TV screen. You consult with your art director on this and figure the costs into your budget. You'll make sure the work is done and corrected product delivered to your production house well before shooting dates. You do the same for special product-related props you're going to need.

You make sure your client delivers the products and props he is obligated to supply in time to meet your production dates. And you don't get just one product package—you get a dozen. Labels become quickly worn and smudged in shooting.

You're responsible for wardrobe, too. If it's extensive, you make sure the production house includes a wardrobe person in the budget. And you make sure they consult with your talent, get sizes, and select a variety of clothing and accessories for your final approval. Early. Most wardrobe items can be returned if not selected for use. If talent is to supply their own wardrobe, you instruct them to bring a variety of items to the shooting so you'll have a choice.

Production Is *Before* Shooting

You're planning and budgeting all the requirements for TV 101-60 *before* you get into actual production. Because you know thorough planning is everything in the making of a good TV commercial. It lets you deliver on time and on budget. When you're already in production, it's too late to discover needs. After the pre-production planning for TV 101-60 has been done, there should be nothing left to do but—*do it*.

Network Clearance—Just In Case

Just to be on the safe side, you submit your commercial to one of the network's Continuity Clearance departments. This has less to do with taste than with proof of advertising claims. Even if TV 101-60 is initially intended only for local station or regional use, you know it's better to have a network reaction at the outset. Otherwise, your client might have to pay for costly revisions if a network on which he subsequently wished to air the commercial demanded proof of claims that couldn't be adequately substantiated in the requisite time.

Working Up Your Production Schedule

Now you work up a complete production schedule. You include casting session, prop delivery, wardrobe fitting, shooting days, editing, recording, mixing, intermediate stage screenings and approval dates, and final client approval deadline. You consult with your writer, art director, and production house people if you need additional input. You make it realistic. You distribute copies to all agency and production house people. You stick to it. This is especially important if you have a firm air date to meet.

The Production Meeting

After your production house has been selected and your budget approved, you call a pre-production meeting with your director and his producer, set designer, prop and effects people, and your agency writer and art director. There you discuss and plan the execution of storyboard and script in complete detail.

You've written up an agenda for the meeting to keep it organized and on target. It begins with a brief description of the commercial's objectives, target audience, advertising promise and benefits to be communicated, visual style, and approach. You discuss sets, props, locations, wardrobe, makeup, shooting techniques, camera angles, special effects, scheduling. When sets are to be designed, you require sketches and elevations for early approval. You keep an eye on costs...you know they can quietly escalate at this stage if you're not careful.

The Perfect Talent Is A Must

Now you arrange the casting. You know the on-screen talent is vitally important to the success of your commercial—they literally represent the client and the product. Each must elicit from the viewer the desired emotional or intellectual response. There must be no compromise. Each must be perfect for the role.

You call a good agent or casting service. You get head shots for pre-selection. You instruct your casting agent *not* to bring in every actor in town. You give your agent or service a good written profile of each character in your commercial and make sure they call only appropriate people.

You audition your cast on videotape. If there's dialogue, you have cue-cards for them to read from. You know you don't get much from an actor whose nose is buried in the script. You screen the tapes with your writer and art director and select not more than three alternate choices for client approval.

When final approvals have been given, you call your agent and put "holds" or "first refusals" on the selected talent for your shooting dates. This gives a little leeway in case of a last-minute change in schedule. A firm "call" commits you to a session fee payment for the date called. The other does not. As soon as shooting dates are ironclad, you give talent firm calls and send them scripts. According to union rules, delivering a script also represents a firm commitment for the talent.

You consult with your cast about wardrobe they'll supply or arrange wardrobe fittings. And you fill out the SAG or AFTRA talent contracts you'll bring to shooting or recording sessions. Your talent will sign them at the beginning of each session.

Go For It!—The Shoot

You've done your pre-production work well. Shooting should go swimmingly—Murphy's law not withstanding.

Just the same, you keep your eye out for cost overruns. You don't let your director get carried away striving for the perfect take on a particular shot...and start running late. You go for a variety of shots and angles. In the editing room, the perfect take may not work and then you're stuck if you have no options. You stick like a leach to daily shooting schedule. While your director's working on one shot, you look ahead to the next, making sure props, wardrobe and talent will be ready.

The Post-Production Process

Now shooting is accomplished. If you shot on film, you transfer your negative to one-inch videotape, then to 3/4-inch tape with visible time code readout. (You might also go to 1/2 inch VHS tape, but 3/4 inch editing systems give you a little more flexibility.) You screen the camera tapes for writer and art director and write down preferred takes for editing reference.

Next, you make a "scratch track" of announcer copy or other narrative voice-over. You either read it yourself into a tape recorder or have someone with a good voice do it for you. No need to hire talent for this since you'll only use it as a guide for your off-line edit. You have the completion studio transfer the scratch track to 3/4-inch videotape (or 1/2 inch VHS, whichever you're using).

Then you sit yourself down in an off-line edit suite with an editor and put the whole thing together in rough form—no transitional effects and no titles. You make a careful list of time-code readouts at the beginning and end of every shot. This is important. It saves time and money during the on-line edit because it lets you locate and edit each desired take quickly and efficiently.

The Very Important Client Approval

You screen the off-line rough edit for everyone involved—writer, art director, account group. You make requested revisions and get approval, Finally, you screen the off-line rough-cut for the client...and get client approval. You make sure he or she understands that NOW is the time to make any changes. For at this stage the cost is negligible. After the on-line edit is done, changes cost. A lot.

With the rough edit approved, you do the big one— the on-line, conforming to your rough-cut and incorporating titles, graphics and electronic effects. TV 101-60 is almost there. But you still have the sound track to finish.

You cast your announcer....select stock music....pick sound effects. You get approvals. You use a good sound recording facility. You record the announcer track to your final picture. If you're using original music, you've selected a good composer or original music house by auditioning music tapes. You may have requested a rough demo tape of the proposed music for preliminary approvals. You pay a moderate additional fee for this.

Your composer screens the finished picture, clocking points at which music will back up or emphasize key visuals. Then he or she will call in musicians and singers and record the music.

Now you do your final track mix. In the mixing studio, with a capable audio engineer, you blend on-camera voices, music, sound-effects, and voice-overs. And you screen the finished TV 101-60 for final agency and client approvals. With everyone presumably deliriously happy, you order your backup duplicate master and air dupes. And you ship.

And that's it—TV 101-60 is conceived, birthed, and delivered. Clearly, a healthy kid. Good luck!

THOMAS I. FORD has held key creative/production positions with three of the leading advertising agencies—senior producer/director/writer, Young & Rubicam; executive producer/production group head, Benton & Bowles; creative producer-director Wells Rich Greene. Earlier, at ABC-TV in New York, Ford directed network and local dramatic and variety programming. Prior to that, at WEWS-TV in Cleveland, he originated, produced and directed a broad range of television programs that spanned the range from opera to Cleveland Indians baseball.

As head of his own company, Tom Ford has written, produced and directed broadcast advertising, industrial and business communications on film and videotape for many of the country's largest corporations. He has also won over fifty top awards at film and advertising festivals in the United States and Europe. He has taught television production and direction at The Graduate School of Drama, Case Western Reserve University, and at the State University of New York at Purchase.

Mr. Ford recently authored a book for the amateur video movie-maker—<u>Pro Techniques of Making Home Video Movies</u>—published by HP Books. He is a graduate with honors of Swarthmore College and completed extensive professional studies at the American Theatre Wing in New York.

Section 2

Other Areas Of Opportunity

11

A Career In Outdoor Advertising Sales: The Billion Dollar Industry You May Have Overlooked!

Robert J. Smith, President
Gateway Outdoor Advertising

This might come as a bit of a shock after 16 years or more of going to school, cramming for exams and highlighting countless textbooks, but the long-term value of any education—especially college—is not the pure information you glean from books or lectures. Rather, it's the process of learning how to successfully deal and communicate with people.

Don't get me wrong—college courses and curriculum are important. There are some practical courses that can prepare you for positions in sales, accounting, finance and other specializations. And in terms of preparing for a career in advertising, courses such as journalism, speech, psychology and sociology (in addition to specific advertising courses) are important. But all of these courses are not "job- or career-specific"—they will help prepare you for most any endeavor. When it comes right down to it, your ability to understand people and communicate with them effectively is the key to success.

Advertising is the business of delivering a message, of communicating, of *persuading*. There are many types of "senders" or "deliverers" of such messages—television, radio, newspaper, outdoor and direct mail are the primary forms.

The Five Thousand Year-Old Billboard

Outdoor advertising is the oldest form of these messengers, and it's probably the most universally misunderstood and misused. To a great extent, that's probably why it's such an interesting field to be involved in—the business is growing, constantly changing, always challenging.

According to the <u>Encyclopedia Americana</u>, "In a sense, advertising began around 3200 B.C. when the Egyptians stenciled inscriptions of the names of kings on the temples being built."

Considering that television, radio, newspaper and direct mail weren't even contemplated then, it can be logically argued that this really marked the beginning of the concept of outdoor advertising.

It was some time before outdoor graduated from these humble beginnings—late in the 19th century, companies began leasing out space on wooden boards for advertising messages or "bills." Hence the term "billboards." Since then, it's grown and evolved not only as an art form, but into a media force.

Today, there are two basic categories of outdoor advertising—*printed or painted bulletins* and *poster panels*. Bulletins are usually 14 x 48 feet, big enough to be visible from relatively far away; these are the billboards you see along expressways and major traffic arteries.

Poster panels are visible along primary and secondary arteries and come in two basic sizes: 12 x 25 feet (a "30-sheet" in industry parlance) or 6 x 12 feet (an "8-sheet").

All three forms—the bulletin, 12 x 25 poster panel and 6 x 12 poster panel—have their place and value in the advertising field and provide alternatives for media placement based on marketing strategy.

Outdoor is probably the purest form of advertising because it's totally involuntary—people don't jump in their cars and drive off to gaze at billboards; you just see them as you drive by. You do, however, turn on a radio to listen to music or the news and, in the process, hear radio advertisements. You turn on the TV and see and hear the commercials. You pick up a newspaper and can't help seeing the ads as you thumb through it.

Outdoor's ability to deliver a strong, brief message at a low cost (relative to the other major media) has caused the industry to grow to close to a billion dollars in sales. The prospects for future growth are excellent—advertisers are always trying to get more "bang for the buck." Obviously, a growing industry offers excellent opportunities for entry-level people.

Entry-Level Opportunities

A sales position in the outdoor advertising field requires a person to make face-to-face contact with professionals on many different levels of authority and responsibility.

On the advertising agency side, you may be calling on the media planner, media buyer, account executive, production director, art or creative director, media director, even the president or general manager of the agency. On the client side, you may be dealing with the secretary who can "get you in the door" to see the advertising manager, the director of marketing or president of the company, or anyone in between. Dealing with such a variety of responsible professionals requires an educated, disciplined, creative, persistent and energetic person. It also means the sales position is constantly changing and ever-challenging.

Though good written and telephone skills are also necessary, face-to-face contact with the decision maker is critical—you must be able to tell your story, both see and hear the response and, most importantly, be a good listener. While direct marketing has it's place and prudent use of both telephone and direct mail contact is all part of the selling process, there still is no substitute for face-to-face contact.

The Personality Traits You Need

I personally do not look for a particular "type" when interviewing people for sales positions, though others in my capacity may and do. It's a matter of philosophy—I believe that a successful sales team is one composed of a number of different personalities with different viewpoints who can, despite their differences, work together toward a common goal. Such a diverse group enables me to match the personalities of particular salespeople to those of my clients—some clients are receptive to a friendly extrovert; others prefer a more serious-type who takes a systematic approach. Matching personalities is crucial.

There are, however, basic *traits* I look for, those I feel are key to any candidate becoming not just a successful salesperson, but someone who can eventually move higher in the organization:

1. Honesty
2. Integrity
3. Perseverance
4. Grit
5. Assertiveness
6. Aggressiveness
7. Ability to communicate
8. Need for self esteem
9. Pride in performance
10. Respect and caring for people
11. Loyalty

Not the entire Boy Scout Code, but close!

What You'll Learn

It's easy to get a job in sales and frankly, I think it's easy to *keep* a job in sales if you work at it. Just remember: ***There's no such thing as a "born salesperson."*** There are however, people who become more successful than others because they possess or develop those traits listed above. There *are* successful salespeople who lack some of these traits; nevertheless, I believe the more of these you possess, the greater your own chances of success.

While it is important you get proper schooling, the *basis for success* in the outdoor advertising business—in fact, in *all business*—is a willingness to learn, make mistakes, work hard and be good at what you do.

In addition to a salesperson having a working knowledge of other facets of the business (operations, accounting, etc.), he or she must develop a working knowledge of other media. So you will be trained not only in basic sales techniques applicable to *any* sales, but also "schooled" in the strengths and weaknesses of other media and how they are bought and sold. Therefore, it helps to be creative and imaginative—a critical consideration in outdoor advertising is the creative execution (or design). This does not mean you need to be an artist—you just need to have vision.

I truly believe that a person who is successful in outdoor sales can be successful in *any* form of advertising sales. Because of the divergent nature of the outdoor business, a salesperson is exposed to so many different circumstances and individuals that he or she becomes well prepared to take the next step. I must warn you though: It's easy to get "hooked" on the business, because it's fun, challenging, ever-changing, rewarding and certainly far from monotonous.

And What You'll Earn

Compensation plans range from straight commission with no benefits to straight salary with full benefits. Most companies offer a base salary plus commission or bonus for special performance and provide benefits, although the movement in the industry is more toward straight commission sales.

A college graduate with no prior sales or work experience typically will earn $10,000—$20,000 in his or her first full year of employment. Keeping the variety of potential compensation plans in mind, it's still reasonable to say that eventually a person can earn as much as he or she is capable of earning. It is not uncommon for a good salesperson to earn $30,000—$60,000 in just a few years. And if you are really good, you can earn more.

A challenging and rewarding opportunity awaits you in the advertising business, and a special opportunity awaits you in the outdoor advertising business. Join us!

Gateway is America's largest 8-sheet outdoor advertising company, with offices in eight markets from New York to Los Angeles. In his present position, which he assumed in June, 1986, at age 38, **ROBERT J. SMITH** oversees all operations and sales. He was previously general manager of Gateway's Chicago office and regional vice president.

A marketing and management graduate of West Virginia University, Mr. Smith successfully operated three different sales territories for Wheeling Corrugating Company and Wheeling-Pittsburgh Steel Company for eight years. In 1978, he switched to advertising sales and quickly became the top performer at Pittsburgh Outdoor Advertising and, subsequently, Foster & Kleiser Outdoor Advertising.

12

Sales Promotion: America's Game

Chris Sutherland, Executive Director
Promotion Marketing Association of America, Inc.

QUESTION: What do basketball, Lee Iacocca and the sales promotion industry have in common?

ANSWER: Despite their distant roots, each is dynamic, very successful and, most of all, uniquely American. The difference is that while Iacocca and basketball do not offer open-door employment opportunities (unless you can sell Chrysler junk bonds or scrape your head on the ceiling with your feet flat on the floor, respectively), sales promotion is booming with opportunity.

The Surprising Dominance Of Sales Promotion

The facts speak for themselves: For every dollar spent on advertising by American consumer product companies, more than *two* dollars is spent on sales promotion. Sales promotion expenditures—over $100 billion—represent the largest single portion of the American marketing budget.

One reason for this surprising dominance lies in the proven ability of sales promotion to motivate purchase. Unlike advertising, which is image based, sales promotion approaches consumers in ways that have an immediate and measurable impact on their decision to purchase. Advertising suggests...promotion motivates.

Sales promotion exists because consumers have a choice, because price is not the only consideration, and because most major consumer goods are marketed on a national basis. Our system of open competition creates a never-ending need on the part of these manufacturers to get and maintain an edge, and sales promotion is the most powerful single force in this endeavor. And while advertising—*aka* "propaganda"—exists in virtually every modern economic environment, sales promotion can only exist in a free enterprise system. In America, consumers celebrate their choice of products, as the seemingly endless flow of product introductions and failures attest.

Perceived quality and brand loyalty are important, but consumers have overwhelmingly demonstrated that they want to be wooed. In supermarkets, for example, studies have shown that fully three out of four purchase decisions are made *after* consumers enter the store! Savvy marketers know that sales promotion is their most effective weapon in the "battle" of the open market place.

This newfound recognition of the power of sales promotion has also led to new challenges and opportunities. The need to manage the business of promotion marketing has created opportunities on the corporate side (to manage, track, evaluate and even create promotions), on the agency side (to create, execute, measure and analyze), and on the supplier side (everything from "low-tech" fulfillment and point-of purchase services to "high-tech" scanner data and analysis). Even advertising agencies have reluctantly accepted the reality (and overwhelming importance) of promotion marketing by buying or creating their own sales promotion agencies or departments.

Putting Promotion Into Perspective

So what is a consumer promotion? It is simply a consumer product or service that is combined with a special offer to motivate immediate or continued purchase. To be considered successful, its effect—the amount of "incremental sales" (those over and above the expected norm during a given period) that can be attributed to a specific promotion—must be measurable and its impact significant.

Sales promotion creates that "edge" through several recognizable vehicles:

Price Off

This seemingly mundane practice—a temporary reduction in the price of a product or group of products—actually has many applications, depending on the promotion goals:

- *"Sales Price"*—the standard deduction of the regular price, usually communicated through advertising, on the package, or at or near where the product is purchased (known in the trade as "point-of-purchase," e.g., an <u>end aisle</u> display in a supermarket).

- *Modified "Sale Price"*—which usually ties the purchase of several products together to create a sale price. For example, instead of simply saying "25% off any tire purchase," tire dealers might try to encourage multiple purchases by saying "Buy Three, Get One Free". The price-off commitment is the same, but a different, more-focused marketing goal is served.

- *Couponing*—Usually delivered through the mail, magazines or newspapers (e.g. via free-standing inserts—"FSIs"— those glossy inserts that always seem to be the first things that fall out of your Sunday newspaper), coupons are the most common sales promotion tool. They are conceptually identical to a sale price, except that they require a redemption process through the retailer (usually serviced by **fulfillment houses**).

    A variation on this theme are *cash rebate programs*, where the consumer must send in product proof-of-purchase (again, administered through a fulfillment house) to receive a rebate check. Because these offers usually involve either multiple purchases or expensive items (e.g., power tools), rebates are generally worth more to the consumer than coupons.

Value Added

As opposed to a price reduction, *"value added"* promotions offer consumers an extra incentive to motivate purchase, one usually not directly related to the product, These promotions may or may not also contain price reductions:

- *Sweepstakes*—possibly the easiest-understood promotion, sweepstakes are simply chance drawings from entries sent in to (guess what?) a fulfillment house, for generally impressive grand prizes of cash, merchandise or travel.

- *Contests*—essentially sweepstakes, except that the contest requires some level of skill and usually is more complicated. Marketers try to involve consumers quickly through contest devices like "Instant Win" and "Match & Win" formats. Sometimes contests can have secondary benefits, like public relations (e.g., themed essay contests), or cross trial (e.g., "winning" game cards that offer a free coupon for a new product line).

- *Free With Proof-Of-Purchase Offers*—offering a free gift as an incentive to purchase. If a single purchase is all that is required, the gift is usually attached to the packaging in some way. Gifts requiring multiple purchases are usually "fulfilled" like other forms of promotion.

- *"Self Liquidators"*—this intriguing term simply refers to promotions that require a cash outlay on the consumer's part in addition to proofs-of-purchase. Because of this shared responsibility, self-liquidated items are usually more expensive than free gifts. This shared cost is also an attractive consideration to the marketer, because cost liabilities don't become a factor until the item is actually ordered (unless pre-purchase is necessary), hence the term "self liquidator".

There are literally hundreds of variations and combinations of these basic elements, and applications only begin with consumer products. Entries into PMAA's Reggie Awards, symbolic of excellence in promotion marketing, have come from the fields of computers, financial services, airlines, auto parts, even building materials.

In other words, over $100 billion worth of creativity, analysis, management, fulfillment, production, etc. spent by companies that need bright people...people like you!

Finding Your Own Niche In Sales Promotion

Where do you find your start in sales promotion? For starters, there are thousands of consumer products, hundreds of companies that market them, hundreds of agencies that service the companies. Wherever you live or want to work, the opportunities are all around you.

Better still, practically every student starts out equal!

That's because there's no MBA in Sales Promotion, no B.A. in Sales Promotion...no degree of any kind in sales promotion. A few universities like Northwestern, Texas and Syracuse offer courses, but marketing's most important new discipline still waits for its first academic department.

Opportunities In Corporate Promotion Departments

In the meantime, the college system's loss can be your gain. Just ask Forest Harwood, former Manager of Sales Promotion for Frito-Lay and Chairman Emeritus of the Promotion Marketing Association of America: "Promotion is the 'fun' part of the marketing mix," explains Harwood. "It's a career where your creative abilities can really shine."

But like many corporate promotion executives, Harwood (president of Harwood Marketing Group) looks for a solid business management background along with versatility in entry-level people: "Be prepared to juggle a variety of project aspects at one time. And remember: They all have to land together. That takes a lot of careful management, advanced planning and flexible perspective. You need to have a 'think fast, think clear, think-on-your-feet' approach to solutions."

Entry-level corporate salaries in promotion departments are about equal to other marketing department positions. Depending on the company, the part of the country, and your qualifications, starting salaries can range from about $22,000 to $45,000 per year.

At the top end, new ground gets broken literally every day. At this writing, General Mills was reportedly offering an estimated package of $250,000 for their newly created Vice President of Promotion position.

Opportunities In Marketing Services Agencies

Where corporate promotion departments can provide relative security and control, marketing services agencies typically offer more excitement, more anxiety and more reward. Under the direction and supervision of corporate promotion managers, sales promotion and related agencies design, create, produce, execute, fulfill and measure the kinds of promotion programs mentioned earlier.

Entry-level people in these agencies typically work with the "nuts and bolts" of sales promotion. Don Roux, President of Roux Marketing Services, looks for people who can be both creative and detailed at the same time: "Client confidence and respect is our main goal, and even our entry-level account coordinators are key to this effort."

But Roux feels that being this close to the action requires a special kind of person: "The *account coordinator* position is at the center of a fast-paced, high-pressure environment, requiring an energetic, anxious to learn, personable individual."

Starting salaries may seem low at between $18,000 and $25,000, but commission and profit sharing can often supplement the base salary. More importantly, advancement can be rapid, because it is often closely tied to your personal performance.

In fact, Roux specifically looks for candidates with advancement potential: "In five years, you should be at the account executive level, where average earnings are $58,000 plus. After ten years, good account executives can be in the six figure area."

Like Harwood, Roux looks for people with solid marketing credentials, although he will also consider communication and finance majors. But bottom line is again often a matter of client perception, according to Roux, and everyone shares in that responsibility: "I look for people who can talk well on their feet, have the ability to see the big picture and to converse both 'knee-to-knee' and by telephone."

As Executive Director of the PMAA, a former vice president of a sales promotion firm, and a manager at Pepsi-Cola USA, I have witnessed the growth of promotion marketing first-hand.

Simply put, sales promotion in the 1980s is to marketing what computers are to information management.

And even if you're not the next Lee Iacocca or Larry Bird, there's still plenty of room for you at Chrysler or in the NBA. Because people have the choice to buy their products, and because Lee and Larry alone aren't always enough incentive, each uses promotion marketing extensively.

And that is truly "America's Game!"

CHRIS SUTHERLAND assumed his current position in September, 1987. Previously, he was vice president at Marketing Equities International, a firm specializing in tie-in promotions, where he worked with Sony, Nabisco and Coca-Cola. He also headed up Sports Concepts, his own sports marketing consultancy.

From 1982 to 1985, he managed the national sports programs for Pepsi-Cola USA. In the public sector, he was responsible for managing all corporate-sponsored sports programs for Los Angeles (CA) County.

A graduate of California State University at Los Angeles, he and his wife, Arlene, reside in Ossining, NY. They have two children.

13

Career Opportunities In Direct Response Agencies

Jonah Gitlitz, President
Direct Marketing Association, Inc.

While direct response advertising agencies—part of the rapidly-growing direct marketing field—offer career opportunities that are similar to those in general advertising agencies, they also offer some unique attractions. But before we discuss these differing opportunities, let's look at the differences between the two kinds of advertising, "traditional" vs. direct response. "Traditional" advertising has typically:

- Supported the marketing of products or services which are of interest to large numbers of people, often millions of them;

- Used broadly-directed media—such as network television—seeking to reach the most potential prospects for the product or service; and,

- Sought to generate sales through geographical outlets (e.g., retail stores, banks, service centers, etc.).

In a typical general advertising program, the sponsoring firm runs extensive media schedules so that potential customers, whoever they may be, will recognize the product, have a positive perception of it, and take action to buy it when they are shopping. In contrast to this approach, direct response advertising:

- Identifies specific people who are most likely to be interested in the product or service;

- Advertises to them, usually through selective media, such as direct mail; and

- Makes an offer (such as a trial period, a premium, a reduced price, etc.) that will move them to inquire or order.

Very likely, the product is then delivered or arrangements for the service are completed through the mail or via telephone contact.

While the overall concept of direct marketing is not new—it goes back at least to the 1870s when mail order catalogs came into vogue—it has been expanding very rapidly in recent years. That has been caused by a combination of social, economic and technological developments. New technologies—notably the computer, the availability of toll-free 800 numbers (as a way to place orders), and the credit card (which makes it easier to arrange payment at a distance)—have combined as strong forces in the growth of the direct marketing field. However, they have also coincided with lifestyle changes that make direct marketing increasingly attractive to many people —women whose careers give them far less time for shopping, senior citizens who find it convenient to shop without leaving home, people who travel frequently, and many others—all of whom find direct shopping ideal for their needs.

As a result of this convergence of technological capability and lifestyle market opportunities, direct marketing has enjoyed substantial expansion. Although precise figures are difficult to pinpoint, observers seem to agree that direct marketing has grown at a rate of at least 10% annually in recent years.

This increasing role for direct marketing has created related growth in opportunities for direct response advertising agencies. These organizations provide services to clients in much the same way that general ad agencies do, but direct response agencies are specialists in that particular type of advertising.

Typically, direct response advertising agencies assist their clients by providing or arranging for research (marketing, opinion, etc.); developing marketing and advertising goals and strategies; recommending media; and creating advertising (by recommending concepts, copy, art, etc.). In these functions, they are similar to general advertising agencies.

However, in part because direct response advertising often includes direct mail programs, other specialized services are also provided. These include: selecting and renting mailing lists, setting up telephone marketing programs, and maintaining computerized databases. Some direct response agencies have "in-house" facilities and operations to produce mailing pieces and send them out (not an inconsiderable service when millions of pieces may be mailed for a single client).

Some agencies have developed extensive computerized database capabilities to store mailing lists, demographic data, lifestyle information, etc. This information can then be used to provide clients with market analyses, to "personalize" mailings (for example, by incorporating the recipient's name in the text of a letter), or other services.

Entry-Level Opportunities In Direct Response Agencies

Most entry-level jobs in direct response advertising agencies fall into one of the three basic organizational areas: *account service, creative* and *media*. And we will go into more detail about these three areas in the next sections. But there are also functions which should be considered as potential areas of opportunities: *mechanical production* (working with printers, lettershops, etc. to prepare mail pieces or advertising material for publications); *traffic* (following client projects through the various departments to expedite and assure that deadlines are met); or *administrative positions* in such areas as accounting. In larger agencies, these functions may offer long-term career tracks; in smaller agencies, they may be a way to gain familiarity with the field and serve, in time, as an "inside track" to the account service, creative or media functions.

Account Service

Account service people are responsible for working directly with client staffers. They serve as the link between the specialized service departments in the agency (creative, media, production, research) and the direct marketing managers, advertising managers, or other prime contacts in the client organization.

They are typically in almost daily contact with clients—in person, by telephone, or in writing—to define marketing and advertising objectives, to explore marketing opportunities or concerns, and to develop campaigns or programs that are aimed at the objectives and appropriate to the opportunities or concerns. Based on these contacts, account people provide information to the agency's service departments so that recommendations can be developed and presented to the client. It is, ideally, a continuous, two-way dialogue.

The typical entry-level job in this area is *assistant account executive,* who is responsible for supporting the day-to-day activities of account management. Duties often include budget control, schedule administration, report writing, trafficking. Essentially, they are account executives "in training."

Creative Services

In a direct response advertising agency, much like general agencies, the creative staff has responsibility for developing concepts and ideas, writing copy, and creating art (layouts, illustrations, etc.) or obtaining it from outside sources.

One of the unique characteristics of direct response advertising, which offers special challenges and satisfactions to creative people—and for that matter, to others in the agency—is the *measurability* of direct response. The response to a mailing piece, a print advertisement with an order coupon, or a TV commercial with a toll-free telephone number—i.e., the number of people who reply to the offer—can be *counted.*

So it is possible to set targets and to determine whether or not they were met. And it is also possible to compare the results of one creative approach to another.

This ability—to almost *immediately* determine results—stands in marked contrast to general advertising, where the measurement of results may be based on slower and usually less-precise opinion studies, audits of product purchases in stores, etc.

A typical entry-level job is *junior copywriter,* who is responsible for generating simple copy (e.g. headlines) for a variety of products, services and/or markets. He or she learns to adapt to creative strategies, formats and/or media. and is, essentially, a copywriter "in training." (Similar positions would be available in allied departments, e.g. art department assistants, TV department assistants, etc.)

In the specialized function of creative material for television, the creative responsibilities and organization are likely to vary, depending on the size of the agency. In nearly all cases, the agency's creative staff develops the *storyboards*—frame-by-frame recommendations for the visual and audio elements of the commercial.

If the agency is a smaller one, most of the steps from there on are likely to be turned over to an outside supplier to arrange for talent, production, direction, music and so forth. In larger agencies, some or all of these responsibilities may be within the agency's own capability or those of a parent general agency.

Media Services

The process of identifying, evaluating and selecting media, as well as negotiating contracts (for broadcast time), placing orders for space, renting mailing lists, etc., is the responsibility of the direct response agency's media staff. It is a function that depends heavily on perceptive analysis and judgement, combined with the ability to successfully administer detailed procedures and recordkeeping systems.

Media people work closely with the account staff, and perhaps with clients, to develop media plans which direct advertising to target audiences with the greatest possible precision and cost efficiency. Because response is measurable, media options can be tested and comparisons made as the agency seeks an "ideal" media mix for a client's campaigns.

There are two typical entry-level positions in a direct response advertising agency media department: media buyer and broadcast buyer.

The *media buyer* is responsible for the day-to-day implementation of media selections within a specialized area (e.g., consumer vs. trade magazines or newspapers vs. magazines, etc.). He or she negotiates suitable positions in the media, purchases space, gathers media research and other pertinent data to support media selections, and releases insertion orders.

The *broadcast buyer* is responsible for purchasing direct response time on a preemptive basis (i.e., at lower rates because the station is given leeway to decide when to run the commercial) for assigned accounts. He or she negotiates rates and clears time, establishes a working rapport with station management, and becomes, essentially, a "market specialist."

Where Are These Agencies Located?

The geographic pattern of direct response agencies tends to parallel that of general agencies. In fact, nearly all of the largest direct response agencies are units of even larger general agencies. The biggest concentration is in New York City, with Chicago also well-represented. But many specialized direct response agencies can be found in such major cities as Los Angeles, Boston and Philadelphia.

However, as interest in direct marketing increases, direct response agency services are being offered in nearly all parts of the country. In medium-sized and smaller cities, there may only be one or two specialized direct response agencies, but many general agencies are establishing departments or other groups within their overall organizational structure to provide such services.

The Advantages Of The Agency Side

College graduates embarking on careers in the direct response field may wonder whether they are best advised to start with a client organization or can develop better experience in an agency. While there are advantages in either course, the most obvious one an agency offers is *diversity*. This is particularly true at the smaller direct response agencies. Newcomers to the field often have the opportunity to be involved with a variety of different accounts, gaining insights from a variety of marketing situations and strategies.

In a similar fashion, there are opportunities in agencies of various sizes to move, in time, from one function to another. For example, someone starting in the media department is likely to develop skills that may later translate into a job in account service. In smaller agencies, where there also fewer staff members, positions are also likely to combine various responsibilities. Thus, an entry-level person in a small agency media department may have responsibilities in both print and broadcast media.

Long-Term Potential

The rapid growth of the direct marketing field over the past decade or so has created a rather severe shortage of experienced people. As a result, capable and well-motivated new people coming into the field have tended to make relatively quick progress, moving from entry-level positions to those with substantial responsibility in a shorter time than one might normally expect at a general ad agency. There are numerous examples in the direct marketing field of men or women who have, within five years of graduation, found themselves in middle-management spots as agency account executives or as list managers, direct marketing managers of departments or product areas on the client side, or in other challenging and rewarding career situations.

We encourage you to explore direct marketing as a career path you may want to pursue. For additional information, please contact the Direct Marketing Educational Foundation, 6 East 43rd Street, New York, NY 10017.

JONAH GITLITZ has been president and CEO of the Direct Marketing Association since February, 1985. He joined DMA in 1981 as senior vice president-public affairs, responsible for the association's extensive government relations programs and public affairs activities. As president, he has continued his deep involvement with government affairs and broad-based public relations efforts to strengthen the field.

Prior to joining DMA, Mr. Gitlitz was executive vice president of the American Advertising Federation for 12 years. While there, he contributed to the development of the National Advertising Review Board, the highly respected, self-regulatory mechanism that deals with national advertising complaints. He was also responsible for the development of the AAF college chapter program and served as president of the Advertising Educational Foundation.

Mr. Gitlitz currently serves as chairman of the American Advertising Federation's Inter-Association Council and on the board of directors of the Council of Better Business Bureaus, the Advertising Council and the American Advertising Federation. He has served on numerous industry and business committees.

A native New Yorker, he is a graduate of the American University, Washington, D.C.

14

Direct Mail: The Personal Medium

C. Rose Harper, Chairman & CEO
The Kleid Company, Inc.

That people buy by mail is beyond dispute. The explosive growth (U.S. and abroad) of direct mail supports this premise. The reasons are as varied as the products sold, though "convenience" appears to be the most common.

The most critical factor affecting receptivity is the type of product or service being offered: It is a combination of the right product with the right message to the *target* prospect that counts. This suggests that mail campaigns must be designed to achieve the required results with the smallest total mailing quantity. The ability to *target market* is a plus for direct mail.

Lists: The "Medium" In Direct Mail

A mailing list consists of the names and addresses of people or companies that have one or more things in common. Such a list is said to represent a *meaningful grouping*.

By selecting the proper list, a direct marketer can mail an offer to prospects who have already demonstrated an interest in a particular type of product or service or have demographic and lifestyle characteristics implying a high probability of interest. For example, someone selling toys would select lists of families with at least one child who had previously bought juvenile items (books, records, magazines, clothing, etc.) or "parenting" products. Lacking demonstrated evidence of children in the home, you might luck out once in every 15 to 20 list tests, but that's very expensive research.

Two Broad Categories Of Lists

Internal lists are a company's files, which may include customers, former customers, prospects, inquiries, sales contacts, warranty cards, etc.

External lists include direct response lists (internal files) and compiled lists.

Review Of Lists By Market Categories

Within these broad categories are a number of defined list markets. And within each of *these* categories, even more well-defined sub-categories:

Category	Number of Lists	Universe (in thousands)
Business & Finance	1,195	338,800
New Technology	374	50,338
Educational/Scientific/Professional	171	15,444
Fund Raising	180	75,755
Hobbies & Special Interests	1,101	299,047
Entertainment	457	144,742
Reading	462	109,193
Self-Improvement/Health/Religious	613	252,774
Women/Home Interest/Family/Gen. Merch.	908	607,031
SUB TOTAL	**5,461**	**1,893,124**
Mixed Media	257	309,350
Telephone Marketing	477	957,939
Compiled	170	265,178
Canadian	394	111,979
Foreign	54	6,191
TOTAL	**6,813**	**3,543,761**

List availability, as you can see, is substantial...which is why mailers need list brokers.

The Players In Direct Mail

Companies that serve both the mailer and the owner are known as *list brokers* (or *list marketing consultants*. They identify the list markets that appear to have an affinity for the products or services of the users (mailers).

Some brokers may also prepare mail plans for clients and project response through cost-per-order. Projecting a direct mail campaign means anticipating what is likely to happen by determining which elements will most likely influence the outcome. Computer technicians, statisticians and mathematicians have devised an impressive array of techniques to accomplish this task.

A *list manager* represents lists on an exclusive basis and is responsible for all promotions of the lists and record keeping.

List compilers are manufacturers, generating lists from a variety of printed sources—directories, trade show registrants, membership rosters, telephone books, auto registrations, college student directories, etc.

Service bureaus process the lists being used in a mailing through a system that identifies duplicate names. No one wants to mail an expensive package to the same person or place more than one time. They may also supply a variety of sophisticated marketing data.

Letter shops are responsible for getting the mailing to the post office on time and in the mailing sequence the post office requires.

Direct response agencies are primarily responsible for the creative function. They create the mailing package, space ads, TV and radio commercials.

List Testing

TEST is the most frequently-used word in the direct mail lexicon; it's rare that any mailer uses a list in its entirety without testing. The proper sample size is determined by two factors: sampling tolerance (or deviation) and the degree of risk that the user is willing to accept. As long as we have perfectly random samples, we can keep sampling tolerance small by taking large samples. This part of the equation is scientific. The risk factor is much harder to deal with because this involves subjective judgements. Some companies can't tolerate much risk.

List testing, unfortunately, is not conducted under laboratory conditions. For starters, we can't get a true random sampling. The best we can do is an "nth" name sample. The universal practice is to reconfirm the test with a larger sample. Actually, this type of sequential sampling is reliable because you can schedule quantities on each successive usage in an orderly fashion, supported by monitored results, thus controlling and minimizing the risk.

Response Analysis

The attractiveness of direct mail is measurability—the moment of truth comes when the results are in. Here is a summary of a magazine publisher's new subscription offer and the various data that is obtained and analyzed:

Actual Mail Quantity	150,040
Number of Orders	3,256
Percent Response	2.17
Package Cost per thousand mailed (M)	$180.00
List Cost per M	$45.56
Total Cost per M	$225.56
Total Cost	$33,843
Gross Cost per Subscriber	$10.39
Percent Credit	90.4
Percent Bad Pay	28.1
Net Subscribers	2,428
Net Percent Response	1.61
Net Cost per Subscriber	$13.93
Total Revenue (on Net)	$43,702
Net Revenue (Total Revenue minus Cost)	$9,859
Net Revenue per Subscriber	$4.06

These discriminants (and more, depending on the product being offered) are calculated on a list-by-list basis.

The big players in direct marketing are: publishers (books, magazines and newsletters); book & record clubs; financial services; insurance companies; catalogs; retailers; business-to-business marketers; and fund-raising organizations. These players are both the "users" and, in most instances, are also list owners. Almost *every* company now uses direct mail.

Opportunities For You In Direct Marketing

Direct mail offers an interesting and diversified choice of career paths. In most instances, entry-level positions are relatively clerical, but afford the opportunity to learn the business. Salary levels range from $18,000 to $23,000, though someone with technical training who could move right into a technical position and earn more.

Where do such entry-level positions lead? At list agencies, list managers, compilers and direct response agencies, job titles would include *account executive, sales representative, data processing manager, manager-information systems* and *copywriter* (particularly in direct response agencies).

At book, magazine and newsletter publishers, insurance and financial services, fund raisers and catalogers, representative jobs are *circulation manager, marketing director, product manager, analyst* and *direct mail manager*.

At a service bureau, you may become an *analyst, manager-information systems* or *data processing manager*.

At most such companies, it would take from three to five years to reach the titles shown above. Salary range: $35,000 to $50,000 or more depending on the ability of the individual.

Recommended college courses include: Direct Marketing, Marketing, Advertising, Finance, Research, Statistics, Computer Science, Mathematics and Liberal Arts (particularly for creative positions).

For Additional Information

Contact any of the following:

Direct Marketing Association, Inc.
6 East 43rd Street—12th Floor
New York, NY 10017

Direct Marketing Educational Foundation, Inc.
6 East 43rd Street—12th Floor
New York, NY 10017

New York University (Center for Direct Marketing)
48 Cooper Square
New York, NY 10003

Note: Some of the material in this article was taken from my book, <u>Mailing List Strategies: A Guide to Direct Mail Success</u>, published by McGraw-Hill in 1986.

C. ROSE HARPER served as chairman of the board of the Direct Marketing Association (DMA) and also four years as treasurer, the first woman to serve in either capacity. She was inducted into the Direct Marketing Hall of Fame in 1985—the first woman so honored. The Kleid Company is considered one of the most professional list marketing consulting firms and is heavily involved in direct mail planning and analysis for many prominent magazines and book publishers.

Mrs. Harper serves on the boards of the Direct Marketing Educational Foundation, Direct Marketing Idea Exchange and the NYU Center for Direct Marketing.

Her book—Mailing List Strategies: A Guide to Direct Mail Success—was published by McGraw-Hill in March, 1986; it is now in its fifth printing. It was selected by *Library Journal* as one of the best business books published in 1986.

15

Career Opportunities In Database Marketing

David Shepard, President
David Shepard Associates, Inc.

Right now, there are probably hundreds of thousands of students who are thinking about a career in business, marketing, advertising or sales. I dare say only a handful of them are considering a career in database marketing.

The reason for this is simple: Database marketing is a relatively new field, one that grew out of the larger but still relatively unheard-of field of direct marketing. If you asked a hundred students if they were familiar with direct marketing, if they knew what people in direct marketing did, I bet the vast majority would look at you with a blank stare.

In fact, nearly everyone *is* familiar with direct marketing—because we're almost all familiar with magazines, book clubs, mail order catalogs and those two-minute television commercials selling unbelievable record collections for only $9.95. All of these businesses and the people who work in them are in the direct marketing business, along with insurance, mutual funds, credit cards, travel, homes, clothing, food, business supplies, computers, copiers, telephone systems. You name the business, and there's a better-than-even chance that direct marketing plays a role in the distribution of that businesses' products and services.

Typical Direct Marketing Problem— Launching A Catalog

I still haven't explained what database marketing is all about, but before I do, let me go on for a little more about direct marketing, specifically direct *mail* marketing. Let's imagine that you have searched far and wide to develop a collection of hard-to-find sports souvenirs—bubble gum cards, programs, baseballs, bats, helmets, basketballs, equipment, old sporting magazines, tickets, uniforms—you name it, anything a sports fan would treasure and buy by mail. Let's further suppose you displayed all of the items you'd managed to find in an attractive catalog. Who would you mail it to?

Deciding What Lists To Rent

"What lists do I rent?" is probably the most important question anyone in direct mail can ask. In the old days, before database marketing, the answer would be relatively simple—you would sit down with a list broker and together decide on which lists to rent. You would then send your catalog to the names on those rented lists, perhaps *Sports Illustrated* subscribers, high school coaches, persons who had bought running shoes by mail, season ticket holders, etc In each case, you would be assuming that someone who bought other sports-related items would probably be interested in your catalog of sports souvenirs.

Keeping Track Of Who Responded

After you mailed your catalog, you would keep careful track of everyone who responded and slowly start building your own list of buyers. The next time you mailed your catalog, you would certainly mail it again to those that responded to it the first time.

Typical Direct Mail Results

This kind of relatively straightforward method typified the direct mail industry for years. Direct mail sellers would rent lists, mail their catalogs, and, if they were successful, receive a response of somewhere between 1% and 3%. When they mailed to previous customers, they would achieve a higher response rate, somewhere between 5% and 10%.

Fortunately mail order sellers could make a profit at these low levels of response.

A Short History Of Database Marketing

In the late 1960s and early '70s, changes began to take place in the computer industry, changes that would radically alter the way direct mail sellers would run their businesses and transform them into database marketers.

Here's just one example: One of the problems with renting lists and mailing to everyone on them is that many people are on more than one list. Many people, for example, subscribe to two, three, five or even more magazines. If you thought magazine subscribers were good candidates for you product, you may have wound up mailing to the same people many times. The computer and sophisticated computer software helped solve this problem. Instead of just renting lists and mailing them, you could rent lots of lists, merge them together, eliminate names that appeared on more than one list and save lots of money.

Turning A List Into A Marketing Database

During the '70s and '80s, some direct marketing companies began to build massive lists of people, lists that included nearly every household in the United States. They contained not only name and address information, but other data like birth dates, the car each person drove, how long he or she had lived at a certain address, the census area he or she lived in, government estimates on the average income of people living in that zip code, how many years of school people in that zip code completed, how they earned their living and on and on.

These massive lists were called databases, and they gave direct marketers access to the detailed information they needed to target their customers as never before. If your research, for example, revealed that of all the people you mailed to, men between the ages of 45 and 55 were by far the best respondents, wouldn't it make sense to target such men in any future mailings? Of course it would. That's *database marketing* or, at least, the tip of the database marketing iceberg.

The process I referred to above—matching your database against someone else's database and adding their information to your database—is referred to as *database enhancement.* There's a whole segment of the direct marketing industry working full-time to make more and more such information available to direct marketers.

Using The Information You Obtain

The central idea of database marketing is that the more information you know about your customers or people you would like to have as customers, the smarter you can be about your marketing activities. You can mail your existing products to people who tend to match the profile of your current customers. And even develop new products to meet the needs of those prospects with characteristics that *differ* from your current customer base.

Database Marketing Today

Today there are hundreds, perhaps even thousands, of direct marketing companies with their own databases of customers. The most sophisticated, advanced companies know a great deal about their customers—what products they bought, when, and in response to which particular direct mail offer or advertisement. They know the promotions their customers received in the past and whether they responded or not. They know a lot of other things about their customers from research questionnaires and by matching their databases with other data bases. And they use all of this information in deciding what offers to make in the future, what products to sell and how to present and price them. This entire process is modern database marketing.

How To Enter The Field

If database marketing sounds interesting and challenging to you, then carefully consider the following points about necessary preparation.

Study General Marketing & Advertising

As with most professions a college education is essential; a graduate degree in business always helps. While not all colleges offer separate courses in direct marketing, most basic marketing courses include sections on direct marketing. So it's advisable to take a broad range of marketing and advertising courses in preparation for a career in direct marketing.

I would also recommend taking one or two courses in market research. More and more direct marketers are adding information gathered from market research to their customer data bases, and it's important to understand how this data is collected and to be able to distinguish good research from bad.

Take Statistics And Computer Courses

But direct marketing *does* differ from general marketing in a number of ways, and these differences mean skills in areas other than general marketing and advertising are required.

For one, direct marketing is very "numbers oriented." General advertisers spend their money on some mix of television, radio, magazine and newspaper ads, hoping that their message gets across and that shoppers buy their products as a result. But no matter which medium they use, it's very hard to measure the effect of each ad or even all of them. Direct marketers have it easy. They know how many catalogs they sent out and how many responses they received. Or how much that couponed magazine cost and how many filled-out coupons they received back. Direct marketing generates *lots* of numbers or statistics.

The best direct marketers are *very* comfortable with numbers and technology. So it's advisable you take at least one (and preferably more) statistics course and to be familiar with computers—how they work and what they can do for you.

Where To Start Your Career

The direct marketing industry is basically divided into two parts: 1) those companies that sell products or services (catalog companies, book and record clubs, magazine publishers, insurance companies, financial services companies, fund raisers, etc.) and 2) those that sell services to the these direct marketing companies (advertising agencies, list brokers, list managers, computer service bureaus, printers, etc.).

My personal recommendation would be to start with a large direct marketing company or advertising agency where you could expect to receive wide exposure to a variety of jobs in a relatively short period of time. After you've gained some experience, you may choose to concentrate in some particular specialty within the direct marketing industry. The Direct Marketing Association maintains compete files on all companies in the industry and is very helpful in assisting students that are interested in a career in any area of direct marketing.

DAVID SHEPARD founded DSA, Inc., a direct marketing consulting firm, in 1976. The company counts among its clients a variety of traditional direct marketing firms, advertising agencies, and many Fortune 500 firms new to the direct marketing business.

Previously, Mr. Shepard held a number of management positions in the Book Club Division of Doubleday & Co., including business manager, director of product management, and vice president-new ventures.

He is a graduate of CCNY and has an M.B.A from Columbia University. Mr. Shepard is a frequent speaker at Direct Marketing Association events, has taught the Direct Marketing Policy course at NYU's School of Continuing Education, and is currently conducting seminars on behalf of the DMA. He was chairman of the DMA's Marketing Council and has written numerous articles on the economics of direct marketing.

16

Getting Into A Corporate Advertising Department

Claudia E. Marshall, Vice President-
Marketing & Communication Services
The Travelers Companies

In some ways, it has never been harder to break into the advertising business, but in *most* ways, it has never been a more exciting business to be in. Over the last 10 to 15 years, the role of advertising agencies has been changing.

In the past, many large corporations looked to their external ad agencies to initiate recommendations about where they should be going and what they should be doing. With business needs changing, becoming increasingly complex, seemingly every day, the client/agency relationship is becoming more of a marketing partnership.

Strategic marketing directions must come from the corporation. The agency must play an increasingly important executional role, focusing on the complexity of creative strategies, media buying and production.

More and more agency account service people who see themselves as broad-gauged marketing people are making the transition to corporations. They see this transition as a way of really getting into a business and having more influence in making advertising work.

If you have already decided that you want to work in a corporate advertising department, there are a couple of routes you can take. First, remember that the primary role of the corporate advertising department is to direct the out-of-house agency, and *that* means you have to know something about the advertising business.

The best way to get that knowledge, obviously, is to work in an agency for a few years in a variety of capacities and learn everything you can. You can also take a more circuitous route—working in a corporate sales or product management support capacity and then moving over to its advertising and marketing services area.

Corporate Advertising Department Setup

The structure of an advertising department varies by company size and other factors. The Travelers department operates on two levels—the corporate advertising program and the in-house agency.

The corporate advertising function develops the positioning strategy for the corporate brand which, in turn, supports the culture and identity of the corporation by reinforcing other product advertising done in the company. Its main responsibility is to direct the out-of-house agency in the development and execution of the corporation's advertising.

The in-house ad agency takes many functions of the ad agency and performs them within the corporate boundaries. Their only client is the corporation and its various lines of business, for which the internal shop produces collateral material, sales promotion and advertising.

The attractiveness of using an in-house agency, rather than "farming everything out" is due to the in-house staff's familiarity with the business, the responsiveness that comes from close proximity, and the ability to maintain close control over costs.

The account service jobs in an in-house operation are essentially the same as those at any ad agency. The titles may vary, but a typical entry-level position is *account coordinator* (or *assistant account executive*), who makes sure each job gets done on time by staying in touch with his or her agency counterparts in creative, traffic and production. Next in line is the *account executive,* also an implementer, but one already starting to get involved in the planning process. Above that is the *account supervisor,* who is accountable for strategic planning on specific portions of a client's business. On top is the *management supervisor* (or *account director*), who takes charge of the overall account and works with the account supervisor on planning, administrative issues, staffing, trouble-shooting and problem-solving.

As you rise through the ranks in account service and the pressure of constant deadlines increases, you will see that advertising is not the glamorous and slick profession that some people think. The long hours and (initially) low pay will test your commitment to the business. If you choose to stick it out, the later rewards—in terms of both personal satisfaction and income potential—can be very gratifying.

The Right Preparation

In most cases, it is pretty difficult to break into a corporate advertising department right out of college because, as I already emphasized, the key role of account service people in a corporate advertising department is to supervise the outside agency. This requires both a good, disciplined, general understanding of marketing and specific knowledge about the business to which you are going to apply it, since the legal and technical problems faced by advertisers have become increasingly important. You also need to have a solid understanding of the technical aspects of advertising—production, media planning, traffic procedures, and how to set advertising objectives.

What I look for when hiring account managers is roughly three to seven years of agency experience. These numbers are not written in stone. A college internship in communications and some extra coursework in marketing or advertising might compensate for less agency time. I strongly urge students who want to work in corporate advertising to get into an agency right out of college. Do anything you can to get in the door—from administrative work to media coordination to research assistant—and use whatever skills you can muster to get exposure to an agency relationship. From there, either keep changing jobs within that agency or move to other agencies in an attempt to keep strengthening your marketing and strategic planning skills and gain exposure to a number of different businesses. As you gain experience, shoot for an account management slot.

The Corporate Route

Depending on your drives and personal ambitions, working your way up from a product management role in a company to its advertising department may be the most logical approach for you. By the time you attempt such a move, you will have been fully steeped in the corporate culture and learned the company's business, products, distribution channels and marketing methodologies.

Your company background can enhance your reputation as a subject-matter expert and boost your credibility with product managers. It may also clarify your perspective about what type of marketing/communications support is needed.

Advertising is the final link in the marketing chain, and it is a logical place in the company for you to round out your marketing career. The buck, in a sense, stops here. The product and pricing setup has been established, and your previous experience in the product area gives you added insight in advising clients about choosing markets, media, and creative strategies.

The Traditional Agency Route

If you really want to get a dose of "street smarts" before coming to work for a client company, I strongly advise you to work on the agency side for a few years. The ability to understand both sides of the fence is, I think, invaluable. After all, from a corporate standpoint, you have to be able to guide the agency in terms of what can and can't be done, where the corporation stands on certain issues, and what business opportunities the corporation wants to push and/or avoid. Accountability is a recurring issue, as your credibility is on the line regularly—with clients, the agency, even your own management.

If you're getting ready to graduate, you might get started in a small or mid-sized agency, working as a "jack (or jill) of all trades." This will enable you to do a little bit of everything and be exposed to as many facets of the business as possible—copywriting, media estimating, strategic planning, and client contact. If you have a graduate business degree, you may be able to get right into a training program in one of the larger agencies where you will receive formal training in various agency departments—media, market research, traffic and production.

Getting a broad smattering of agency experience—print and broadcast, packaged goods, etc.— and handling a variety of accounts, from breakfast cereals to liquor to real estate, will make you increasingly "merchandisable." The real-life experience you gain working for different clients and learning about different businesses will serve you well on the corporate side. After all, there is nothing wrong with going to work for a financial services company and applying a communications strategy that worked well for the razor blade account your agency worked on!

Broad and varied agency experience will teach you how to provide solid marketing communications support for any kind of business.

Personal Traits

An equally important skill you acquire from agency life is *flexible people skills*. This comes in handy in a corporate setting where you interact with a large assortment of people, some of whom support your area and some of whom do *not*. Always remember that advertising is a service business—your success depends on your cooperation with and sensitivity to many different kinds of people.

A high level of *adaptability* is also called for. If you are moving to the corporate side in search of a haven of stability and a respite from the high pressure and long hours of agency life, you may be disappointed. Mergers, acquisitions, and extensive new product development are becoming everyday facts of life in corporations, so you must be amenable to change.

You'll need an *even temperament* to manage and give direction to a broad range of people, bring order to frequently chaotic situations, and deal with ambiguity. You must also be adept at selling ideas and translating vague concepts into specific directions for creative people.

Strong *analytical skills*, perhaps honed in an agency's media department, will help you decipher technical product information so you can communicate intelligently with clients about their business.

The ability to *listen* well is also an asset. You must be able to get clients to open up with you about their marketing objectives and strategies in order to design the most effective marketing communications plan for them, one that helps them position their products in the marketplace and distinguish them from competitors'. What do we want people to think about us when they see our advertising?

Whether you are developing the overall corporate advertising campaign or promoting one of the company's product lines, you have to be willing to *take risks*. You must be willing to support the agency's recommendations, even if they seem radical, if it has followed through on your directions. Similarly, you must be able to send the agency back to the drawing board when you think it is off the mark. That means having *confidence* in your own judgment and being *knowledgeable* about what is going on in the company and in the marketplace.

Education

An undergraduate degree with a major in communications or business, especially marketing, is good preparation for an advertising career. If you choose to go the business route— which will set you ahead in terms of basic business knowledge—be sure to include some technical communications courses like advertising, journalism, broadcasting and public relations. Similarly, if you decide to concentrate in the liberal arts, perhaps majoring in English or history, be sure to supplement them with courses in technical communications and marketing.

If you choose to pursue an advanced degree in either business or communications, I strongly urge you to get some "practical" experience first in an ad agency. This will not only expose you to the business and show you what skills you need to develop further, but should help you decide what area of specialization is best for you. It may also convince you to pick another profession!

A Typical Day Is Atypical

It's hard to describe a "typical" day in a corporate advertising department. There are client consultations, "blue sky" sessions with the agency, time spent with associates in creative, production and traffic, and meetings with your management. There is a great deal of time and energy spent on getting approvals, on everything from strategies to final artwork. In some ways, you could look upon the corporate advertising function as the great gatekeeper for the approval process.

In her current position, **CLAUDIA E. MARSHALL** manages over 100 marketing and communications professionals serving the corporation and its products. She joined The Travelers in 1983 as vice president of advertising and marketing services.

Prior to joining Travelers, she was vice president at Chase Manhattan Bank in New York. She was with the bank for 11 years in a number of executive marketing and communications positions. Ms. Marshall also worked as a marketing representative for the IBM Corporation in the New York financial area.

Ms. Marshall is a nationally known speaker in the marketing and communication field. She is a director of the Association of National Advertisers, a trustee of the Marketing Science Institute, and a steering committee director of the American Marketing Association. She has published numerous books and articles, including Developing New Services (1983) and Creativity in Services Marketing (1985).

She holds an M.B.A. in finance from New York University and a B.A. in mathematics and English (cum laude) from Cedar Crest College. She also received an M.A. in communication from Michigan State University, where she was a professor of mass communication and research methods.

Section 3

The Advertising Scene Outside New York

17

Boston: A City Of Tradition In Transition

George J. Hill III, Chairman/Worldwide Creative Director
Hill, Holliday, Connors, Cosmopulos, Inc.

There are about 2,250,000 people in the Greater Boston area.

Most of them wouldn't want to be anyplace else.

Because Boston is, above all, a livable city. But you already knew that.

More importantly, it's a city of tradition that has always been involved in the process of change. Boston is not just liveable—it's adjustable; it's demonstrated over and over how to adjust and prosper in the face of all kinds of social and economic conditions.

This constant change has strengthened the character of native Bostonians, even as it has attracted a steady flow of newcomers into the region.

What's Great About Boston...

Boston is no longer defined by city or county lines. It is a state of mind—an attitude of success—whose work force relies just as strongly on commuters from southern New Hampshire as it does on residents of the Back Bay.

There is a legacy of education that gives Boston a cosmopolitan cultural heritage. On any given night, presidential candidates may be gathering at Harvard's Kennedy School for an evening of political platforming; across the bridge at Boston University, a ballet ensemble from China is offering its only American performance; down the road a bit, at Boston College, a forum on global economic interdependence is about to begin; in the Fens, 300 business leaders from all parts of the country have assembled at Simmons College to evaluate the role woken play in industrial management.

It's a typical night in Boston. And, typically, there are also sellout crowds at Symphony Hall, Boston Garden, the Wang Opera Center and Fenway Park.

The movie theaters—current and revival—are offering two evening shows. The bookstores are open late. There are new (affordable) restaurants all over the South End. Jake Wirth's is handing out the same special brew dark beer it has served to generations of Bostonians. And, at Durgin Park, waitresses are handing out the insults they've featured as a *specialite de maison* for the last 50 years.

The remarkable fact is that the entire populace will recover from this nighttime spontaneity and arrive at the office bushy-tailed (if not bright-eyed) the next morning.

If you want all the rewards Boston has to offer, you should count yourself among the early risers. The city's universities attract students as well as evening-seminar audiences. And many of the good ones decide they like the place well enough to stick around for a few formative years.

They enter the job market with a head start: Some of them have had internships; they've all been able to make interview appointments and get an early line on some of the better positions. If they pay attention to the local press—*Adweek*/New England can be found in most school libraries and both the *Globe* and *Herald* regularly cover the advertising scene—they already know who's hot (and hiring).

...And The Boston Advertising Scene

They also will have learned that Boston is a city of three large agencies and about 30 terrific smaller ones. And they all know each other. In other advertising centers, agency people tend to hang out in small corporate clusters. There's a BBDO bar, a JWT restaurant, an Ogilvy coffee shop. Boston is much looser. With a strong advertising club as an organizational force, there are monthly lunches where names can be attached to faces. After work, a place like Joe's American Bar & Grill will probably have customers from a couple of dozen different agencies. As fierce as their business competition during the day, by night they're swapping war stories and picking up one another's tab.

The familiarity is not contemptuous. These people from disparate agencies not only unwind together, they've often spent a great deal of time working together. Leaving one agency for another is not an occasion for self-immunization, as it often is in other parts of the world. Indeed, there's a civilized conviviality that allows former colleagues to quietly toast their comrades' successes.

If there's one characteristic that separates Boston advertising from work done in other parts of the country, it's the superior brand of creative work done for regional accounts. The great work is not just being done for the national advertiser who throws a gargantuan budget at a network television campaign. In New England, the gourmet grocery chain gets terrific work from its local advertising agency, as does the local car dealership association or the hometown newspaper.

Boston is a young city and one of young businesses—10% of its advertising agencies have been in business less than two years; another 30% were founded after 1980. Only a third of the advertising agencies were around before 1970. As the New England economy has thrived on entrepreneurial energies, so has the agency business. And the funds are there to encourage further growth and expansion.

The Advertising Club of Boston has sampled its membership for the last five years, with specific emphasis on billings growth. Last year, the responding agencies represented approximately two thirds of the Greater Boston advertising community. They reported handling a total of $1,071,700,000 in billings—a 22.5% growth over the previous year.

"This strong growth rate indicates that the advertising community has successfully reacted to the downturn experienced by one of the industries (high tech) responsible for its growth," the Ad Club reported.

The dollar volume was generated by a mix of clients that reflects the diversity of the larger New England economy. Over 30 Boston agencies handle communications services for over 100 of the *"Fortune* 500" and "Service 500" accounts. Most agencies handle three or fewer of these premium pieces of business. In fact, only four agencies reported that they handled more than seven such accounts.

By and large, these agencies are not only Boston-born, but tend to stay in town, too—only 16% of the Ad Club agencies reported that they had any offices outside the city.

"This data indicates that agencies operating in the area entered the advertising industry in the Greater Boston area and have remained in the region," the Ad Club notes. "This indicates an optimism about the ability of the region's economy to provide future growth for agencies serving industries located in the Greater Boston area."

A very precise 2,144 people last year found employment at the 50 agencies included in the Ad Club survey. Nearly three quarters of the agencies employed fewer than 20 people. One fifth (22%) had fewer than ten people on their full-time payroll. Some 40% were in the mid-size range, with staffs of 20 - 65 people. More than half of the employees in the Greater Boston advertising community were accounted for by just five agencies, each with more than 100 people on staff.

Those are the parameters. But parameters certainly won't get you a job. The fact that the agency business is thriving in Boston doesn't do you much good if you find your only source of remuneration on the unemployment line.

How To Get A Job By The Bay

With your first appointment, make an impression. And that means more than showing up with a resume and a bunch of references from marketing professors.

Study local advertising. Find stuff that you like. Spend an afternoon at the Boston Public Library with The Standard Directory of Advertisers; an index at the front of this formidable red tome makes the information inside easily accessible. If you like an ad, use the Directory to find out who created it. Come up with a list of advertising agencies you respect, whose work you believe in, whose product most impresses you.

Use that list (and the important information in the *Job Opportunities Databank* in the back of this *Career Directory)* as your starting point. Then get on the telephone and make some appointments. The larger offices will have personnel offices (sometimes under the heady title of "human resources"). The smaller shops will have someone knowledgeable at the switchboard. If you've been particularly impressed for the work they've done for Sam's Restaurant, ask to speak to someone who works on the Sam's account.

By and large, they'll be flattered to learn that the source of your phone call is admiration for their work, not the reference of a second cousin on an account executive's mother's side. Sure, you are bound to get your head chewed off by some people, but they're the ones who've forgotten that *they* once had to go out and look for a first job.

The lesson is simple: Arrive at an office with more than just a few facts about yourself—show up with an educated interest in your potential employer.

Because the Boston advertising community is tight, a good first impression can take you a long way. If the people who handle Sam's don't have any jobs, they may well know of an agency down the street that has a few openings.

Jot down the name of the agency and head over to the offices of *ADWEEK*/New England. Treat yourself to a copy of the <u>New England Advertising Agency Directory</u>. Learn as much as you can about this other agency down the street. See who their clients are; find out what different kinds of communications services they provide.

You arrive on their doorstep not just with the recommendation from the people at Sam's agency, but with some smarts...only to find out that they want a writer and you only have a portfolio of art. Don't despair: As long as you keep informed, you'll keep building referrals. And that's a lot more interesting than the unemployment lines. Or becoming just another worker in industrial management.

A graduate of Harvard, **GEORGE J. HILL, III** began his career at BBDO. In 1968, he was a founding partner of Hill, Holliday, Connors, Cosmopulos, where he has spent the rest of his career.

18

Ad Makin' Town: The Advertising Scene In Chicago

Hall "Cap" Adams, Jr., Chairman & CEO
Leo Burnett Company, Inc.

Back in 1961, Leo Burnett penned a speech to his employees titled "Ad Makin' Town." It was a dissertation which proclaimed that Chicago was a force to be reckoned with. To quote Mr. Burnett:

"Unlike New York...which was a mythical place...Chicago is *real*. Now I don't intend to argue that Chicago is in any way a worthier city than say, New York. But I *am* suggesting our sod-busting delivery, our loose-limbed stand, and our wide-eyed perspective make it easier for us to create ads that talk turkey to the majority of Americans—that's all."

Hard hitting perhaps, but this chapter is about Chicago. And like me, Leo Burnett was in love with this city.

Chicago is the third largest advertising center in the world, ranked behind New York and Tokyo. But bigger does not necessarily mean better. And Chicago is plenty big enough.

In many ways, Chicago is no different than any other major advertising city, larger or smaller. Chicago advertising agencies create terrific advertising for their clients. Chicago advertising agencies recruit the best people available. And the Chicago advertising business is a tough one to break into.

A lot of noise was made a while back about Chicago's style of advertising. Back in July 1986, a headline from our own *Crain's Chicago Business* states: "If it's friendly and family, it's from Chicago." The story went on to describe the differences in advertising from Chicago, New York and Los Angeles.

At one time, I might have agreed with the theory of Chicago-style advertising. But today I challenge you to watch a reel of the nation's best advertising and pick out the individual ads produced in New York, Chicago or Los Angeles!

You see, another look will tell you that Chicago is no longer Carl Sandburg's "hog butchering capital of the world." We're a contemporary, progressive city—that's why major corporations have established worldwide headquarters within our city limits over the years. And Chicago agencies service many major national accounts, whether those clients operate out of neighborhood or from distant headquarters, companies like Anheuser Busch, Adolph Coors, General Mills, S.C. Johnson & Son, Kraft, Sears, McDonald's, Procter & Gamble, Philip Morris and Wrigley. The list goes on and on—you can find it in the <u>Advertiser Red Book</u>.

I mention just a few major accounts to emphasize that major advertisers have no reservations about trusting their products to Chicago agencies. If you come to work in this city, you will handle the same demanding national accounts as you would in New York.

What about finding a job in Chicago? The jobs are here. Chicago has more than 200 full-service advertising agencies. Foote Cone & Belding employs 650 people in its Chicago office, J. Walter Thompson 380, DDB Needham 600, Young & Rubicam 100, just to name a few. Burnett currently employs 2,050 people in its Chicago headquarters.

The same tough expectations exist here as anywhere else advertising is created,: If you are looking for a job on the account management side of the business, you are going to need a strong background in liberal arts or business. If you are looking for a job in creative, you're going to need a portfolio full of big ideas.

Of course, dynamic people study all sorts of things in college. What we look for is leadership. People who are active and successful in a lot of different areas.

Chicago is no longer considered the "advertising stepping-stone" to the "big time" of New York. If you come to Chicago, come to stay, and come prepared to play in the big leagues.

You might want to consider a few other Chicago realities. We are a city of extremes. Our August temperatures often reach 100 degrees and stay there for days. In January, wind-chill factors send the temperature plummeting, sometimes to less than 50 degrees below zero. However, in spite of such horror stories, Chicago's average temperature is a relatively moderate 49.2 degrees.

The average cost for a home in the Chicago metro area is $118,000. Average rent, $495.

There are some other things you should know before you buy your one-way ticket to the Windy City. For one thing, we are *not* the biggest city in the world. And while that may mean we're shy one or two major department stores, it also means we're more accessible. Our O'Hare Airport is one the of busiest in the world, and we are serviced by major train and bus lines.

What does that mean? It means that with a buck and a C.T.A. map, you can get from almost any point in our city to any other. That includes most of our suburbs. And because Chicago is smaller, our advertising row is more condensed: Most agencies are lined up along or adjacent to Michigan Avenue's Magnificent Mile.

In other words, pounding Chicago's pavement might be a little easier on your oxfords than in other major cities.

If you accept a job in Chicago, you can expect to spend an average of 60 minutes commuting daily. Of course, our Lincoln Park people can get to work within minutes. But our Barrington (a far-western suburb) and Indiana employees can spend as much as two hours traveling...one way.

So there you have it: A general overview of Chicago's climate, advertising and otherwise.

Naturally, the location you choose to live in is a matter of strict personal preference.

You should spend some time in any city you consider settling in.

Talk to the people who live there.

Compare.

Contrast.

Then move to Chicago.

And good luck!

HALL "CAP" ADAMS, JR. has been chairman and chief executive officer of Leo Burnett Company, Inc. since January 1, 1987. Previously he was chairman and CEO of the company's USA division, a position he assumed in 1982. Mr. Adams has been a member of the Leo Burnett Company's Board of Directors since 1977 and serves as chairman of its executive committee.

Mr. Adams, whose entire business career has been with Leo Burnett, started as a media research analyst in 1956. He was elected vice president in 1969, senior vice president in 1973, group vice president in 1979 and executive vice president/marketing services in 1981.

He is a director of the Advertising Council, the 4A's, the Chicago Council of Foreign Relations, Rush-Presbyterian St. Luke's Medical Center and Junior Achievement of Chicago. He is a member of the Chicago Central Area Committee and Northwestern University Associates, and is serving on the advisory council for the J.L. Kellogg Graduate School of Management.

A graduate of Williams College, Williamstown, Massachusetts, he served in the U.S. Army for two years. He is a resident of Winnetka, Illinois, and is married with two children.

19

Advertising In The Motor City

W. B. "Brod" Doner, Founder, Chairman—Executive Committee
W. B. Doner & Company Advertising

Our agency's largest office is in Detroit, Michigan, which immediately conjures up a singular impression—the automotive industry. No argument—it's a big part of Detroit's reputation and identity.

Admittedly, Detroit doesn't get very good press, and some of that criticism is justified. But it is a superb and affordable area in which to live, the cultural stimuli are marvelous, and there are excellent school systems and recreational facilities in many parts of Greater Detroit.

Detroit is a city bordered on one side by the Great Lakes and on the other by many inland lakes. If you fly low over Northwest Detroit, you will swear there is more water than land.

With few exceptions, our personnel live within 30 minutes of the agency; about half of them are no more than ten minutes away. It's a convenient place to work.

What Makes Our Agency Unique

In a town so identified with a single industry, there always has been a question whether a Detroit-based agency could prosper and grow *without* an automotive account.

We've done it. Of course, it took many years—over 50—which seems a long time to someone young enough to be looking for an entry-level position in the advertising business.

But we are a maverick agency in many ways. Nearly a hundred accounts, for example, contribute to our $50,000,000 in billing. Obviously, our average account is not huge according to the standards of a J. Walter Thompson, Saatchi & Saatchi, or Young & Rubicam, but we have variety. Creatives don't get burned out because they're stuck on one account.

We are also unusual in that we have used Detroit and Baltimore as our base, developed our talents, and then "distributed" those talents into other parts of North America and, now, overseas.

We are like the old vaudevillians who, rather than changing their acts, perfected them and then changed the *audience* by moving from city to city.

W. B. Doner & Co. presently employs about 575 people, 335 of whom are in the Detroit office, 145 in our Baltimore co-headquarters, the rest in our seven other offices (located in Boston, Chicago, Cleveland, London, Montreal, St. Petersburg, and Toronto).

Emphasis On Retailers

We like retail accounts—perhaps 40% of our billing represents retail advertising.

How do we define retail? Broadly speaking, a retailer is someone who sells through his or her own outlets, rather than distributing through others. According to that definition, not only is a drugstore, a supermarket or a hardware store a retailer, but so is a bank, an insurance company and a petroleum company.

In representing clients who qualify under the above definition, we have developed a "next-day" business mentality. Retail advertising is the most *accountable* kind of advertising —the product or service either sells or it doesn't. We often say to our retailers that while we must do investigative research and copy research and tracking research, their ultimate research tool is the cash register. Retailers lovingly embrace this theory.

It's natural to think that an agency with retail clients would spend a great deal of its time and talent figuring out ways to run a sale or lay out circulars replete with exclamatory headlines and sunburst price features. But there is another important difference in our agency—more than 80% of our work for retailers is in broadcast. Except to flesh out a theme we have developed for broadcast, we involve ourselves only rarely with retail print advertising.

Even when we do run a sale—or, more importantly, when we're establishing a conceptual theme for a retailer—we apply the same creative juices and the same zest for the right creative thrust as we do for our consumer product manufacturers or financial service clientele.

There are several aspects to our philosophy of advertising:

1. Simple Ideas Have Great Power

That holds true whether the advertising campaign is for Hygrade's Ball Park Franks ("They plump when you cook 'em" campaign we've run for 30 years) or for Highland Superstores, a chain of electronic stores, whose campaign for many years was, "Everything you never expected from an appliance store."

These are simple ideas, kept simple by the constant exercise of will power.

2. Likeable Advertising Sells

We have proven over and over again that if people like your advertising, they will like you and your product or store...and people like to buy from people they like.

3. In order to do likeable advertising that is effective, you must apply the Head, the Heart and The Funnybone

Getting Your Start In Detroit

What does all of this mean to someone seeking a career in advertising?

After considering our philosophy and account mix, determine for yourself whether you're at all interested in our kind of agency. While I have outlined a few areas in which we are unusual or maverick, that doesn't mean we are *absolutely* unique. There are other agencies that subscribe to the same or a similar philosophy, even a number of them right here in Detroit. If you *don't* want to work for an agency like ours, identify the kind(s) of agency you *do* want to work for and search them out.

Some Job Interview Pointers

Let's assume you have decided to apply for a job at Doner. This means you want to be with an agency where the emphasis is on creativity, where, for the most part, you won't begin by working on mega-sized accounts (we only have a few) and where you can be sure you'll work your butt off.

In preparation for a successful job interview at our company, work your butt off *now*. Sit down and <u>cram</u> as if you were going to take one of the most important exams of your life—because you *are*. Learn about our agency—its clients, its creative product, even the reputation of its research, marketing and media departments.

The most successful job interview which I held was with a new college graduate who got an appointment with me by asking his uncle (an old friend) to introduce him. I do not think such methods devious or weak. In fact, I admire them—an applicant who gets a third-party introduction to me may be resourceful enough to do the same when he or she becomes part of our new business team.

Fortunately, this young man had no intention of getting a job through connections alone— he had crammed so successfully that he knew our accounts and the nature of our agency better than many people who had been with us for years. I interviewed him, and he interviewed me. I asked him questions about himself, and he asked me many questions about events going on at the agency, about specific current accounts, even about prospects whose names he had seen in trade magazine reports.

I have not been surprised at all that this young man went from trainee to assistant account executive to account supervisor in a period of less than three years. And he applies the same thoughtful, ingratiating technique in dealing with our clientele that he used on me.

Know What You Want To Do

While we are not a huge agency, our departmentalization is quite well-defined, something you'll find true of many medium-sized shops and most large ones. So be sure to decide in advance whether you are best suited for copywriting, art directing, print or broadcast production, marketing, research, account service, media planning, media buying, media research, accounting, etc. Don't expect the interviewer to decide where you'd fit.

On the other hand, once in a great while we do succumb to someone who says, "I think I have the ability and the talent, but I want to learn about this business. If you can start me in the mailroom, in the secretarial pool, or anyplace else where I can absorb the atmosphere and the routine of this agency, I'll take anything you've got until you and my department head decide where I can best serve the agency."

And Learn About Our Industry *Now*

As for education, we have no rigid rules, but we favor those graduates with a liberal arts foundation and a marketing or advertising major. There are relatively few schools with a serious advertising program, but those few who do make a great contribution to our industry.

I suggest you subscribe to the advertising trade papers, particularly *Advertising Age* and *Adweek*. Canada's *Marketing Magazine* and London's *Campaign* are also useful and fascinating.

Look at advertising continuously. Don't just thumb through magazines and newspapers—*study* the ads, *compare* the ads. Develop your tastes, both from a sales effectiveness standpoint and an aesthetic one. They are of equal importance.

Whether you're inclined toward the marketing side or the creative side, think about advertising *ideas*. Try them on your friends. Use people in the advertising business as sounding boards.

Find An Internship

If you have the qualifications, you can get a summer internship with us or with other similar-sized agencies. We are not interested in those who want to make a few bucks and keep themselves occupied for the summer. If you don't intend to go into advertising after graduation, then you're a poor investment for us, in terms of both the money we'd pay and the time and energy we'd expend training you.

If you're both good and determined, get in touch with us—virtually anyone who demonstrates a genuine desire to break into advertising can get an interview.

W.B. "BROD" DONER's advertising career began in 1936. It ended on January 4, 1990, when after completing his last phone call of the day, he passed away quietly.

Founder and chairman of the executive committee of W. B Doner Company, Mr. Doner was born in Detroit and lived there all his life except for college (University of Wisconsin) and World War II.

Doner turned down the family business after graduation and instead joined a local advertising agency. Fired along with several other staff members after 18 months—and unable to find another agency job in the midst of the Depression—Doner started his own agency in March, 1937, with two employees.

Today, with more than 500 employees in offices in Baltimore, Boston, Chicago, Cleveland, Detroit, London, Montreal, St. Petersburg and Toronto, W. B. Doner & Co. is one of the top 30 agencies in North America. Its client list ranges from pickles to hot dogs, from gasoline to supermarkets. The agency celebrated its 50th anniversary in 1987 with the founder still active.

Doner was a director of the National Multiple Sclerosis Society and the International MS Society. He was a lifetime member of the Adcraft Club of Detroit and a member of the Detroit Club, Detroit Athletic Club, Rennaissance Club of Detroit, Harmonie Club of New York and Franklin Hills Country Club. He and his wife Rolla had six children and thirteen grandchildren.

Herb Fried, the agency's chief executive officer and chairman of the board, has assumed the position as head of W.B. Doner & Company.

20

The Advertising Scene In Texas

Robert H. Bloom, Chairman & CEO
The Bloom Companies, Inc.

First of all, I must state that I see absolutely *no* difference in the way advertising is practiced in Dallas or New York. While significant differences may have existed in the earlier stages of our development, the advertising industry has truly come of age in Texas.

Atlanta was once the dominant Sunbelt advertising center. Today that position belongs to Dallas. Our biggest accounts used to be local businesses; now the major agencies in Dallas service national clients in cities all over the map. A lot of award-winning advertising is coming out of the Lone Star State. And the best and brightest of Madison Avenue are sending their books and resumes *to Texas*. Good advertising, coupled with the "good life," make for a powerful lure.

Predictably, the major Texas ad agencies are grouped in the metropolitan areas. Dallas leads the pack with Houston, San Antonio, Fort Worth and Austin coming up behind. In Dallas, the three largest agencies are Tracy-Locke, owned by BBDO; Bozell; and Bloom, the largest independent ad agency in the South and one of the 25 largest independent agencies in the country.

The Houston advertising scene is dominated by branches of the big New York shops, such as Ogilvy & Mather and McCann-Erickson. Traditionally, Houston accounts are predominantly industrial, while Dallas concentrates on consumer business.

Aside from other full-service shops, San Antonio has several agencies specializing in Hispanic advertising—a by-product of the composition of the city's population. And they're creating that advertising for national clients.

So Why Texas? The Good And The Bad

The economy in Texas right now is very difficult. Texas agencies are down-sizing and/or merging in an attempt to stay alive. Those agencies totally dependent on oil accounts probably won't make it. But while the weaker ones will fail, the strong shops will emerge even stronger.

Here at Bloom, we are extremely optimistic about the future. In our opinion, there has never been a better time for an independent advertising agency specializing in consumer product and service accounts.

People also seem to forget the number of national (non-energy) advertisers based in Texas. Dallas, for example, is the home of American Airlines, Dr. Pepper, Frito-Lay, and Southland Corporation.

Being based in Dallas was once considered a handicap. It isn't anymore. With the addition of DFW Airport, Dallas has emerged as one of the easiest places to get in and out of. You can "day trip" almost anywhere. We serve the Carnation Company (Los Angeles, CA), Nestle Foods (Purchase, NY) and Maybelline Cosmetics (Memphis, TN) from Dallas.

The time has also passed when a Texas agency has to go out-of-state to do all of its production. We now have a Las Colinas production facility with state-of-the-art capabilities in Dallas, with similar facilities in other cities around the state. Texas has an advantage over other national advertising centers—an exceptionally good quality of life. The state's cities have developed some wonderful art museums, good theater, ballet companies and superior symphonies. The Texas of today is definitely not the "land of the cowpoke," as we have been historically depicted.

Texans also live by the basic work ethic of "come in early, work hard, and stay late if you have to." It's the no-nonsense approach practiced by people who tend to be very honest and direct. The bottom line is to <u>win.</u> Everyone understands it and everyone works hard to do it. You "go for it," whatever "it" may be. And when you work in an agency, you'll find yourself surrounded by transplanted New Yorkers, Californians and Midwesterners. The state has evolved into the "third coast," and Dallas has emerged as one of the nation's major agency centers.

Breaking In—It's Hard Here, Too!

But breaking into advertising in Texas isn't easy. When you're starting out, there are some basic rules I think you should follow, rules that will help ensure your eventual career success.

1. *Assess your interests, strengths and weaknesses* in order to determine what agency department you want to work in. Moving from one area to another is not always easy; in the mid- or large-sized agencies, it's frequently impossible. I personally believe you should get a career aptitude testing service evaluation such as AIMS. By coupling the aptitude test information with your own self-knowledge, you'll find it easier to match your interests and talents to opportunities within the increasingly segmented departments of the larger agency organizations.

2. *Be patient and be persistent.* Entry-level jobs are extremely difficult to get in *any* part of the country, because the national advertising agency community is small, and overall agency employment isn't growing. The current trend toward consolidation through merger is further reducing career opportunities. Texas is no exception. There are very few entry-level positions available in any year; to secure one of them, you must be *very* aggressive and *very* patient.

3. *What kind of agency you work for*—in terms of its client roster and management style/ philosophy—*is much more important than its geographic location.* It would be better to work for Bloom/Dallas than a small New York agency. And it would be better to work at a *big* New York agency than a small one there. Frankly, there are simply more opportunities to learn, better teachers, a greater variety of brands and bigger clients. Finally, the bigger agency has more disciplines. I feel very strongly that a larger, more sophisticated environment is a better starting place, although it might not necessarily be the best *ending* place.

4. *Starting with packaged goods clients is essential.* Although some entry-level account service, creative, media and research people may not *want* to work on packaged goods accounts—now

or *ever*—there are disciplines available *only* in packaged goods that must be learned right from the start; they're very difficult to pick up later on.

5. *Be prepared to do the "grunt work" associated with any starting positions, particularly with packaged goods accounts.* It won't last forever. But that kind of early learning is essential to understanding almost any other kind of advertising. It's also transferable to most other kinds of clients' businesses and to different types of advertising agencies.

6. *Try to select the "right" person to work for...*it may well be the third most critical element (after the size and kinds of clients you'll be exposed to). How good a teacher will he or she be? How smart is he or she? How much training and guidance is he or she willing to provide? All are critical questions; the answers should strongly influence your choice of an entry-level position.

7. *If any key element doesn't meet your expectations, get out fast!* If you start to work at an agency or on an account that turns out to be less than ideal or for a person who falls far short of great, you need to get out of that environment as fast as you can without sacrificing your ethics or being inconsiderate of your employer. Meet your obligations to that employer, but if things just aren't right, then move on to the right kind of agency, teacher and/or client—just as fast as you possibly can.

8. *Don't overlook opportunities in the media department.* Too many people do. Yet it's the one agency department that's drastically changing, because of computerization, complexity of media decisions, and the rapid changes in the media themselves (i.e., segmented publications, cable, etc.).

In conclusion, I recommend the Texas market as a wonderful place to both learn and practice the craft of advertising. It will take patience and persistence. But with heavy doses of both, if you are *determined* to succeed in Texas, you *will* succeed. And, at the same time, you'll enjoy a sensational quality of life. Remember: Advertising is no different in Texas than it is in New York City. I should certainly know—I spend half my week in Dallas and the other half in New York...every week. This is hard but fun, challenging and stimulating. Just like the agency business itself!

ROBERT H. BLOOM attended Duke University and graduated from the University of Oklahoma with a Bachelor of Science degree. In 1957, after serving an an officer in the U.S. Navy, he joined The Bloom Agency (now The Bloom Companies), the agency formed by his father in 1951. He was named president in 1962 and chairman/CE0 in 1980.

Today, The Bloom Companies ranks as one of the nation's 25 largest independent agencies with over $180 million in annual billings and 250 employees. Its roster of domestic consumer advertisers include: Airwick Industries, Pentax Cameras, Sandoz Pharmaceuticals Corporation, Associated Importers, Romanoff International, Scott Paper Company, Witco Corporation, Carter Wallace Corporation and the City of New York Cultural Commission in the New York office; Block Drug, Campbell Taggart, Carnation, Dallas Convention and Visitor's Bureau, Team Bank, Liggett & Myers, Nestle Foods, Owens Country Sausage, Ross Laboratories, Schering-Plough, and Skaggs Alpha Beta in the Dallas office.

Bob Bloom has served on the Board of the American Association of Advertising Agencies, as well as a number of other local and national civic organizations.

21

Go West, Young Person!

**Phillip Joanou, Chairman and Chief Executive
Dailey & Associates Advertising**

If you live in the West, are interested in advertising, and ask your professors or counselors about how to get started in the agency business, you'll probably be told: Go to New York. Because in New York, such advisors think, you'll find:

- Big league creative;
- Leadership and innovation;
- Major national agencies;
- A fast pace;
- Opportunities to work for major clients.

And, of course, "New York is the advertising center of the world. It's where things start. Others follow"...or so you will be told. "Spend a few years in New York, get an impressive resume. Then, if you wish, return to the West, get a terrific job, and kick back." As if all this weren't enough, you also get to enjoy great museums, wonderful restaurants, fabulous plays, and be with dynamic, charge-ahead people.

All of this, of course, is absolutely true. But if you were to ask *my* advice on where to go to begin your advertising career, I would simply point out that you don't *have* to go to New York to get many (if not all) of the same opportunities and experiences. If you would really prefer to live and work in the West, but feel compelled to go to New York because everyone says that's the smart thing to do, *don't*. Things have changed—if you like the West, stay in the West, because today you will find:

- Big league creative;
- Leadership and innovation;
- Major national agencies;
- A fast pace;
- Opportunities to work for major clients.

There are a few additions I feel make the West special: a great climate, fabulous beaches, mountains and deserts, excellent theater, more championship sports than anywhere in the country; the world's leading trend-setting restaurants, terrific museums, and friendly, outgoing, hard-working people.

Let's look at some of the factors that might influence your decision and help you realize that working in the West is a more than viable career choice.

Western Creative Is Breakthrough

What about major league creative?

Paul Goldberger, architecture critic for *The New York Times*, recently wrote: "Los Angeles is forever destined to be compared to New York, and often in the manner of a child with a talented older sibling. Why does it not do everything correctly, the way its older brother did? Why does it not play by the rules? It is no secret, of course, that the child who goes his own way often turns out, upon maturity, to be the more creative, and so it is with Los Angeles—as an artistic center it is very much coming into its own in this decade, and its creative energies seem nearly limitless. There is less self-consciousness to the Los Angelenos, less of a sense of self-importance, less of a sense that there is a set of rules governing the making of architecture. It is right to speak of the architecture being produced here in terms of freestyle. In the hands of its best practitioners it is disciplined, but this discipline is self-imposed, not ordained from above."

Replace the word "architecture" with "advertising" and you have the difference between East and West.

The West offers a freer, creative climate, one that has produced some of the most innovative, talked-about advertising of the last decade. People are still arguing, for example, about Chiat/Day's "1984" commercial for Apple Computer. No other commercial—by *any* agency *any*where—caused as much interest and controversy. keye/donna/pearlstein has done brilliant work for a number of clients. Few would argue about the creative skills of Hal Riney in San Francisco. Roger Livingston in Seattle has probably won more Clios and New York awards than any agency its size in America. Cliff Einstein, at Dailey & Associates, is one of the most highly regarded creative directors in the United States.

There are many other powerful, highly creative, strong agencies headquartered in the West whose work holds up with *any* work being done by *any* agency *any*where in the world.

The West Leads In Innovation

Is New York still the center for leadership and innovation? John (Megatrends) Naisbett's group collects detailed data on a vast number of information categories from all across the country. They then search for the patterns—"globally," regionally, locally—hiding within this statistical torrent. The results can be fascinating. For example, he has learned that there are five states in which most social invention occurs in this country. The other forty five are, in effect, followers. Not surprisingly, *California is the key indicator state.* Florida is second, followed by the Western states of Washington and Colorado. Way back in the pack is New York: *a definite trend follower, not the trend setter many might have of think it is.*

> "The Mediterranean is the ocean of the past, the Atlantic the ocean of the present, and the Pacific the ocean of the future."
> — Roger Skrentny

The West Is Big Business

What about the size of the Western market?

If the Western states were a separate nation, its 1985 GNP—$839 billion—would rank fourth in the world behind the United States, USSR and Japan, and far ahead of Canada, Italy, and Spain.

21 of the top 100 advertisers in America are headquartered or have a major division on the West Coast. Large corporations with large advertising budgets demand and expect the highest levels of sophistication and professionalism.

Carpenter and Associates recently predicted that bank deposits in California will exceed total deposits in New York banks in 1990. (California the financial center of America?)

Today 44% of all venture capital funds generated in the U.S. come into California. "Attitudes in New York and California are completely reversed," states one analyst. "In New York, if a person says he's going to go out and start his own business, become an entrepreneur, people will look at him and think, 'This guy has lost his job.' In California, people will look at him and say: 'He should have done that five years ago.'"

According to *Inc.* magazine's listing of the "500 Fastest-Growing Private Companies," eight of the top 20 are from California alone. (Tomorrow's big new advertising spenders.)

Forbes' listing of the 500 largest companies in the United States shows that 109 are in the West, 50 in Southern California alone.

According to the U.S. Census Bureau, California residents have a higher per capita personal income than New York residents. (Advertising salaries in the large Western markets are comparable to New York.)

Unlike much of the country, the West does not depend on older, more vulnerable heavy industry. Rather, it harbors the largest concentration of high technology enterprise in the world and a diversity of other manufacturing, agricultural and raw materials industries. Such diversity gives the West the capacity to continue to grow.

The Myth Of The "Laid Back" West

New York's pace is dictated by commuting schedules, since virtually everyone commutes into "The City." People have to get up very early to get to work late. And leave work early to get home late. This creates a very fast physical pace. Do not, however, confuse motion with action.

Westerners control their own commute. Everyone drives. If you want to stay late, you don't worry about trains. You don't have to get cranky and aggressive because you are running out of time. You control time. Results are what count, not frenetic motion. This makes some harassed Easterners believe the pace is slow and easy out here. When people like this come West to manage branches of Eastern agencies, they quite often fail, because, in fact, the competition is fierce, the quality second to none. So if you are not prepared to work very hard to succeed, stay away from the agency business, East *or* West.

The West Has Major Clients

The West offers you chances to work on large national and international clients, too. These major corporations require large, full-service agencies that can provide them with the best advertising available. If they weren't getting the kind and calibre of professional work they needed, it stands to reason that they would simply transfer their accounts East.

Corporations like Carnation, Beatrice Hunt-Wesson, Honda, Mazda, Levi Strauss, Disney, Nike, Lockheed, Atlantic Richfield, Taco Bell, Toyota, Clorox, Apple, Gallo, Hilton, to name just a few, demand the best from their agencies...and they get it. There are more than enough "major league, world class" clients in the West to keep you busy for a lifetime.

Don't misunderstand me. New York is a great city, and if you like it, a great place for an advertising career. But it isn't *better*, just *different*.

Some Pitfalls

There *are* some "downsides" you should be aware of if you're thinking about a West coast advertising career. First, with the exception of Los Angeles and San Francisco, there is less job mobility in most markets. Many people are willing to accept this risk for the lifestyle available in cities like San Diego, Portland or Seattle. There are good jobs in all of these markets. There are excellent agencies headquartered in the West, but there are *not* a lot of them.

Another possible disadvantage: A good number of agency offices are branches of New York-headquartered companies. In many of these, major decisions are made in New York, so working on the West coast leaves you far away from the real seat of power.

For some of these companies, advancement means moving to corporate headquarters in New York. This, of course, defeats the purpose of building a career in the West.

One thing you would *not* have to give up is money, at least in the Los Angeles market. All surveys I've seen show that salaries in Southern California are equal to those paid in the agency business in New York.

What To Do Next

All the advice in this *Career Directory* that is pertinent to getting an agency job in New York or Chicago or Detroit applies to the agency business out West: Read and use this excellent volume. Get out the Agency Red Book. Talk to your professors for advice and leads. Write to agency heads. Follow up with phone calls.

What are the best companies—anywhere—looking for? Intelligence. Honesty. High energy. If you possess these, present yourself well, and don't give up, you *will* find the job you want... *where* you want it.

PHILIP JOANOU has an extensive background in marketing consumer goods and services, and has been a major contributor to the growth of Dailey & Associates, the largest international agency headquartered in the West.

He has managed several major national accounts, including brands for Ralston Purina, Carnation, Lipton, Hill Brothers, Beatrice-Hunt-Wesson, American Honda, Great Western Savings, and Transamerica.

A graduate of the University of Arizona, Mr. Joanou has taught undergraduate marketing at the University of Southern California, served as director of the 4A's Institute of Advanced Studies at USC, and has lectured at UCLA, the Art Center, and various professional organizations. He has served as a governor of the 4A's and is current a director on their national board. He has been director of the Los Angeles Advertising Club and director and president of the Western States Advertising Agencies Association, which named him "Advertising Man Of the Year" in 1983. Mr. Joanou is also active in community affairs with a number of civic and fraternal organizations. He is the originator and architect of the Partnership for a Drug Free America.

In 1972, Mr. Joanou joined Peter Dailey in Washington, D.C. as executive vice president of the November Group, creating the advertising campaign for President Nixon's re-election. He later worked on the presidential campaigns of Gerald Ford and Ronald Reagan.

He is listed in Who's Who in Advertising, Who's Who in the World, and Who's Who in America. He has lived in La Canada for the past 20 years with his wife, Michelle, and their children, Janet, Phillip, Jennifer and Kathy.

22

The Advertising Scene
In Canada

Charles Abrams, Vice-Chairman/Executive Creative Director
Backer Spielvogel Bates Canada Inc.

If you *can't* make it in New York, Chicago, Minneapolis, Boston, or any other advertising center in the States, don't assume you can show your driver's license to a customs official, cross the border, and have Canadian advertising agencies anxiously awaiting you with open arms. They won't be.

While it may have been more benevolent a few years ago, the fact is the Canadian advertising industry is evolving to world-class status. The colleges, universities and art schools are filled with people who are determined to get into advertising. The competition, in other words, is fierce.

Add to that the fact that Canadian agencies have not been immune to mergers and acquisitions. Practically every major U. S. and U. K. agency has an office here—Saatchi & Saatchi, Backer Spielvogel Bates, WPP Group (J. Walter Thompson, Ogilvy & Mather), DDB Needham (which recently merged with Canadian agency Carder Grey), Y & R, McLaren Lintas, McCann-Erickson, Scali McCabe Sloves and Chiat Day Mojo, Baker Lovic (BBDO), McKim (NW Ayer with a minority interest). It may be just a matter of time before Canadian-owned agencies such as Vickers & Benson and Cossette Communications align themselves with multinational shops.

What all this means is that job opportunities will diminish. But not if you have the talent and determination to fight your way into this business. And many do just that—and not just from the States, but the U. K., South Africa, Australia, Scotland, Ireland and Hong Kong, as well.

And where exactly are they heading? Toronto!

Why Toronto?

Toronto is the New York of Canada. Virtually every major advertising agency is located here, and practically every major Canadian advertiser spends its advertising dollars here. And when I say major advertisers, I mean just that—McDonalds, Procter & Gamble, Warner Lambert,

GM, Ford, Chrysler, Toyota, Nissan, Honda, General Foods, Campbell's, Ralston Purina—the list goes on. Less familiar, though more important, are the big Canadian advertisers such as Petro Canada, Loblaw's Supermarkets (the first North American company responsible for starting the green marketing revolution), Canadian Airlines, Labatts and Molson breweries (Molson being second only to the Canadian government in ad dollars spent).

Toronto has everything a major advertising centre needs and more. Thousands of people move to greater Toronto every year, adding to the 3.2 million people who already live here.

Dynamic, cosmopolitan, sophisticated and clean are words that best describe Toronto, the capital of Ontario, which lies on the northwest shore of Lake Ontario, just across from Buffalo, New York. A mere one-hour flight from New York City or Chicago. It has become an international centre of business, finance, communications, the arts and medical research.

Toronto offers an abundance of excellent shopping and schools, first-class public transportation, diverse housing options, and a healthy economic base. One of the most exciting features of the city is its ethnic diversity, as is illustrated by the publication of official announcements in the *six* most frequently spoken languages in Toronto—English, French, Italian, Portugese, Chinese and Greek.

The city has become a favorite locale for shooting feature films, TV mini-series and commercials. It has a financial district and a vibrant theatre district. If you want chic and expensive, just head uptown to the Bloor and Bay area. Boutiques, galleries and world-class restaurants abound. Many of the city's advertising firms are located here. Canada's largest university, the University of Toronto, is right in the heart of the city.

Toronto has outgrown its past nicknames ("Hogtown" and "Muddy York"). It's a live, vibrant, growing city designed for people. It's safe, sane and civilized.

But a note of caution: In a recent survey, it was reported that Toronto has become the most expensive city in the Western Hemisphere, outstripping pricey locales like New York, Chicago and Lima, Peru. Calgary and Montreal were both in the Top Twelve. And housing costs, which are astronomical, were not taken into account! The good news is that Toronto ranked 28th worldwide.

Just how big is the advertising scene in Canada?

At last count, there were over 260 advertising agencies in operation *in Toronto alone*. If you add the branch offices coast-to-coast, the one- and two-man shops, the promotion houses, and the retail and direct response agencies from Halifax to Victoria—to say nothing of Winnipeg, Windsor, Waterloo, Whitehorse and Yellowknife!—the list grows to well over 500.

But 15% of these shops do 85% of the business. The major mergers of the last few years have seen a shrinking of the power base down to five or six multinationals, each with two or more offshoots or commonly-held sister shops. These are followed by a few strong-and-holding-out Canadian agencies, then by a plethora of smallish, regional and special-interest shops.

The Differences You'll Find

Are the American and Canadian advertising industries very different from each other? Well, yes and no. As an American who was raised on the New York ad scene, I've seen the best and the worst of Madison Avenue and had the opportunity to work with some of the most brilliant names in the business. When I was asked to take this post in Canada, I knew there would be some adjustments, but, in truth, found that the differences between the two countries' ad businesses to be more a matter of geography, language, and government than of people or modus operandi. Advertising people are as dedicated, hard-working, professional, caring, creative and crazy in Toronto as they are in Tucson...or New York or Detroit or Dallas or Seattle. Clients are clients regardless of where they're from. And the creative process of thinking, writing, art directing, presenting and producing really doesn't differ much on either side of the border.

So people aside, here are the differences:

1) Canada has essentially one-tenth the population of the U. S. Hence, one-tenth the advertising budgets and one-tenth the purchasing power. We tend to have to work with tighter budgets, and (generally speaking) our campaigns have to last longer. Creative people have to be generalists—the creative director who is overseeing a big car shoot one day can be writing a small print ad for bird seed the next. In the U. S., particularly in New York, you'll find job titles such as "TV copywriter" and "print art director." Not so in Canada, where *everybody* in Creative has to be adept at creating ads for *every* kind of media.

2) We have two official languages: English and French. 27% of the Canadian population lives in the (French-speaking) Province of Quebec. All government documents must be printed in two languages. As must the labels on every can of soup. So our already-smaller budgets must be stretched even further to accommodate the translations and adaptations needed. And speaking of those, merely "switching" an English-language approach won't necessarily satisfy the cultural nuances of the French language. Consequently, American-based advertisers whose message would fly nicely in the rest of Canada could be faced with major overhauls if they wanted to run the same ad in Quebec.

3) We have incredible government intervention into what we can and can't say about our clients' products in the broadcast media, especially TV. Food is governed by a commission in Ottawa which must approve every word and every picture in a TV spot. Proprietary medicines, cough syrups, other non-prescription drugs, and even sugarless gums fall under the Health Protection Branch (protecting the public from us, I assume), and their TV claims are governed accordingly. In the case of beer and wine advertising, there are no less than *five* Federal approval committees, in addition to the individual rules and guidelines from ten separate provinces. Hence lead times in Canada have to be longer so the government bodies can bestow their stamps of approval on our creative. Which, I might add, is challenged to the maximum every time out.

Now For The Good News

Despite the government restrictions, the Canadian advertising industry is turning out work that is excellent...world-class...exemplary.

Despite the two languages, Canadian agencies, through their affiliates in Quebec, can offer their clients consistently national coverage with well-thought-out, appropriate, market-smart communications.

And despite the smaller population and matching budgets, fresh, innovative concepts—where the idea is bigger than the estimate—are developed, presented and sold every day.

Finally, as far as the commercial film industry is concerned, Canadian production values are highly regarded throughout the world.

Which is why I get literally dozens of phone calls and letters and resumes and portfolios every week. From people like you. Who want, more than anything else in the world, to break into advertising.

Getting Into The Creative Department

Creative is more than a part of the agency; it's the heart of the agency. Oh, sure, we all work together—Creative, Media, Account Management. But the scripts, storyboards, ads, and ideas turned out in the Creative department are, in truth, the *product* of the agency. It's what we *do*. It's what we *sell*. So if my biased viewpoint on the importance of Creative comes from the heart, this fact comes from statistics: Creative receives more applications for employment, *more* letters, *more* phone calls, *more* requests, for interviews *than any other department in any other business in any other industry...in the world.*

Now, please read this. I'm going to say it only once, and then I'm going to go on as if I never said it:

Only one in 500 applicants will be successful in landing an entry-level Creative position in a Canadian agency.

You have to be better than good to get in—you have to be outstanding. You have to make yourself noticed. And you have to have substance behind your approach.

Agencies are not waiting with open arms to hire you. Most of them won't even see you. It's simply easier for them to go with someone with experience than to train a newcomer.

Knowing this, plan your strategy accordingly.

That said, here's some specific advice for you would-be copywriters and art directors.

If You Want To Be A Copywriter

It's very important to realize that a copywriter has different talents than a literary writer. The finest prose in the world is useless to a client who needs to move a brand in six short words on a billboard. The most eloquent screenplay styling must be set aside when the client's product must be seen and sold in 15 seconds.

A copywriter is a specialist. A person with the verbal abilities to hone an idea down to its bare bones and present that idea on the silver platter of originality.

If you want to get started in copywriting, you must, first and foremost, prove that you can *write*. Secondly, and just as important, you must prove that you can write *ads*. Prepare more than your resume. Write a letter or brief essay explaining why you want so badly to work in advertising. Write, write, write ads. Make ads for nonexistent products. Prepare TV scripts for current products and for services you admire. Make up a portfolio of ads and scripts that show you understand the communications art of advertising. If you write an ad, prepare a TV commercial to go along with it and a billboard to complete the campaign. Beg an artist friend to sketch up your ideas. Or make a collage of pictures to illustrate your message.

There is no such thing as a "copywriting school." Apart from having a superb command of language, knowing how to spell (please!), and having skill in grammar and sentence structure, a copywriter can come from almost any academic background. Life experience, people skills, sales-manship, and the power of persuasion are the finest talents a beginning copywriter can have.

If You Want To Be An Art Director

Aspiring art directors usually come with formal training from an Art College or University; they will have been trained in layout, typography, illustration, and the graphic arts in general. Unlike copywriters, they will emerge from school with a portfolio of school projects on which they have been graded.

If you have such a portfolio, don't depend on it alone to get you an interview. Add to it. Make ads. Design your own campaigns. Let the potential interviewer see first-hand that you have something to contribute. That you are more than a talented "wrist." That you can think. That you are an ad-maker.

Getting started as an art director is only slightly different than the task facing the would-be copywriter. In your case, however, you don't necessarily have to start in an agency proper. A year or two at a design studio, paste-up shop or type house will give you some experience from which to springboard into a "real shop." Like the copywriter, however, make the rounds with your portfolio, write to creative directors, and be persistent. Your talent will be immediately visible the second your portfolio is opened. So make those opening pages as dynamic as possible.

You Still Want To Work In Advertising?

You've absorbed my blunt caveats stated earlier. You *know* that only a handful of applicants make it in the Creative Department in any given year. But you still have the guts and the hopes to try to break into advertising. Here is some closing advice I hope will make it easier for you:

- Arm yourself with all possible information about obtaining work in Canada. Write to Employment & Immigration Canada, Central C.I.C., 443 University Avenue, Toronto, Ontario M5G 2H6, and ask them to send you their pamphlets on obtaining an Employment Authorization. Your prospective employer/agency will have to show just cause why a Canadian could not be hired for the same job for which you're applying. Difficult, but *not* hopeless.

- Do your homework. Learn all you can about the industry, the agen-cy business, and the accounts those agencies service. For each agency in which you're interested, find out exactly what it does. How it operates. What its reputation is. What accounts it handles. What accounts it has recently won. Or lost. Read the industry journals; find out about mergers, acquisitions, and staffing changes.

- Go to the library and read everything you can find on the business of advertising—Bill Bernbach's Book by Bob Levenson, Playing in Traffic on Madison Avenue by David Herzburn, When Advertising Tried Harder by Larry Dubrow, and others of the same ilk.

- Write to MacLean Hunter Publications (777 Bay Street, Toronto, Ontario, M5W 1A7), subscribe to *Marketing* magazine, Canada's pre-miere weekly "what's going on in advertising" journal, and ask them to send you a copy of their annual Awards Issue.

- You may also want to subscribe to *Playback*, a bi-weekly newspaper tabloid published by Brunico Communications, Inc. (111 Queen Street East, Suite 330, Toronto, Ontario M5C 1S2).

- If you can't afford any subscriptions, many of the above publications should be available in the reading room of your local library.

- Avail yourself of a wonderful little *free* booklet entitled, So You Want To Be In An Advertising Agency, published by the Institute for Canadian Advertising (30 Soudan Avenue, Toronto, Ontario M4S 1V6). This member-council has possibly the best library of advertising-related publications in the country. I drew heavily upon their material when preparing this article!

- Hang in there. Consider your job search as the most important job you have. Be persistent, polite and passionate in your approach to the people who hold the keys to your career. If the top ten agencies you try don't pan out, try the next ten on your list. And the next ten. And the next. Just keep trying.

- Now here's the big one: ***Take the first job offered to you.*** Regardless of its humble stature. Regardless of its seeming distance from what you *really* want to do.

  Be willing to work in the mailroom.

  Be willing to carry someone's portfolio.

  Be willing to be willing. And wait like a cat for the chance to move up,.

Good luck!

CHARLES ABRAMS recently arrived in Canada from New York, where he was executive vice-president and a member of both the executive committee and the board of directors of Backer's sister agency, Saatchi & Saatchi Compton.

His career spans over 20 years, starting with Doyle Dane Bernbach in 1968, the agency responsible for igniting the creative revolution in the 1960s with its work for Volkswagon and AVIS. In 1983, he joined DDB's International Division as vice president/head art director, creating Pan-European campaigns for Polaroid, Atari and Seagram Corp.

Mr. Abrams has won numerous creative awards throughout his career, and while at Saatchi received accolades for his work on British Airways and New York City's first and highly controversial AIDS prevention campaign.

Section 4

The Job Search Process

23

Getting Started: Self Evaluation And Career Objectives

Getting a job may be a relatively simple one-step or couple-of weeks-process or a complex, months-long operation.

Starting, nurturing and developing a career (or even a series of careers) is a lifelong process.

What we'll be talking about in the five chapters that together form our Job Search Process are those basic steps to take, assumptions to make, things to think about if you want a job—especially a first job in an ad agency. But when these steps—this process—are applied and expanded over a lifetime, most if not all of them are the same procedures, carried out over and over again, that are necessary to develop a successful, lifelong, professional career.

What does all this have to do with putting together a resume and portfolio, writing a cover letter, heading off for interviews, and the other "traditional" steps necessary to get a job? Whether your college graduation is just around the corner or a far-distant memory, you will continuously need to focus, evaluate and re-evaluate your response to the ever-changing challenge of your future: Just what do you want to do with the rest of your life? Whether you like it or not, you're all looking for that "entry-level opportunity."

You're already one or two steps ahead of the competition—you're sure (pretty sure?) you want to pursue a career in advertising. By heeding the advice of the many professionals who have written chapters for this *Career Directory*—and utilizing the extensive entry-level job, organization and publication listings we've included—you're well on your way to fulfilling that dream. But there are some key decisions and time-consuming preparations to make if you want to transform that hopeful dream into a real, live job.

The actual process of finding the right agency, right career path, and, most importantly, the right first job, begins long before you start mailing out resumes to potential employers. The choices and decisions you make now are not irrevocable, but this first job will have a definite impact on the career options you leave yourself. To help you make some of the right decisions and choices along the way (and avoid the most notable traps and pitfalls), the following chapters will lead you through a series of organized steps. If the entire job search process we are recommending here is properly executed, it will undoubtedly help you land exactly the job you want.

If you're currently in high school and hope, after college, to land a job in advertising, then attending the right college, choosing the right major, and getting the summer work experience many agencies look for are all important steps. Read the section of this *Career Directory* that covers the particular job specialty in which you're interested—many of the contributors have recommended colleges or graduate programs they favor.

If you're hoping to jump right into any of these jobs with*out* a college degree or other professional training, our best and only advice is—don't do it. As you'll soon see in the detailed information included in the *Job Opportunities Databank*, there are not *that* many job openings for students without a college degree. Those that do exist are generally clerical and will only rarely lead to promising careers.

The Concept Of A Job Search *Process*

These are the key steps in the detailed job search process we will cover in this and the following four chapters:

1. *Evaluating yourself*: Know thyself. What skills and abilities can you offer a prospective employer? What do you enjoy doing? What are your strengths and weaknesses? What do you *want* to do?

2. *Establishing your career objectives*: Where do you want to be next year, three years, five years from now? What do you ultimately want to accomplish in your career and your life?

3. *Creating an agency target list*: How to prepare a "Hit List" of potential employers—researching them, matching their needs with your skills, and starting your job search assault. Preparing agency information sheets and evaluating your chances.

4. *Networking for success:* Learning how to utilize every contact, every friend, every relative, and anyone else you can think of to break down the barriers facing any would-be agency professional. How to organize your home office to keep track of your communications and stay on top of your job campaign.

5. *Preparing your resume:* How to encapsulate years of school and little actual work experience into a professional, selling resume. Learning when and how to use it.

6. *Preparing cover letters:* The many ordinary and the all-too-few extraordinary cover letters, the kind that land interviews and jobs.

7. *Interviewing:* How to make the interview process work for you—from the first "hello" to the first day on the job.

We won't try to kid you—it *is* a lot of work. To do it right, you have to get started early, probably quite a bit earlier than you'd planned. Frankly, we recommend beginning this process one full year prior to the day you plan to start work.

So if you're in college, the end of your junior year is the right time to begin your research and preparations. That should give you enough time during summer vacation to set up your files and begin your library research.

Whether you're in college or graduate school, one item may need to be planned even earlier—allowing enough free time in your schedule of classes for interview preparations and appointments. Waiting until your senior year to "make some time" is already too late. Searching for a full-time job is itself a full-time job! Though you're naturally restricted by your schedule, it's not difficult to plan ahead and prepare for your upcoming job search. Try to leave at least a couple of free mornings or afternoons a week. A day or even two without classes is even better.

Otherwise, you'll find yourself, crazed and distracted, trying to prepare for an interview in the ten-minute period between your Advertising Ethics lecture and your Layout & Design seminar. Not the best way to make a first impression and certainly not the way you want to approach an important meeting.

The Self-Evaluation Process

Learning about who you are, what you want to be, what you *can* be, are critical first steps in the job search process and, unfortunately, the ones most often ignored by job seekers everywhere, especially students eager to leave the ivy behind and plunge into the "real world." But avoiding this crucial self evaluation can hinder your progress and even damage some decent prospects.

Why? Because in order to land a job with a agency at which you'll actually be happy, you need to be able to identify those agencies and/or job descriptions that best match your own skills, likes and strengths. The more you know about yourself, the more you'll bring to this process and the more accurate the "match-ups." You'll be able to structure your presentation (resume, cover letter, interviews) to stress your most marketable skills and talents (and, dare we say it, conveniently avoid your weaknesses?). Later, you'll be able to evaluate potential employers and job offers on the basis of your own needs and desires. This spells the difference between waking up in the morning ready to enthusiastically tackle a new day of challenges and shutting off the alarm in the hopes the day (and your job) will just disappear.

Creating Your Self-Evaluation Form

Take a sheet of lined notebook paper. Set up eight columns across the top—Strengths, Weaknesses, Skills, Hobbies, Courses, Experience, Likes, Dislikes.

Now, fill in each of these columns according to these guidelines:

Strengths: Describe personality traits you consider your strengths (and try to look at them as an employer would)—e.g., persistence, organization, ambition, intelligence, logic, assertiveness, aggression, leadership, etc.

Weaknesses: The traits you consider glaring weaknesses—e.g., impatience, conceit, etc. (And remember: Look at these as a potential employer would. Don't assume that the personal traits you consider weaknesses will necessarily be considered negatives in the business world. You may be "easily bored," a trait that led to lousy grades early on because teachers couldn't keep you interested in the subjects they were teaching. Well, many entrepreneurs need ever-changing challenges. Strength or weakness?)

Skills: Any skill you have, whether you think it's marketable or not. Everything from basic business skills—like typing, word processing and stenography—to computer, accounting or teaching experience and foreign language literacy. Don't forget possibly obscure but marketable skills like "good telephone voice."

Hobbies: The things you enjoy doing that, more than likely, have no overt connection to career objectives. These should be distinct from the skills listed above, and may include activities such as reading, games, travel, sports and the like. While these may not be marketable in any general sense, they may well be useful in specific circumstances. (If you love travel, you may be perfect for that entry-level job as liaison for the International Dept. And your "hobbies"—and the knowledge and expertise they've given you—may just get it for you!)

Courses: All the general subject areas (history, literature, etc.) and/or specific courses you've taken which may be marketable, you really enjoyed, or both.

Experience: Just the specific functions you performed at any part-time (school year) or full-time (summer) jobs. Entries may include "General Office" (typing, filing, answering phones, etc.), "Creative Writing," "Product Marketing," "Graphic Design," etc.

Likes: List all your "likes"—those important considerations that you haven't listed anywhere else yet. These might include the types of people you like to be with, the kind of environment you prefer (city, country, large places, small places, quiet, loud, fast-paced, slow-paced), and anything else which hasn't shown up somewhere on this form. However, try not to include entries which refer to specific jobs or agencies. We'll list those on another form.

Dislikes: All the people, places and things you can easily live without.

Now assess the "marketability" of each item you've listed. In other words, are some of your likes, skills or courses easier to match to a specific job description, or do they have little to do with a specific job or agency? Mark highly marketable skills with an "H." Use "M" to characterize those skills which may be marketable in a particular set of circumstances, "L" for those with minimal potential application to any job.

Referring back to the same list, decide if you'd enjoy using your marketable skills or talents as part of your everyday job—"Y" for yes, "N" for no. You may type 80 words a minute but truly despise typing or worry that stressing it too much will land you on the permanent clerical staff. If so, mark typing with an "N." (Keep one thing in mind—just because you dislike typing shouldn't mean you absolutely won't accept a job that requires it. Many do.)

Now, go over the entire form carefully and look for inconsistencies.

The Value Of A Second Opinion

There is a familiar misconception about the self-evaluation process that gets in the way of many new job applicants—the belief that it is a process which must be accomplished in isolation. Nothing could be further from the truth. Just because the family doctor tells you you need an operation doesn't mean you run right off to the hospital. Prudence dictates that you check out the opinion with another physician. Getting such a "second opinion"—someone else's, not just your own—is a valuable practice throughout the job search process, as well.

So after you've completed the various exercises in this chapter, review them with a friend, relative or parent. These second opinions may reveal some aspects of your self description on which you and the rest of the world differ. If so, discuss them, learn from them, and, if necessary, change some conclusions. Should everyone concur with your self evaluation, you will be reassured that your choices are on target.

Establishing Your Career Objectives

For better or worse, you now know something more of who and what you are. But we've yet to establish and evaluate another important area—your overall needs, desires and goals. Where are you going? What do you want to accomplish?

If you're getting ready to graduate from college or graduate school, the next five years are the most critical period of your whole career. You need to make the initial transition from college to the workplace, establish yourself in a new and completely unfamiliar agency environment, and begin to build the professional credentials necessary to achieve your career goals.

If that strikes you as a pretty tall order, well, it *is*. Unless you've narrowly prepared yourself for a specific profession, you're probably most *ill*-prepared for any real job. Instead, you've (hopefully) learned some basic principles—research and analytical skills that are necessary for success at almost any level—and, more or less, how to think. Maybe how to write...a little. Or draw...a little less. Or type.

It's tough to face, but face it you must: No matter what your college, major or degree, all you represent right now is potential. How you package that potential and what you eventually make of it is completely up to you. And it's an unfortunate fact that many agencies will take a professional with barely a year or two experience over *any* newcomer, no matter how promising. Smaller shops, especially, can rarely afford to hire someone who can't begin contributing immediately.

So you have to be prepared to take your comparatively modest skills and experience and package them in a way that will get you interviewed and hired. Quite a challenge.

But Is Advertising Right For *You?*

Presuming you now have a much better idea of yourself and where you'd like to be—job-, career- and life-wise in the foreseeable future—let's make sure some of your basic assumptions are right. We presume you purchased this *Career Directory* because you're considering a career in some area of the agency business. Are you sure? Do you know enough about the industry as a whole and the particular part you're heading for to decide whether it's right for you? Probably not. So start your research *now*—learn as much about your potential career as you now know about

In Appendix A, we've listed all the trade organizations associated with the advertising business. Where possible, we've included details on educational information available from these associations, but you should certainly consider writing each of the pertinent ones, letting them know you're interested in a career in their area of specialization, and that you would appreciate whatever help and advice they're willing to impart. You'll find many sponsor seminars and conferences throughout the country, some of which you may be able to attend.

In Appendix B, we've listed the trade publications dedicated to the highly specific interests of the various areas of the advertising community. These magazines are generally not available at newsstands (unless you live in or near New York City), but you may be able to obtain back issues at your local library (most major libraries have extensive collections of such journals) or by writing to the magazines' circulation/subscription departments.

You may also try writing to the publishers and/or editors of these publications. State in your cover letter what area of the agency business you're considering and ask them for whatever help and advice they can offer. But be specific. These are busy professionals and they do not have the time or the inclination to simply "tell me everything you can about becoming an AE."

If you can afford it now, we strongly suggest subscribing to whichever trade magazines are applicable to the specialty you're considering. If you can't subscribe to all of them, make it a point to regularly read the copies that arrive at your local public or college library.

These publications may well provide the most imaginative and far-reaching information for your job search. Even a quick perusal of an issue or two will give you an excellent "feel" for the industry. After reading only a few articles, you'll already get a handle on what's happening in the field and some of the industry's peculiar and particular jargon. Later, more detailed study will aid you in your search for a specific job.

Authors of the articles themselves may well turn out to be important resources. If an article is directly related to your chosen specialty, why not call the author and ask some questions? You'd be amazed how willing many of these professionals will be to talk to you and answer your questions. They may even tell you about job openings at their agencies! (But *do* use common sense—authors will not *always* respond graciously to your invitation to "chat about the business." And don't be *too* aggressive here.)

You'll find such research to be a double-edged sword. In addition to helping you get a handle on whether the area you've chosen is really right for you, you'll slowly learn enough about particular specialties, agencies, campaigns, the industry, etc., to actually sound like you know what you're talking about when you hit the pavement looking for your first job. And nothing is better than sounding like a pro...except being one.

Advertising Is It. Now What?

After all this research, we're going to assume you've reached that final decision—you really *do* want a career in advertising. It is with this vague certainty that all too many of you will race off, hunting for any agency willing to give you a job. You'll manage to get interviews at a couple and, smiling brightly, tell everyone you meet, "I want a career in advertising." The interviewers, unfortunately, will all ask the same awkward question—"What *exactly* do you want to do at our agency?"—and that will be the end of that.

It is simply not enough to narrow your job search to a specific industry. And so far, that's all you've done. You must now establish a specific career objective—the job you want to start, the career you want to pursue. Just knowing that you "want to get into advertising" doesn't mean anything to anybody. If that's all you can tell an interviewer, it demonstrates a lack of research into the industry itself and your failure to think ahead.

Interviewers will *not* welcome you with open arms if you're still vague about your career goals. If you've managed to get an "informational interview" with an executive whose agency currently has no job openings, what is he supposed to do with your resume after you leave? Who should he send it to for future consideration? Since *you* don't seem to know exactly what you want to do, how's *he* going to figure it out? Worse, he'll probably resent your asking him to function as your personal career counselor.

Remember, the more specific your career objective, the better your chances of finding a job. It's that simple and that important. Naturally, before you declare your objective to the world, check once again to make sure your specific job target matches the skills and interests you defined in your self evaluation. Eventually, you may want to state such an objective on your resume and "To obtain an entry-level position as an assistant account executive at a metropolitan advertising agency" is quite a bit better than "I want a career in advertising." Do not consider this step final until you can summarize your job/career objective in a single, short, accurate sentence.

24

Targeting Prospective Employers & Networking For Success

As you move along the job search path, one fact will quickly become crystal clear—it is primarily a process of **elimination**: Your task is to consider and research as many options as possible, then—for good reasons—*eliminate* as many as possible, attempting to continually narrow your focus.

The essential first step is to establish some criteria to evaluate potential employers. This will enable you to identify your target agencies, those for whom you'd really like to work. (This process, as we've pointed out, is not specific to any industry or field; the same steps, with perhaps some research resource variations, are applicable to any job, any company, any industry.)

Take a sheet of blank paper and divide it into three vertical columns. Title it "Target Agency —Ideal Profile." Call the left-hand column "Musts," the middle column "Preferences," and the right-hand column "Nevers."

We've listed a series of questions below. After considering each question, decide whether a particular criteria *must* be met, whether you would simply *prefer* it, or *never* would consider it at all. If there are other criteria you consider important, feel free to add them to the list below and mark them accordingly on your Profile.

1. What are your geographical preferences? U. S.? Canada? Europe? Anywhere you can get a job???

2. If you prefer to work in the U.S. or Canada, what area, state(s) or province(s)? If overseas, what area or countries?

3. Do you prefer a large city, small city, town, or somewhere as far away from civilization as possible?

4. In regard to question 3, any specific preferences?

5. Do you prefer a warm or cold climate?

6. Do you prefer a large or small agency? Define your terms (by billings, income, employees, offices, number or types of accounts, etc.).

7. Do you mind relocating right now? Do you want to work for an agency or **agency** group with a reputation for *frequently* relocating top people?

8. Do you mind travelling frequently? What percent do you consider reasonable? (Make sure this matches the normal requirements of the job specialization **you're** considering.)

9. What salary would you *like* to receive (put in the "Preference" column)? **What's** the *lowest* salary you'll accept (in the "Must" column)?

10. Are there any benefits (such as an expense account, medical and/or dental insurance, company car, etc.) you must or would like to have?

11. Are you planning to attend graduate school at some point in the future; if so, **is a** tuition reimbursement plan important to you?

12. Do you feel a formal training program necessary?

13. If applicable, what kinds of specific accounts would you prefer to work with? **What** specific types of advertising do you wish to be involved in (direct response/mail, print, TV, radio, retail, national, trade, consumer, etc.)?

It's important to keep revising this new form, just as you should continue to **update your** Self-Evaluation Form. After all, it contains the criteria by which you will judge **every potential** employer. Armed with a complete list of such criteria, you're now ready to find **all the agencies** that match them.

Targeting Individual Agencies

To begin creating your initial list of targeted ad agencies, start with the *Job Opportunities Databank*. We've listed every major U. S. agency—and more than a few smaller ones—plus, for the first time, opportunities at small and large agencies across Canada. These **agencies completed** questionnaires we supplied, providing us (and you!) with a plethora of data concerning **their over-** all operations, hiring practices, and other important information on entry-level job **opportunities.** This latter information includes key contacts (names), the average number of **entry-level people** they hire each year, along with complete job descriptions and requirements. All of **the detailed** information in these chapters was provided by the agencies themselves. To our **knowledge, it is** available *only* in this *Career Directory.*

We have attempted to include information on those large and medium-sized **ad agencies** that represent most of the entry-level jobs out there. But there are, of course, **many other agencies** of all sizes and shapes that you may also wish to research. In the next section, we **will discuss some** other reference books you can use to obtain more information on the agencies we've **listed, as well** as those we haven't.

Other Reference Tools

In order to obtain some of the detailed information you need, you will **probably need to do** further research, either in the library or by meeting and chatting with people **familiar with the** shops in which you're interested.

If you want to check out some additional agencies, use the <u>Standard Directory of Adver-</u> <u>tising Agencies</u> (also known, because of its bright cover, as the <u>Agency Red Book</u>). **Your local library** will probably have a copy (and, given its exorbitant cost, you probably shouldn't think of actually buying one). Even if you want to work for one of the "majors" and have found all your target agencies in our listings, you will find the Agency Red Book to be an invaluable research tool. Use it to check the correct spellings of agency executives' names (including all pertinent department heads). It will also supply you with a complete list of accounts for each listed agency (and they list thousands).

The most helpful book for you to study if you're hoping to go to work on the client side of the business (in addition to our own Marketing & Sales Career Directory) is probably the Standard Directory of Advertisers (the Advertiser Red Book). With listings of over 17,000 companies in two editions (classified and geographical), it is nearly four times the size of its sister publication.

As you narrow your target list, you may want to check other sources, both advertising-oriented and general directories. The annual Ad Dollar Summary (available from Leading National Advertisers, 130 Madison Ave., 5th Floor, New York, NY 10002) is the book the industry uses to chart exact ad spending in all media (TV, radio, newspapers, magazines and outdoor). If you are considering a specific advertiser company, this book will give you a good feel for the amount they spend and the type of advertising you'd wind up working on.

A regionalized series of books which contains extensive information on both agencies and clients is Adweek's Directory of Advertising. It lists agencies, brands and client companies, media companies, and service companies. It may well supply some additional information on targeted agencies or companies and should be available in your local library. There are six regional editions: West, Midwest, East, New England, Southwest and Southeast.

For more general research (pertinent to all companies), you might want to start with How To Find Information About Companies (Washington Researchers); the Encyclopedia of Business Information Sources (Gale Research, Book Tower, Detroit, MI 48226); and/or the Guide to American Directories (B. Klein Publications, P.O. Box 8503, Coral Springs, FL 33065), which lists directories for over 3,000 fields.

If you want to work for one of the associations which serves the agency business, we've listed all those in Appendix A. Other associations may be researched in the Encyclopedia of Associations (Gale Research Co.) or National Trade and Professional Associations of the United States (Columbia Books, Inc., 777 14th St., NW, Suite 236, Washington, DC 20005).

There are, in addition, many general corporate directories, biographical indexes, statistical abstracts, etc., etc.—from Gale Research, Dun & Bradstreet, Standard & Poor's, Ward's and others— which may give you additional information on major agencies and their executives. These volumes—and more such directories seem to be published every month—should all be available in the reference (and/or business) section of your local library.

The trade magazines which you've been studying (and to which you've already subscribed) will offer a steady stream of information. Become as familiar as possible with individual agencies, accounts, products, ad campaigns, issues, jargon, topics covered, etc.

One last note on potential sources of leads:

The Oxbridge Directory of Newsletters, 7th Edition (available from Oxbridge Communications, 150 Fifth Ave., Suite 301, New York, NY 10011) lists details of more than 17,000 newsletters in a plethora of industries and might well give you some ideas and names.

And the Professional Exhibits Directory (Gale Research Co.) lists more than 2,000 trade shows and conventions. Such shows are excellent places to "run into" account execs, media buyers, etc., and offer unexpected opportunities to learn about the business "from the horse's mouth."

Ask The Person Who Owns One

Some years ago, this advice was used as the theme for a highly successful automobile advertising campaign. The prospective car buyer was encouraged to find out about the product by asking the (supposedly) most trustworthy judge of all—someone who was already an owner.

You can use the same approach in your job search. You all have relatives or friends already out in the workplace—these are your best sources of information about those industries. Cast your net in as wide a circle as possible. Contact these valuable resources. You'll be amazed at how readily they will answer your questions. I suggest you check the criteria list at the beginning of this chapter to formulate your own list of pertinent questions. Ideally and minimally you will want to learn: how the industry is doing, what its long-term prospects are, the kinds of personalities they favor (aggressive, low key), rate of employee turnover, and the availability of training.

The Other Side Of The Iceberg

You are now better prepared to choose those agencies that meet your own list of criteria. But a word of caution about these now-"obvious" requirements—they are not the only ones you need to take into consideration. And you probably won't be able to find all or many of the answers to this second set of questions in any reference book—they *are* known, however, by those persons already at work in the industry. Here is the list you will want to follow:

Promotion—If you are aggressive about your career plans, you'll want to know if you have a shot at the top. Look for agencies that traditionally promote from within.

Training—Look for agencies in which your early tenure will actually be a period of on-the-job training, hopefully ones in which training remains part of the long-term process. As new techniques and technologies enter the workplace, you must make sure you are updated on these skills. Most importantly, look for training that is craft- or function-oriented—these are the so-called **transferrable skills**, ones you can easily bring along with you from job-to-job, company-to-company, sometimes industry-to-industry.

Salary—Some industries are generally high paying, some not. But even an industry with a tradition of paying abnormally low salaries may have particular companies or job functions (like sales) within companies that command high remuneration. But it's important you know what the industry standard is.

Benefits—Look for agencies in which health insurance, vacation pay, retirement plans, stock purchase opportunities, and other important employee benefits are extensive...and company paid. If you have to pay for basic benefits like medical coverage yourself, you'll be surprised at how expensive they are. An exceptional benefit package may even lead you to accept a lower-than-usual salary.

Unions—Make sure you know about the union situation in each industry you research. Periodic, union-mandated salary increases are one benefit non-union workers may find hard to match.

Making Friends And Influencing People

Networking is a term you have probably heard; it is definitely a key aspect of any successful job search and a process you must master.

Informational interviews and **job interviews** are the two primary outgrowths of successful networking.

Referrals, an aspect of the networking process, entail using someone else's name, credentials and recommendation to set up a receptive environment when seeking a job interview.

All of these terms have one thing in common: Each depends on the actions of other people to put them in motion.

So what *is* networking? *How* do you build your own network? And *why* do you need one in the first place? The balance of this chapter answers all of those questions and more.

Get your telephone ready. It's time to make some friends.

Not The World's Oldest Profession, But...

As Gekko, the high-rolling corporate raider, sneers in the movie *Wall Street:* "Any schmuck can analyze stock charts. What separates the players from the sheep is **information.**" Networking is the process of creating your own group of relatives, friends and acquaintances who can feed you the information *you* need to find a job—identifying where the jobs are and giving you the personal introductions and background data necessary to pursue them.

If the job market were so well-organized that details on all employment opportunities were immediately available to all applicants, there would be no need for such a process. Rest assured the job market is *not* such a smooth-running machine—most applicants are left very much to their own devices. Build and use your own network wisely and you'll be amazed at the amount of useful job intelligence you will turn up.

While the term networking didn't gain prominence until the 1970s, it is by no means a new phenomenon. A selection process that connects people of similar skills, backgrounds and/or attitudes—in other words, networking—has been in existence in a variety of forms for centuries. Attend any Ivy League school and you're automatically part of its very special centuries-old network.

Major law firms are known to favor candidates from a preferred list of law schools—the same ones the senior partners attended. Washington, D.C. and Corporate America have their own network—the same corporate bigwigs move back and forth from boardroom to Cabinet Room. The Academia-Washington connection is just as strong—notice the number of Harvard professors (e.g., Henry Kissinger, John Kenneth Galbraith) who call Washington their second home? No matter which party is in power, certain names just keep surfacing as Secretary of This or Undersecretary of That. No, networking is not new. It's just left its ivory tower and become a well-publicized process *anyone* can and should utilize in their lifelong career development.

And it works. Remember your own reaction when you were asked to recommend someone for a job, club or school office? You certainly didn't want to look foolish, so you gave it some thought and tried to recommend the best-qualified person that you thought would "fit in" with the rest of the group. It's a built-in screening process—what's more natural than recommending someone who's "our kind of _____?"

Creating The Ideal Network

As in most endeavors, there's a wrong way and a right way to network. The following tips will help you construct your own wide-ranging, information-gathering, interview-generating group—*your* network.

Diversify

Unlike the Harvard or Princeton network—confined to former graduates of each school—*your* network should be as diversified and wide-ranging as possible. You never know who might be in a position to help, so don't limit your group of friends. The more diverse they are, the greater the variety of information they may supply you with.

Don't Forget...

...to include everyone you know in your initial networking list: friends, relatives, social acquaintances, classmates, college alumni, professors, teachers; your dentist, doctor, family lawyer, insurance agent, banker, travel agent; elected officials in your community; ministers; fellow church members; local tradesmen; local business or social club officers. And everybody *they* know!

Be Specific

Make a list of the kinds of assistance you will require from those in your network, then make specific requests of each. Do they know of jobs at their company? Can they introduce you to the proper executives? Have they heard something about or know someone at the company you're planning to interview with next week?

The more organized you are, the easier it will be to target the information you need and figure out who might have it. Calling everyone and simply asking for "whatever help you can give me" is unfair to the people you're calling and a less effective way to garner information you need.

Learn The Difference...

...between an **informational** interview and a **job** interview. The former requires you to cast yourself in the role of information gatherer; *you* are the interviewer and knowledge is your goal—about an industry, company, job function, key executive, etc. Such a meeting with someone already doing what you soon *hope* to be doing is by far the best way to find out everything you need to know...before you walk through the door and sit down for a formal job interview, at which time your purpose is more sharply defined: to get the job you're interviewing for.

If you learn of a specific job opening during an informational interview, you are in a position to find out details about the job, identify the interviewer and, possibly, even learn some things about him or her. In addition, presuming you get your contact's permission, you may be able to use his or her name as a referral. Calling up the interviewer and saying, "Joan Smith in your Media department suggested I contact you regarding openings for assistant copywriters," is far superior to "Hello. Do you have any job openings at your agency?"

(Be careful about referring to a specific job opening, even if your contact told you about it. It may not be something you're supposed to know about. By presenting your query as an open-ended question, you give your prospective employer the option of exploring your background without further commitment. If there is a job for which you're qualified, you'll find out soon enough.)

Don't Waste A Contact

Not everyone you call on your highly-diversified networking list will know about a job opening. It would be surprising if each one did. But what about *their* friends and colleagues? It's amazing how everyone knows someone who knows someone. Ask—you'll find that someone.

Value Your Contacts

If someone has provided you with helpful information or an introduction to a friend or colleague, keep him or her informed about how it all turns out. A referral that's panned out should be reported to the person who opened the door for you in the first place. Such courtesy will be appreciated...and may lead to more contacts. If someone has nothing to offer today, a call back in the future is still appropriate and may pay off.

The lesson is clear: Keep your options open, your contact list alive. Detailed records of your network—whom you spoke with, when, what transpired, etc.—will help you keep track of your overall progress and organize what can be a complicated and involved process.

Informational Interviews

You were, of course, smart enough to include John Fredericks, the bank officer who handled your dad's mortgage, on your original contact list. He knew you as a bright and concientious college senior; in fact, your perfect three-year repayment record on the loan you took out to buy that '77 Plymouth impressed him. When you called him, he was happy to refer you to his golfing buddy, Bob Jones, a management supervisor at Ad Agency, Inc. Armed with permission to use Fredericks' name and recommendation, you wrote a letter to Bob Jones, the gist of which went something like this:

> I am writing at the suggestion of Mr. Fredericks at Fidelity National Bank. He knows of my interest in the agency business and, given your position at Ad Agency, Inc., thought you may be able to help me get a clearer understanding of it and how I might eventually be able to fit in.
>
> While I am majoring in marketing and minoring in English, I know I need to speak with professionals such as yourself to get a better understanding of the "big picture." If you could spare a half hour to meet with me, I'm certain I would be able to get enough information to give me the direction I need.
>
> I'll call your office next week in the hope that we can schedule a meeting.

Send a copy of this letter to Mr. Fredericks at the bank—it will refresh his memory should Mr. Jones call to inqure about you. Next step: the follow-up phone call. After you get Mr. Jones' secretary on the line, it will, with luck, go something like this:

> "Hello, I'm Mr. Paul Smith. I'm calling in reference to a letter I wrote to Mr. Jones requesting an appointment."
>
> "Oh, yes. You're the young man interested in our account executive training program. Mr. Jones can see you on June 23rd. Will 10 A.M. be satisfactory?"
>
> "That's fine. I'll be there."

Well, the appointed day arrives. Well-scrubbed and dressed in your best (and most conservative) suit, you are ushered into Mr. Jones' office. He offers you coffee (you decline) and says that it is okay to light up if you smoke (you decline). The conversation might go something like this:

> **You:** "Thank you for seeing me, Mr. Jones. I know you are busy and appreciate your taking the time to talk with me."
>
> **Jones:** "Well it's my pleasure since you come so highly recommended. I'm always pleased to meet someone interested in my field."

You: "As I stated in my letter, my interest in the agency business is very real, but I'm having trouble seeing how all of my studies fit into the big picture. I think I'll be much better prepared to evaluate future job offers if I can learn how everything fits. May I ask you a few questions about the account executive function at Ad Agency, Inc.?"

Mr. Jones relaxes. He realizes this is a knowledge hunt you are on, not a thinly-veiled job interview. Your approach has kept him off the spot—he doesn't have to be concerned with making a hiring decision. You've already gotten high marks for not putting him on the defensive. From this point on, you will be able to ask anything and everything you need to find out—not just about the account executive function at "ad agencies" in general, but specifically about the training program at Ad Agency, Inc. (which is what you're really interested in).

You should have made a detailed list of the questions you want answers to. Ask away. Take notes. What's happening in the field? What's happening at his agency? Where can you fit in?—Don't be afraid to ask pointed questions like, "Given my course work (hand him your resume), where would I best fit in at an agency like yours?"

After The Interview

The next step should be obvious: *Two* thank-you letters are required, one to Mr. Jones, the second to Mr. Fredericks. Get them both out immediately. (And see the next chapter if you need help writing them.)

Keeping Track of The Interview Trail

Let's talk about record keeping again. If your networking works the way it's supposed to, this was only the first of many such interviews. Experts have estimated that the average person could develop a contact list of 250 people. Even if we limit your initial list to only 100, if each of them gave you one referral, your list would suddenly have 200 names. Presuming that it will not be necessary or helpful to see all of them, it's certainly possible that such a list could lead to 100 informational and/or job interviews! Unless you keep accurate records, by the time you're on No. 50, you won't even remember the first dozen!

So get the results of each interview down on paper. Use whatever format with which you are comfortable. You should create some kind of file, folder or note card that is an "Interview Recap Record." It should be set up and contain something like the following:

Name: Ad Agency Inc.
Address: 333 Broad St., NY, NY 10000
Phone: (212) 666-6666
Contact: Robert L. Jones
Type of Business: Ad Agency—primarily business-to-business accounts
Referral Contact: Mr. Fredericks, Fidelity National Bank
Date: June 23, 1990

At this point, you should add a one- or two-paragraph summary of what you found out at the meeting. Since these comments are for your eyes only, you should be both objective and subjective. State the facts—what you found out in response to your specific questions—but include your impressions—your estimate of the opportunities for further discussions, your chances for future consideration for employment.

"I Was Just Calling To..."

Find any logical opportunity to stay in touch with Mr. Jones. You may, for example, let him know when you graduate and tell him your Grade Point Average, carbon him on any letters you write to Mr. Fredericks, even send a congratulatory note if his agency's year-end financial results are positive or if you read something in the local paper about his department, one of his accounts or one of his campaigns. This type of follow up has the all-important effect of keeping you and your name in the forefront of others' minds. Out of sight *is* out of mind. No matter how talented you may be or how good an impression you made, you'll have to work hard to "stay visible."

There Are Rules, Just Like Any Game

It should already be obvious that the networking process is not only effective, but also quite deliberate in its objectives. There are two specific groups of people you must attempt to target: those who can give you information about an industry or career area and those who are potential employers. The line between these groups may often blur. Don't be concerned—you'll soon learn when (and how) to shift the focus from interview*er* to interview*ee*.

To simplify this process, follow a single rule: Show interest in the field or job area under discussion, but wait to be asked about actually working for that agency. During your informational interviews, you will be surprised at the number of times the person you're interviewing turns to you and asks, "Would you be interested in...?" Consider carefully what's being asked and, if you *would* be interested in the position under discussion, make your feelings known.

What's It All About (Alfie)?

- To unearth current information about the industry, agency and pertinent job functions. Remember: Your knowledge and understanding of broad industry trends, financial health, hiring opportunities, and the competitive picture are key.
- To investigate each agency's hiring policies—who makes the decisions, who the key players are (personnel, staff managers), whether there's a hiring season, if they prefer applicants going direct or through recruiters, etc.
- To sell yourself—discuss your interests and research activities—and leave your calling card, your resume.
- To seek out advice on refining your job search process.
- To obtain the names of other persons (referrals) who can give you additional information on where the jobs are and what the market conditions are like.
- To develop a list of follow-up activities that will keep you visible to key contacts.

If The Process Scares You

Some of you will undoutedly be hesitant about, even fear, the networking process. It is not an unusual response—it is very human to want to accomplish things "on your own," without anyone's help. Understandable and commendable as such independence might seem, it is, in reality, an impediment if it limits your involvement in this important process. Networking has such universal application because *there is no other effective way to bridge the gap between job applicant and job.* Employers are grateful for its existence. You should be, too.

Whether you are a first-time applicant or reentering the work force now that the children are grown, the networking process will more than likely be your point of entry. Sending out mass mailings of your resume and answering the help wanted ads may well be less personal (and, therefore, "easier") approaches, but they will also be far less effective. The natural selection process of the networking phenomenon is your assurance that water does indeed seek its own level—you will be matched up with companies and job opportunities in which there is a mutual fit.

Six Good Reasons To Network

Many people fear the networking process because they think they are "bothering" others with their own selfish demands. Nonsense! There are good reasons—six of them, at least—why the people on your networking list will be *happy* to help you:

1) *Some day you will get to return the favor.* An ace insurance salesman built a successful business by offering low-cost coverage to first-year medical students. Ten years later, these now-successful practitioners remembered the company (and person) that helped them when they were just getting started. He gets new referrals every day.

2) *They, too, are seeking information.* If you sense that your "brain is being picked" about the latest case studies being used in your marketing courses, be forthcoming with your information. Why not let the interviewer "audit" your course? It may be the reason he or she agreed to see you in the first place.

3) *Internal politics*—Some people will see you simply to make themselves appear powerful, implying to others in their organization that they have the authority to hire (they may or may not), an envied prerogative.

4) *They're "saving for a rainy day"*—Executives know that it never hurts to look and that maintaining a backlog of qualified candidates is a big asset when the floodgates open and supervisors are forced to hire quickly.

5) *They're just plain nice*—Some people will see you simply because they feel it's the decent thing to do or because they just can't say "no."

6) *They are looking themselves*—Some people will see you because they are anxious to do a friend (whoever referred you) a favor. Or because they have another friend seeking new talent, in which case you represent a referral *they* can make (part of their own continuing network process). You see, networking never *does* stop—it helps them and it helps you.

Before you proceed to the next chapter, begin making your contact list. You may wish to keep a separate sheet of paper or note card on each person (especially the dozen or so you think are most important), even a separate telephone list to make your communications easier and more efficient. However you set up your list, be sure to keep it up to date—it won't be long before you'll be calling each and every name on the list.

25

Preparing Your Resume

    Your resume is a one- or two-page summary of you—your education, skills, employment experience, and career objective(s). It is *not* a biography—just a quick way to identify and describe you to potential employers. Most importantly, its *real* purpose is to *sell* you to the company you want to work for. It must set you apart from all the other applicants (those competitors) out there.

    So, as you sit down to formulate your resume, remember you're trying to present the pertinent information in a format and manner that will convince an executive to grant you an interview, the prelude to any job offer. (If you feel you need more help in resume preparation, or even in the entire job search area, we recommend <u>Your First Resume</u> by Ronald W. Fry.)

An Overview Of Resume Preparation

- **Know what you're doing**—your resume is a personal billboard of accomplishments. It must communicate your specific worth to a prospective employer.

- **Your language should be action-oriented,** full of "doing"-type words. And less is better than more. Be concise and direct; don't worry about complete sentences.

- **Be persuasive.** In those sections that allow you the freedom to do so, don't hesitate to communicate your worth in the strongest language. This does *not* mean a long list of self-congratulatory superlatives; it *does* mean truthful claims about your abilities and the evidence (educational, experiential) that supports them.

- **Don't be cheap or gaudy.** Don't hesitate to spend the few extra dollars necessary to present a professional-looking resume. Do avoid outlandish (and generally ineffective) gimmicks like over-sized or brightly-colored paper.

- **Find an editor.** Every good writer needs one, and you are *writing* your resume. At the very least, it will offer you a second set of eyes proofreading for embarrassing typos. But if you are fortunate enough to have a professional in the field—a recruiter or personnel executive—critique a draft, grab the opportunity.

- **If you're the next Michaelangelo,** so multi-talented that you can easily qualify for jobs in different career areas, don't hesitate to prepare two or more completely different resumes. This will enable you to change the emphasis on your education and skills according to the specific career objective on each resume, a necessary alteration that will correctly target each one.

- **Choose the proper format.** There are only three we recommend—chronological, functional and combination. It's important you use the one that's right for you.

The Records You Need

The resume-writing process begins with the assembly and organization of all the personal, educational and employment data from which you will choose the pieces that actually end up on paper. If this information is properly organized, writing your resume will be a relatively easy task, a simple process of just shifting data from one format (record-keeping sheets) to another (the resume format you'll use later in this chapter, including a fill-in-the-blanks form).

As you will soon see, there is a lot of information you'll need to keep track of. In order to avoid a fevered search for important information, take the time right now to designate a single location in which to store all your records. My recommendation is either a filing cabinet or an expandable pocket portfolio. The latter is less expensive, yet it will still enable you to sort your records into an unlimited number of more-manageable categories.

Losing important report cards, citations, letters, etc., is easy to do if your life's history is scattered throughout your room or, even worse, your house! While copies of many of these items may be obtainable, why put yourself through all that extra work? Making good organization a habit will ensure that all the records you need to prepare your resume will be right where you need them *when* you need them.

For each of the categories summarized below, designate a separate file drawer or, at the very least, file folder in which pertinent records can be kept. Your own notes are important, but keeping actual report cards, award citations, letters, etc. is even more so. Here's what your record-keeping system should include:

Transcripts (Including GPA And Class Rank Information)

Transcripts are your school's official record of your academic history, usually available, on request, from your high school's guidance office or college registrar's office.

Your college may charge you for copies and "on request" doesn't mean "whenever you want"—you may have to wait some time for your request to be processed (so *don't* wait until the last minute!).

Your school-calculated GPA (Grade Point Average) is on the transcript. Most schools calculate this by multiplying the credit hours assigned to each course times a numerical grade equivalent (e.g., "A" = 4.0, "B" = 3.0, etc.), then dividing by total credits/courses taken. Class rank is simply a listing of GPAs, from highest to lowest.

Employment Records

Details on every part-time or full-time job you've held, including:

- Each employer's name, address and telephone number
- Name of supervisor
- Exact dates worked
- Approximate numbers of hours per week
- Specific duties and responsibilities
- Specific skills utilized
- Accomplishments, honors
- Copies of awards, letters of recommendation

Volunteer Activities

Just because you weren't paid for a specific job—stuffing envelopes for the local Republican candidate, running a car wash to raise money for the homeless, manning a drug hotline—doesn't mean that it wasn't significant or that you shouldn't include it on your resume. So keep the same detailed notes on these volunteer activities as you have on the jobs you've held:

- Each organization's name, address and telephone number
- Name of supervisor
- Exact dates worked
- Approximate numbers of hours per week
- Specific duties and responsibilities
- Specific skills utilized
- Accomplishments, honors
- Copies of awards, letters of recommendation

Extracurricular Activities

List all sports, clubs or other activities in which you've participated, either inside or outside school. For each, you should include:

- Name of activity/club/group
- Office(s) held
- Purpose of club/activity
- Specific duties/responsibilities
- Achievements, accomplishments, awards

Honors And Awards

Even if some of these honors are previously listed, the following specific data on every honor or award you receive should be kept in your awards folder:

- Award name
- Date and from whom received
- What it was for
- Any pertinent details

Military Records

Complete military history, if pertinent, including:

- Dates of service
- Final rank awarded
- Duties and responsibilities
- All citations and awards
- Details on specific training and/or special schooling
- Skills developed
- Specific accomplishments

Creating Your First Resume

There are a lot of options about what to include or leave out. In general, we suggest you always include the following data:

- Your name, address and telephone number
- Pertinent educational history (grades, class rank, activities, etc.)
- Pertinent work history
- Academic honors
- Memberships in organizations
- Military service history (if applicable)

You have the option of including the following:

- Your career objective
- Personal data
- Hobbies
- Summary of qualifications

And you should *never* include the following:

- Photographs or illustrations (of yourself or anything else) unless they are required by your profession—e.g., actors' composites
- Why you left past jobs
- References
- Salary history or present salary objectives/requirements (if salary history is requested in an ad, include it in your cover letter)
- Feelings about travel or relocation

Special note: There is definitely a school of thought that discourages any mention of personal data—marital status, health, etc.—on a resume. While I am not vehemently opposed to including such information, I am not convinced it is particularly necessary, either.

As far as hobbies go, I would only include such information if it were in some way pertinent to the job/career you're targeting. Your love of reading is pertinent if, for example, you are applying for a part-time job at a library. But including details on the joys of "hiking, long walks with my dog and Isaac Asimov short stories" is rarely correct.

Maximizing Form And Substance

Your resume should be limited to a single page if possible, two at most. When you're laying out the resume, try to leave a reasonable amount of "white space"—generous margins all around and spacing between entries. It should be typed or printed (not Xeroxed) on 8 1/2" x 11" white, cream or ivory stock. The ink should be black or, at most, a royal blue.

Don't scrimp on the paper quality—use the best bond you can afford. And since printing 100 or even 200 copies will cost little more than 50, if you do decide to print your resume, *over*estimate your needs, and opt for the highest quantity you think you may need. Prices at various "quick print" shops are not exorbitant; the quality look printing affords will leave the right impression.

Use Power Words For Impact

Be brief. Use phraseology rather than complete sentences. Your resume is a summary of your talents, not a term paper. Choose your words carefully and use "power words" whenever possible. "Organized" is more powerful than "put together;" "supervised" better than "oversaw;" "formulated" better than "thought up."

Strong words like these can make the most mundane clerical work sound like a series of responsible, professional positions. And, of course, they will tend to make your resume stand out. Here's a starter list of words that you may want to use in your resume:

achieved	administered	advised
analyzed	applied	arranged
budgeted	calculated	classified
communicated	completed	computed
conceptualized	coordinated	critiqued
delegated	determined	developed
devised	directed	established
evaluated	executed	formulated
gathered	generated	guided
implemented	improved	initiated
instituted	instructed	introduced
invented	issued	launched
lectured	litigated	lobbied
managed	negotiated	operated
organized	overhauled	planned
prepared	presented	presided
programmed	promoted	recommended
researched	reviewed	revised
reorganized	regulated	selected
solved	scheduled	supervised
systematized	taught	tested
trained	updated	utilized

Choose The Right Format

There is not a lot of mystery here—your background will generally lead you to the right format. For an entry-level job applicant with limited work experience, the **chronological** format, which organizes your educational and employment history by date (most recent first) is the obvious choice.

For older or more experienced applicants, either the **functional**—which emphasizes the duties and responsibilities of all your jobs over the course of your career—or **combination**—halfway between chronological and functional—may be more suitable. While I have tended to emphasize the chronological format in this chapter, one of the other two may well be the right one for you.

Here's What To Avoid

In case we didn't stress them enough, here are some reminders of what to avoid:

- **Be brief and to the point**—Two pages if absolutely necessary, one page if at all possible. Never longer!

- **Don't be fancy.** Multi-colored paper and all-italic type won't impress employers, just make your resume harder to read (and easier to discard). Use plain white or ivory paper, blue or black ink and an easy-to-read standard typeface.

- **Forget rules about sentences.** Say what you need to say in the fewest words possible; use phrases, not drawn-out sentences.

- **Stick to the facts.** Don't talk about your dog, vacation, etc.

- **Resumes should never be blind.** A cover letter should *always* accompany a resume and that letter should always be directed to a specific person.

- **Almost doesn't count.** Your resume *must* be perfect—proofread everything as many times as necessary to catch any misspellings, grammatical errors, strange hyphenations or typos.

- **This is your sales tool.** Your resume is, in many cases, as close to you as an employer will ever get. Make sure it includes the information necessary to sell yourself the way you want to be sold!

- **Spend the money for good printing.** Soiled, tattered or poorly reproduced copies speak poorly of your own self-image. Spend the money and take the time to make sure your resume is the best presentation you've ever made.

- **Help the reader,** by organizing your resume in a clear-cut manner so key points are easily gleaned.

On the following pages, I've included a "fill-in-the-blanks" resume form so you can construct your own resume, plus a couple of samples of well-constructed student resumes.

Fill-In-The-Blanks Resume Form

Name : _____

Address : _____

City, state, zip code : _____

Telephone number : _____

OBJECTIVE :_____

_____

_____

_____

SUMMARY OF QUALIFICATIONS: _____

_____

_____

_____

_____

_____

_____

EDUCATION:

Graduate School : _____

Address : _____

Address: _____

Expected graduation date : _____   Grade point average : _____

Degree earned (expected): _____   Class rank : _____

Important classes you have taken, especially those that relate to your targeted career:

_____

_____

_____

_____

_____

_____

_____

COLLEGE:_____

Address : _____

Address: _____

Expected graduation date : _____Grade point average : _____

Class rank : _____   Major:_____   Minor: _____

Important classes you have taken, especially those that relate to your expected career:

_____

_____

_____

_____

_____

_____

_____

HIGH SCHOOL:_____

Address : _____

Address: _____

Expected graduation date : _____Grade point average : _____

Class rank : _____

Important classes you have taken, especially those that relate to your expected career:

_____

_____

_____

_____

_____

_____

HOBBIES AND OTHER INTERESTS (OPTIONAL)

_____

_____

_____

_____

_____

_____

_____

_____

EXTRACURRICULAR ACTIVITIES (Activity name, dates participated, duties and responsibilities, offices held, accomplishments):

_____

_____

_____

_____

_____

_____

_____

AWARDS AND HONORS (Award name, from whom and date received, significance of the award, any other pertinent details):

_____

_____

_____

_____

_____

_____

WORK EXPERIENCE Include job title, name of business, address and phone number, dates of employment, supervisor's name and title, your major responsibilities, accomplishments and any awards won. Include volunteer experience in this category. List your experiences with the most recent dates first, even if you later decide not to use a chronological format

_____

_____

_____

_____

_____

_____

_____

_____

_____

_____

_____

_____

_____

_____

_____

_____

REFERENCES Though you should *not* include references in your resume, you do need to prepare a separate list of at least three people who know you fairly well and will, you believe, recommend you highly to prospective employers. For each, include job title, company name, address and telephone number. Before you include anyone on this list, make sure you have their permission to use their name as a reference and confirm what they intend to say about you to a potential employer.

1. _____

_____

_____

_____

2. _____

_____

_____

_____

3. _____

_____

_____

_____

4. _____

_____

_____

_____

5. _____

_____

_____

_____

6. _____

_____

_____

_____

Sample Chronological Resume

LINDSAY TAYLOR FRY

HOME ADDRESS:	SCHOOL ADDRESS:
80 Stemmons Freeway,	4240 Hill St.,
Dallas, TX 87540	Los Angeles, CA 90410
(214)788-0000	(213)001-0100

OBJECTIVE   A position offering challenge and responsibility in agency marketing research

EDUCATION

1986-1990

U.C.L.A., Los Angeles, CA

Graduating in June, 1990, with a B.A. degree (Marketing); Deans List four years; Summa cum laude.

Fields of study include: marketing and advertising theory, research, business law, economics, mass communications, statistical analysis and research methodology.

Graduate courses in advertising theory and policies, consumer behavioral theory, sales management.

1982-1986

Greg Wright High School, Los Angeles, CA

National Honor Society; Senior Class President; United Way Club Head Fund Raiser.

**WORK
EXPERIENCE**

(Summers)

1989: JIM CANNON, INC., Los Angeles, CA

Administrative assistant in Research Department: Trained in behavioral research techniques; Responsible for record keeping, expense reports, public relations, lab report dissemination, correspondence.

1986 - 1988: KISCHTRONICS, San Diego, CA

Basic sales and management training at this major research and development facility. Duties included billing, inventory control, shipping and distribution, lab maintenance and delivery schedules.

Sample Functional Resume

JIM BEAM
76 Cortlandt St.,
New York, NY 10017
(212)555-1111

Career Objective: A position as an entry-level account executive
at a major metropolitan ad agency

SUMMARY

I am completing my degree in journalism, specializing in marketing, at University State. For two summers, I interned as an assistant account executive (with copywriting responsibilities) for a local advertising agency. I also have two year's experience selling advertising space (and supervising a staff of three salespeople) on my college newspaper and one year's experience in a bookstore. All of these jobs have convinced me I will be successful in advertising account work.

EXPERIENCE

Summer, 1988 & 89: Intern, Kay Silver & Associates, Inc.
Summer, 1987 : Intern, Committee to Re-elect Kim Kerr

1988/89 & 1989/90 school years: Ad Director, *The Daily Planet*
1987/88 school year: Salesman, Joe's University Book Store

EDUCATION

B.A. Journalism (Marketing) University State - June, 1990
(summa cum laude)

PROFESSIONAL MEMBERSHIPS AND BUSINESS SKILLS

Member of the Young Professionals Division of the Advertising Club of New York.
Skills: Sales, media placement, typing (50 wpm), word processing, computer literate.

PERSONAL

Age: 21
Health: Excellent
Language Skills: Fluent (read/write/speak) in German and French

References Available Upon Request

26

Writing Better Letters

Stop for a moment and review your resume draft. It is undoubtedly (by now) a near-perfect document that instantly tells the reader the kind of job you want and why you are qualified. But does it say anything personal about you? Any amplification of your talents? Any words that are ideally "you?" Any hint of the kind of person who stands behind that resume?

If you've prepared it properly, the answers should be a series of ringing "no's"—your resume should be a mere sketch of your life, a bare-bones summary of your skills, education and experience.

To the general we must add the specific. That's what your letters must accomplish—adding the lines, colors and shading that will help fill out your self portrait. This chapter will cover the kinds of letters you will most often be called upon to prepare in your job search. There are essentially nine different types you will utilize again and again, based primarily on what each is trying to accomplish. I've included at least one well-written example of each at the end of this chapter.

Before you put pencil to paper to compose any letter, there are five key questions you must ask yourself:

- **Why** are you writing it?
- To **Whom**?
- **What** are you trying to accomplish?.
- **Which** lead will get the reader's attention?
- **How** do you organize the letter to best accomplish your objectives?

Why?

There should be a single, easily-definable reason you are writing any letter. This reason will often dictate what and how you write—the tone and flavor of the letter—as well as what you include or leave out.

Have you been asked in an ad to amplify your qualifications for a job, provide a salary history and college transcripts? Then that (minimally) is your objective in writing. Limit yourself to following instructions and do a little personal selling—but very little. Including everything asked for and a simple, adequate cover letter is better than writing a "knock-'em, sock-'em" letter and omitting your salary history.

If, however, you are on a networking search, the objective of your letter is to seek out contacts who will refer you for possible informational or job interviews. In this case, getting a name and address—a referral—is your stated purpose for writing. You have to be specific and ask for this action.

You will no doubt follow up with a phone call, but be certain the letter conveys what you are after. Being vague or oblique won't help you. You are after a definite yes or no when it comes to contact assistance. The recipient of your letter should know this. As they say in the world of selling, at some point you have to ask for the order.

Who?

Using the proper "tone" in a letter is as important as the content—you wouldn't write a letter to your television repairman using the same words and style you would employ in a letter to the director of personnel of a major company. Properly addressing the person or persons you are writing is as important as what you say to them.

Some hints to utilize: the recipient's job title and level, his or her hiring clout (if they are just a pass along conduit, save your selling for the next step up the ladder), the kind of person they are (based on your knowledge of their area of involvement).

For example, it pays to sound technical with technical people—in other words, use the kinds of words and language which they use on the job. If you have had the opportunity to speak with them, it will be easy for you. If not, and you have formed some opinions as to their types then use these as the basis of the language you employ. The cardinal rule is to say it in words you think the recipient will be comfortable hearing, not in the words you might otherwise personally choose.

What?

What do you have to offer that company? What do you have to contribute to the job, process or work situation that is unique and/or of particular benefit to the recipient of your letter?

For example, if you were applying for a sales position and recently ranked number one in a summer sales job, then conveying this benefit is logical and desirable. It is a factor you may have left off your resume. Even if it was listed in your skills/accomplishment section of the resume, you can underscore and call attention to it in your letter. Repetition, when it is properly focused, can be a good thing.

Which?

Of all the opening sentences you can compose, which will immediately get the reader's attention? If your opening sentence is dynamic, you are already fifty percent of the way to your end objective—having your entire letter read. Don't slide into it. Know the point you are trying to make and come right to it.

How?

While a good opening is essential, how do you organize your letter so that it is easy for the recipient to read in its entirety? This is a question of *flow*—the way the words and sentences naturally lead one to another, holding the reader's interest until he or she reaches your signature.

If you have your objective clearly in mind, this task is easier than it sounds: Simply convey your message(s) in a logical sequence. End your letter by stating what the next steps are—yours and/or the reader's.

One More Time

Pay attention to the small things. Neatness still counts. Have your letters typed. Spend a few extra dollars and have some personal stationary printed.

And most important, make certain that your correspondence goes out quickly. The general rule is to get a letter in the mail during the week in which the project comes to your attention or in which you have had some contact with the organization. I personally attempt to mail follow-up letters the same day as the contact; at worst, within 24 hours.

When To Write

- To answer an ad
- To prospect (many companies)
- To inquire about specific openings (single company)
- To obtain a referral
- To obtain an informational interview
- To obtain a job interview
- To say "thank you"
- To accept or reject a job offer
- To withdraw from consideration for a job

In some cases, the letter will accompany your resume; in others, it will need to stand alone. Each of the above circumstance is described in the pages that follow. I have included at least one sample of each type of letter at the end of this chapter.

Answering An Ad

Your eye catches an ad in the Positions Available Section of the Sunday paper for an assistant publicist. It tells you that the position is in a large publishing company and that, though some experience would be desirable, it is not required. Well, you possess *those* skills. The ad asks that you send a letter and resume to a Post Office Box. No salary is indicated, no phone number given. You decide to reply.

Your purpose in writing—the objective (why?)—is to secure a job interview. Since no individual is singled out for receipt of the ad, and since it is a large company, you assume it will be screened by Personnel.

Adopt a professional, formal tone. You are answering a "blind" ad, so you have to play it safe. In your first sentence, refer to the ad—including the place and date of publication and the position outlined. (Chances are this company is running more than one ad on the same date and in the same paper, so you need to identify the one to which you are replying.) Tell the reader what (specifically) you have to offer that company. Include your resume, phone number and the times it is easiest to reach you. Ask for the order—tell them you'd like to have an appointment.

Blanket Prospecting Letter

In June of this year you will graduate from a specialized four-year insurance college. You seek a position (internship or full-time employment) in a major insurer's underwriting department. You have decided to write to fifty top insurance companies, sending each a copy of your resume. You don't know which, if any, have job openings.

Such blanket mailings are effective given two circumstances: 1) You must have an exemplary record and a resume which reflects it, and 2) You must send out a goodly number of packages, since the response rate to such mailings is very low.

A blanket mailing doesn't mean an impersonal one—you should *always* be writing to a specific executive. If you have a referral, send a personalized letter to that person. If not, do *not* simply mail a package to the Personnel department; identify the department head and *then* send a personalized letter. And make sure you get on the phone and follow up each letter within about ten days. Don't just sit back and wait for everyone to call you. They won't.

Just Inquiring

The inquiry letter is a step above the blanket prospecting letter; it's a "cold-calling" device with a twist. You have earmarked a company (and a person) as a possibility in your job search based on something you have read about them. Your general research tells you that it is a good place to work. Although you are not aware of any specific openings, you know that they employ entry-level personnel with your credentials.

While ostensibly inquiring about any openings, you are really just "referring yourself" to them in order to place your resume in front of the right person. This is what I would call a "why not?" attempt at securing a job interview. Its effectiveness depends on their actually having been in the news. This, after all, is your "excuse" for writing.

Networking

It's time to get out that folder marked "Contacts" and prepare a draft networking letter. The lead sentence should be very specific, referring immediately to the friend, colleague, etc. "who suggested I write you about..." Remember: Your objective is to secure an informational interview, pave the way for a job interview, and/or get referred to still other contacts.

This type of letter should not place the recipient in a position where a decision is necessary; rather, the request should be couched in terms of "career advice." The second paragraph can then inform the reader of your level of experience. Finally, be specific about seeking an appointment.

Unless you have been specifically asked by the referring person to do so, you will probably not be including a resume with such letters. So the letter itself must highlight your credentials, enabling the reader to gauge your relative level of experience. For entry-level personnel, education, of course, will be most important.

For An Informational Interview

Though the objectives of this letter are similar to those of the networking letter, they are not as personal. These are "knowledge quests" on your part and the recipient will most likely not be someone you have been referred to. The idea is to convince the reader of the sincerity of your research effort. Whatever selling you do, if you do any at all, will arise as a consequence of the meeting, not beforehand. A positive response to this type of request is in itself a good step forward. It is, after all, exposure, and amazing things can develop when people in authority agree to see you.

Thank-You Letters

Although it may not always seem so, manners *do* count in the job world. But what counts even more are the simple gestures that show you actually care—like writing a thank-you letter. A well-executed, timely thank-you note tells more about your personality than anything else you may have sent. It says something about the way you were brought up—whatever else your resume tells them, you are, at least, polite, courteous and thoughtful.

Thank-you letters may well become the beginning of an all-important dialogue that leads directly to a job. So be extra careful in composing them, and make certain that they are custom made for each occasion and person.

The following are the primary situations in which you will be called upon to write some variation of thank-you letter:

- After a job interview

- After an informational interview

- Accepting a job offer

- Responding to rejection: While optional, such a letter is appropriate if you have been among the finalists in a job search or were rejected due to limited experience. Remember: Some day you'll *have* enough experience; make the interviewer want to stay in touch.

- Withdrawing from consideration: Used when you decide you are no longer interested in a particular position. (A variation is usable for declining an actual job offer.) Whatever the reason for writing such a letter, it's wise to do so and thus keep future lines of communication open.

In Response To An Ad

10 E. 89th Street
New York, N.Y. 10028
December 3, 1990

The <u>New York Times</u>
P.O. Box 7520
New York, N.Y. 10128

Dear Sir or Madam:

This letter is in response to your advertisement for an assistant publicist which appeared in the December 2nd issue of the *New York Times*.

I have the qualifications you are seeking. I graduated magna cum laude from Emerson Junior College with a degree in public relations and a minor in journalism.

I wrote for the Emerson newspaper—the <u>Collegian</u>—during all four years. During my senior year, when I was editor-in-chief, we won four awards for editorial excellence—three more than Emerson had ever won before.

For the past three summers, I have worked for Little Local PR, a firm specializing in publishing accounts. This position has provided me with hands-on experience in the public relations field, as well as the chance to use and hone my writing, communication and interpersonal skills.

My resume is enclosed. I would like to have the opportunity to meet with you personally to discuss your requirements for the position. I can be reached at (212) 785-1225 between 8:00 a.m. and 5:00 p.m. and at (212) 785-4221 after 5:00 p.m. I look forward to hearing from you.

Sincerely,

Karen Weber

Enclosure: Resume, Clips

Prospecting Letter

```
Kim Kerr
8 Robutuck Hwy.
Hammond, IN 54054
555-875-2392
```

December 14, 1990

Mr. Fred Jones
Vice President—Underwriting
Alcott & Alcott
One Lakeshore Drive
Chicago, Illinois

Dear Mr. Jones:

The name of Alcott & Alcott continually pops up in our classroom discussions of outstanding insurance companies. Given my interest in insurance as a career and underwriting as a specialty, I've taken the liberty of enclosing my resume.

As you can see, I have just completed a very comprehensive four years of study at the College of Insurance which included courses in all lines of insurance, underwriting, rating, etc. Though my resume does not indicate it, I will be graduating in the top 10% of my class, with honors.

I will be in the Chicago area on June 29 and will call your office to see when it is convenient to arrange an appointment.

Sincerely yours,

Kim Kerr

Inquiry Letter

42 7th Street
Ski City, Vermont 85722
September 30, 1990

Ms. Crystal Igotmine
President
Really Big Ad & PR, Inc.
521 West Elm Street
Indianapolis, IN   83230

Dear Ms. Igotmine:

I just completed reading the article in the October issue of <u>Fortune</u> on your company's record-breaking quarter. Congratulations!

Your innovative approach to recruiting minorities is of particular interest to me because of my background in advertising and minority recruitment.

I am interested in learning more about your work as well as the possibilities of joining your firm. My qualifications include:

- B.A. in Psychology
- Research on minority recruitment
- Publicity Seminar participation (Univ. of Virginia)
- Reports preparation on creative writing, education and minorities

I will be in Connecticut during the week of October 10 and hope your schedule will permit us to meet briefly to discuss our mutual interests. I will call your office next week to see if such a meeting can be arranged.

I appreciate your consideration.

Sincerely yours,

Ronald W. Sodidie

Networking Letter

Richard A. Starky
42 Bach St., Musical City, IN 20202   **317-555-1515**

May 14, 1990

Ms. Michelle Fleming
Vice President
Financial Planning Associates
42 Jenkins Avenue
Fulton, Mississippi 23232

Dear Ms. Fleming:

Sam Kinnison suggested I write you. I am interested in an entry-level editorial position, but <u>not</u> with a publishing company. Sam felt it would be mutually beneficial for us to meet and talk.

I have been educated and trained as an accountant and have just over two years' part-time experience in bookkeeping, accounting, auditing and tax work. But I also worked on the college newspaper throughout my undergraduate career. I am particularly interested in finding a way to mesh my interest in journalism with my training in finance.

I know from Sam how similar our backgrounds are— thc same training, the same interest in journalism. And, of course, I am aware of how successfully you have managed to mesh these interests— fourteen awards for newsletter excellence in fifteen years!

As I begin my job search during the next few months, I am certain your advice would help me. Would it be possible for us to meet briefly? My resume is enclosed.

I will call your office next week to see when your schedule would permit such a meeting.

Sincerely,

Richard A. Starky

To Obtain An Informational Interview

16 NW 128th Street
Raleigh, North Carolina 75755
December 2, 1990

Mr. Johnson B. McClure
Vice President—Trading
SellThemGoldMines Brokerage, Inc.
484 Smithers Road
Awkmont, North Carolina 76857

Dear Mr. McClure:

I'm sure a good deal of the credit for your company's 23% jump in trading volume last year is attributable to the highly-motivated sales staff you have recruited during the last three years. I hope to obtain an entry-level position for a company just as committed to growth.

I have four years of sterling sales results to boast of, experience acquired while working my way through college. I believe my familiarity with the precious metals market, sales experience and Bachelor's degree in economics from American University have properly prepared me for a career in precious metals trading.

As I begin my job search, I am trying to gather as much information and advice as possible before applying for positions. Could I take a few minutes of your time next week to discuss my career plans? I will call your office on Monday, December 12, to see if such a meeting can be arranged.

I appreciate your consideration and look forward to meeting you.

Sincerely,

Karen R. Burns

After An Informational Interview

LAZELLE WRIGHT
921 West Fourth Street
Steamboat, Colorado 72105
303-303-3030

May 21, 1990

Mr. James R. Payne
Marketing Manager
Proctor's Gamble, Inc.
241 Snowridge
Ogden, Utah 72108

Dear Mr. Payne:

Jinny Bastienelli was right when she said you would be most helpful in advising me on a career in consumer product marketing.

I appreciated your taking the time from your busy schedule to meet with me. Your advice was most helpful and I have incorporated your suggestions into my resume. I will send you a copy next week.

Again, thanks so much for your assistance. As you suggested, I will contact Joe Simmons at Conglomerate, Inc. next week in regards to a possible opening with his company.

Sincerely,

Lazelle Wright

After A Job Interview

1497 Lilac Street
Old Adams, MA 01281
October 5, 1990

Mr. Rudy Delacort
Director of Personnel
We Publish Everything, Inc.
175 Boylston Avenue
Ribbit, Massachusetts 02857

Dear Mr. Delacort:

Thank you for the opportunity to interview yesterday for the sales trainee position. I enjoyed meeting you and Cliff Stoudt and learning more about WPEI.

Your organization appears to be growing in a direction which parallels my interests and career goals. The interview with you and your staff confirmed my initial positive impressions of WPEI, and I want to reiterate my strong interest in working for you.

I am convinced my prior experience as ad sales director for my school's daily newspaper, my Business College training in marketing and finance, and my summer sales experience working with a variety of products would enable me to progress steadily through your training program and become a productive member of your sales team.

Again, thank you for your consideration. If you need any additional information from me, please feel free to call.

Yours truly,

Hugh Beaumont

cc: Mr. Cliff Stoudt
New Projects Unit

Accepting A Job Offer

1497 Lilac Street
Old Adams, MA 01281
October 5, 1990

Mr. Rudy Delacort
Director of Personnel
We Publish Everything Inc.
175 Boylston Avenue
Ribbit, Massachusetts 02857

Dear Mr. Delacort:

I want to thank you and Mr. Stoudt for giving me the opportunity to work for WPEI. I am very pleased to accept the position as a sales rep trainee with your New Projects Unit. The position entails exactly the kind of work I want to do, and I know that I will do a good job for you.

As we discussed, I shall begin work on January 5, 1991. In the interim I shall complete all the necessary employment forms, obtain the required physical examination and locate housing.

I plan to be in Ribbit within the next two weeks and would like to deliver the paperwork to you personally. At that time, we could handle any remaining items pertaining to my employment. I'll call next week to schedule an appointment with you.

Sincerely yours,

Edward J. Haskell

cc: Mr. Cliff Stoudt
    New Projects Unit

Withdrawing From Consideration

1497 Lilac Street
Old Adams, MA 01281
October 5, 1990

Mr. Rudy Delacort
Director of Personnel
We Publish Everything, Inc.
175 Boylston Avenue
Ribbit, Massachusetts 02857

Dear Mr. Delacort:

It was indeed a pleasure meeting with you and Mr. Stoudt last week to discuss your needs for a sales rep trainee in your New Projects Unit. Our time together was most enjoyable and informative.

As I discussed with you during our meetings, I believe one purpose of preliminary interviews is to explore areas of mutual interest and to assess the fit between the individual and the position. After careful consideration, I have decided to withdraw from consideration for the position.

My decision is based primarily upon the one factor we discussed in some detail—the position would simply require more travel than I am able to accept, given my other responsibilities.

I want to thank you for interviewing me and giving me the opportunity to learn about your needs. You have a fine staff and and I would have enjoyed working with them.

Yours truly,

Barbara Billingsly

cc: Mr. Cliff Stoudt
    New Projects Unit

In Response To Rejection

1497 Lilac Street
Old Adams, MA 01281
October 5, 1990

Mr. Rudy Delacort
Director of Personnel
We Publish Everything, Inc.
175 Boylston Avenue
Ribbit, Massachusetts   02857

Dear Mr. Delacort:

Thank you for giving me the opportunity to interview for the sales rep trainee position. I appreciate your consideration and interest in me.

Although I am disappointed in not being selected for your current vacancy, I want you to know that I appreciated the courtesy and professionalism shown to me during the entire selection process. I enjoyed meeting you, Cliff Stoudt, and the other members of your sales staff. My meetings confirmed that WPEI would be an exciting place to work and build a career.

I want to reiterate my strong interest in working for you. Please keep me in mind if a similar position becomes available in the near future.

Again, thank you for the opportunity to interview and best wishes to you and your staff.

Sincerely yours,

Anthony Dow

cc: Mr. Cliff Stoudt
    New Projects Unit

27

Questions For You,
Questions For Them

You've done days of research, contacted everyone you've known since kindergarten, compiled a professional-looking and -sounding resume, and written brilliant letters to the handful of companies your research has revealed are perfect matches for your own strengths, interests and abilities. Unfortunately, all of this preparatory work will be meaningless if you are unable to suc-cessfully convince one of those firms to hire you.

If you were able set up an initial meeting at one of these companies, your resume and cover letter obviously peaked *someone's* interest. Now you have to traverse the last minefield—the job interview itself. It's time to make all that preparation pay off.

This chapter will attempt to put the interview process in perspective, giving you the "inside story" on what to expect and how to handle the questions and circumstances that arise during the course of a normal interview...and even many of those that surface in the bizarre interview situations we have all sometimes experienced.

Why Interviews Shouldn't Scare You

Interviews shouldn't scare you. The concept of two (or more) persons meeting to determine if they are right for each other is a relatively logical and certainly not apparently frightening idea. As important as research, resumes, letters and phone calls are, they are inherently impersonal. The interview is your chance to really see and feel the company firsthand—"up close and personal," as Howard Cosell used to crow—so think of it as a positive opportunity, your chance to succeed.

That said, many of you will still be put off by the inherently inquisitive nature of the process. Though many questions *will* be asked, interviews are essentially experiments in chemistry. Are you right for the company? Is the company right for you? Not just on paper—*in the flesh*. If you decide the company *is* right for you, *your* purpose is simple and clearcut—to convince the interviewer that you are the right person for the job, that you will fit in, and that you will be an asset to the company now and in the future. The interviewer's purpose is equally simple—to decide whether he or she should buy what you're selling.

This chapter will focus on the kinds of questions you are likely to be asked, how to answer them, and the questions you should be ready to ask of the interviewer. By removing the workings of the interview process from the "unknown" category, you will reduce the fear it engenders.

But all the preparation in the world won't completely eliminate your sweaty palms, unless you can convince yourself that the interview is an important, positive life experience from which you will benefit...even if you don't get the job. Approach it with a little enthusiasm, calm yourself, and let your personality do the rest. You will undoubtedly spend an interesting hour, one that will teach you more about yourself. It's just another step in the learning process you've undertaken.

What To Do First

Start by setting up a calendar on which you can enter and track all your scheduled appointments. When you schedule an interview with a company, ask them how much time you should allow for the appointment. Some require all new applicants to fill out numerous forms and/or complete a battery of intelligence or psychological tests—all before the first interview. If you've only allowed an hour for the interview—and scheduled another at a nearby firm ten minutes later—the first time you confront a three-hour test series will effectively destroy any schedule.

Some companies, especially if the first interview is very positive, like to keep applicants around to talk to other executives. This process may be planned or, in a lot of cases, a spontaneous decision by an interviewer who likes you and wants you to meet some other key decision makers. Other companies will tend to schedule such a series of second interviews on a separate day. Find out, if you can, how the company you're planning to visit generally operates. Otherwise, especially if you've traveled to another city to interview with a number of firms in a short period of time, a schedule that's too tight will fall apart in no time at all.

If you need to travel out-of-state to interview with a company, be sure to ask if they will be paying some or all of your travel expenses. (It's generally expected that you'll be paying your own way to firms within your home state.) If they don't offer—and you don't ask—presume you're paying the freight.

Even if the company agrees to reimburse you, make sure you have enough money to pay all the expenses yourself. While some may reimburse you immediately, the majority of firms may take from a week to a month to forward you an expense check.

What Color Shirts Does He Like?

The research you did to find these companies is nothing compared to the research you need to do now that you're beginning to narrow your search. If you followed our detailed suggestions when you started targeting these firms in the first place, you've already amassed a lot of information about them. If you didn't do the research *then*, you sure better decide to do it *now*. Study each company as if you were going to be tested on your detailed knowledge of their organization and operations. Here's what you should know about each company you plan to visit:

The Basics

1. The address of (and directions to) the office you're visiting
2. Headquarters location (if different)
3. Some idea of domestic and international branches

4. Relative size (compared to other similar companies)
5. Annual billings, sales and/or income (last two years)
6. Subsidiary companies; specialized divisions
7. Departments (overall structure)
8. Major accounts, products or services

The Subtleties

1. History of the firm (specialties, honors, awards, famous names)
2. Names, titles and backgrounds of top management
3. Existence (and type) of training program
4. Relocation policy
5. Relative salaries (compared to other companies in field or by size)
6. Recent developments concerning the the company and its products or services (from your trade magazine and newspaper reading)
7. Everything you can learn about the career, likes and dislikes of the person(s) interviewing you

The amount of time and work necessary to be *this* well prepared for an interview is considerable. It will not be accomplished the day before the interview. You may even find some of the information you need to be unavailable on short notice.

(Is it really so important to do all this? Well, **somebody out there is going to.** *And if you happen to be interviewing for the same job as that other, well-prepared, knowledgeable candidate, who do* **you** *think will impress the interviewer more?)*

As we've already discussed, if you give yourself enough time, most of this information is surprisingly easy to obtain. In addition to the reference sources we previously covered (see Appendix B, too), the company itself can probably supply you with a great deal of data. A firm's annual report—which all publicly-owned companies must publish yearly for their stockholders—is a virtual treasure trove of information. Write each company and request copies of their last two annual reports. A comparison of sales, income and other data over this period may enable you to discover some interesting things about their overall financial health and growth potential. Many libraries also have collections of annual reports from major corporations.

Attempting to learn about your interviewer is a chore, the importance of which is underestimated by most applicants (who then, of course, don't bother to do it). Being one of the exceptions may get you a job. Use the biographical references available in your local library. If he or she is listed in any of these sources, you'll be able to learn an awful lot about his or her background. In addition, find out if he or she has written any articles that have appeared in the trade press or, even better, books on his or her area(s) of expertise. Referring to these writings during the course of an interview, without making it *too* obvious a compliment, can be very effective. We all have egos and we all like people to talk about us. The interviewer is no different from the rest of us. You might also check to see if any of your networking contacts worked with him or her at his current (or a previous) company and can help "fill you in."

Selection Vs. Screening Interviews

The process to which the majority of this chapter is devoted is the actual *selection interview*, usually conducted by the person to whom the new hire will be reporting. But there is another process—the *screening interview*—which many of you may have to survive first.

Screening interviews are usually conducted by a member of the personnel department. Though they may not be empowered to hire, they *are* in a position to screen out or eliminate those candidates they feel (based on the facts) are not qualified to handle the job. These decisions are not usually made on the basis of personality, appearance, eloquence, persuasiveness or any other subjective criteria, but rather by clicking off yes or no answers against a checklist of skills. If you don't have the requisite number, you will be eliminated from further consideration. This may seem arbitrary, but it is a realistic and often necessary way for corporations to minimize the time and dollars involved in filling even the lowest jobs on the corporate ladder.

Remember, screening personnel are not looking for reasons to *hire* you; they're trying to find ways to *eliminate* you from the job search pack. Resumes sent blindly to the personnel department will usually be subjected to such screening; you will be eliminated without any personal contact (an excellent reason to construct a superior resume and *not* send out blind mailings).

If you are contacted, it will most likely be by telephone. When you are responding to such a call, keep these three things in mind: 1). It *is* an interview; be on your guard. 2). Answer all questions honestly. And 3). Be enthusiastic. You will get the standard questions from the interviewer—his or her attempts to "flesh out" the information included on your resume and/or cover letter. Strictly speaking, they are seeking out any negatives which may exist. If your resume is honest and factual (and it should be), you have no reason to be anxious, because you have nothing to hide.

Don't be nervous—be glad you were called and remember your objective: to get past this screening phase so you can get on to the real interview.

The Day Of The Interview

On the day of the interview, wear a conservative (not funereal) business suit—*not* a sports coat, *not* a "nice" blouse and skirt. Shoes should be shined, nails cleaned, hair cut and in place. And no low-cut or tight-fitting dresses (especially on the men).

It's not unusual for resumes and cover letters to head in different directions when a company starts passing them around to a number of executives. If you sent them, both may even be long gone. So bring along extra copies of your resume and your own copy of the cover letter that originally accompanied it.

Whether or not you make them available, we suggest you prepare a neatly-typed list of references (including the name, title, company, address and phone number of each person). You may want to bring along a copy of your high school or college transcript, especially if it's something to brag about. (Once you get your first job, you'll probably never use it—or be asked for it—again, so enjoy it while you can!)

On Time Means Fifteen Minutes Early

Plan to arrive fifteen minutes before your scheduled appointment. If you're in an unfamiliar city or have a long drive to their offices, allow extra time for the unexpected delays that seem to occur with mind-numbing regularity on important days.

Arriving early will give you some time to check your appearance, catch your breath, check in with the receptionist, learn how to correctly pronounce the interviewer's name, and get yourself organized and battle ready.

Arriving late does not make a sterling first impression. If you are only a few minutes late, it's probably best not to mention it or even excuse yourself. With a little luck, everybody else is behind schedule and no one will notice. However, if you're more than fifteen minutes late, have an honest (or at least *serviceable*) explanation ready and offer it at your first opportunity. Then drop the subject as quickly as possible and move on to the interview.

The Eyes Have It

When you meet the interviewer, shake hands firmly. People notice handshakes and often form a first impression based solely on them.

Ask for a business card. This will make sure you get the person's name and title right when you write your follow-up letter. You can staple it to the company file for easy reference as you continue your networking.

Try to maintain eye contact with the interviewer as you talk. This will indicate you're interested in what he or she has to say. Sit straight. Avoid smoking.

Should coffee or a soft drink be offered, you may accept (but should do so only if the interviewer is joining you).

Keep your voice at a comfortable level, and try to sound enthusiastic (without imitating Charleen Cheerleader). Be confident and poised, and provide direct, accurate and honest answers to the trickiest questions.

And, as you try to remember all this, just be yourself, and try to act like you're comfortable and almost enjoying this whole process!

Don't Name Drop...Conspicuously

A friendly relationship with other company employees may have provided you with valuable information prior to the interview, but don't flaunt such relationships. The interviewer is interested only in how you will relate to him or her and how well he or she surmises you will fit in with the rest of the staff. Name dropping may smack of favoritism. And you are in no position to know who the interviewer's favorite (or *least* favorite) people are.

On the other hand, if you have established a complex network of professionals through informational interviews, attending trade shows, reading trade magazines, etc., it is perfectly permissable to refer to these people, their companies, conversations you've had, whatever. It may even impress the interviewer with the extensiveness of your preparation.

Fork On The Left, Knife On The Right

Interviews are sometimes conducted over lunch, though this is not usually the case with entry-level people. If it does happen to you, though, try to order something in the middle price range, neither filet mignon nor a cheeseburger.

Do not order alcohol. If your interviewer orders a carafe of wine, you may share it. Otherwise, alcohol should be considered *verboten*, under any and all circumstances. Then hope your mother taught you the correct way to eat and talk at the same time. If not, just do your best to maintain your poise.

The Importance Of *Last* Impressions

There are some things interviewers will always view with displeasure: street language, complete lack of eye contact, insufficient or vague explanations or answers, a noticeable lack of energy, poor interpersonal skills (i.e., not listening or the basic inability to carry on an intelligent conversation), and a demonstrable lack of motivation.

Every impression may count. And the very *last* impression an interviewer has may outweigh everything else. So, before you allow an interview to end, summarize why you want the job, why you are qualified, and what, *in particular*, you can offer their company.

Then, take some action. If the interviewer hasn't told you about the rest of the interview process and/or where you stand, ask him or her. Will you be seeing other people that day? If so, ask for some background on anyone else with whom you'll be interviewing. If there are no other meetings that day, what's the next step? When can you expect to hear from them about coming back?

When you return home, file all the business cards, copies of correspondence and notes from the interview(s) with each company in the appropriate files. Finally, but most importantly, ask yourself which firms you really want to work for and which you are no longer interested in. This will quickly determine how far you want the process at each to develop before you politely tell them to stop considering you for the job.

Immediately send a thank-you letter to each executive you met. These should, of course, be neatly-typed business letters, not handwritten notes (unless you are most friendly, indeed, with the interviewer and want to *stress* the "informal" nature of your note). If you are still interested in pursuing a position at their company, tell them in no uncertain terms. Reiterate why you feel you're the best candidate and tell each of the executives when you hope (expect?) to hear from them.

On The 8th Day God Created Interviewers

Though most interviews will follow a relatively standard format, there will undoubtedly be a wide disparity in the skills of the interviewers you meet. Many of these executives (with the exception of the Personnel staff) will most likely not have extensive interviewing experience, have limited knowledge of interviewing techniques, use them infrequently, be hurried or harried by the press of other duties or not even view your interview as critically important.

Rather than studying standardized test results or utilizing professional evaluation skills developed over many years of practice, these non-professionals react intuitively—their initial (first five minutes) impressions are often the lasting and overriding factors they remember. So you must sell yourself ...fast.

The best way to do this is to try to achieve a comfort level with your interviewer. Isn't establishing rapport—through words, gestures, appearance common interests, etc. —what you try to do in *any* social situation? It's just trying to know one another better. Against this backdrop, the questions and answers will flow in a more natural way.

The Set Sequence

Irrespective of the competence levels of the interviewer, you can anticipate an interview sequence roughly as follows:

- Greetings
- Social niceties (small talk)
- Purpose of meeting (let's get down to business)
- Broad questions/answers

- Specific questions/answers
- In-depth discussion of company, job and opportunity
- Summarizing information given & received
- Possible salary probe (dependent upon level of achievement)
- Summary/indication as to next steps

When you look at this sequence closely, it is obvious that once you have gotten past the greeting, social niceties and some explanation of the job (in the "getting down to business" section), the bulk of the interview will be questions—yours and the interviewer's. In this question and answer session, there are not necessarily any right or wrong answers, only good and bad ones.

It's Time To Play Q & A

You can't control the "chemistry" between you and the interviewer—do you seem to "hit it off" right from the start or never connect at all? Since you *can't* control such a subjective problem, it pays to focus on what you *can* —the questions you will be asked, your answers and the questions *you* had better be prepared to ask.

Not surprisingly, many of the same questions pop up in interview after interview, regardless of company size, type or location. I have chosen the thirteen most common—along with appropriate hints and answers for each—for inclusion in this chapter. Remember: There are no right or wrong answers to these questions, only good and bad ones.

Substance counts more than speed when answering questions. Take your time and make sure that you listen to each question—there is nothing quite as disquieting as a lengthy, well-thoughtout answer that is completely irrelevant to the question asked. You wind up looking like a programmed clone with stock answers to dozens of questions who has, unfortunately, pulled the wrong one out of the grab bag.

Once you have adequately answered a specific question, it *is* permissible to go beyond it and add more information if doing so adds something to the discussion and/or highlights a particular strength, skill, course, etc. But avoid making lengthy speeches just for the sake of sounding off.

Study the list of questions (and hints) that follow, and prepare at least one solid, concise answer for each. Practice with a friend until your answers to these most-asked questions sound intelligent, professional and, most important, unmemorized and unrehearsed.

"Why do you want to be in this field?"

Using your knowledge and understanding of the particular field, explain why you find the business exciting and where and how you see yourself fitting in.

"Why do you think you will be successful in this business?"

Using the information from your self evaluation and the research you did on that particular company, formulate an answer which marries your strengths to theirs and to the characteristics of the position for which you're applying.

"Why did you choose our company?"

This is an excellent opportunity to explain the extensive process of education and research you've undertaken. Tell them about your strengths and how you match up with their firm. Emphasize specific things about their company that led you to seek an interview. Be a salesperson—be convincing.

"What can you do for us?"

Construct an answer that essentially lists your strengths, the experience you have which will contribute to your job performance, and any other unique qualifications that will place you at the head of the applicant pack. Be careful: This is a question specifically designed to *eliminate* some of that pack. Sell yourself. Be one of the few called back for a second interview.

"What position here interests you?"

If you're interviewing for a specific position, answer accordingly. If you want to make sure you don't close the door on other opportunities of which you might be unaware, you can follow up with your own question: "I'm here to apply for your Sales Training Program. Is there another position open for which you feel I'm qualified?"

If you've arranged an interview with a company without knowing of any specific openings, use the answer to this question to describe the kind of work you'd like to do and why you're qualified to do it. Avoid a specific job title, since they will tend to vary from firm to firm.

If you're on a first interview with the personnel department, just answer the question. They only want to figure out where to send you.

"What jobs have you held and why did you leave them?"

Or the direct approach: "Have you ever been fired?" Take this opportunity to expand on your resume, rather than precisely answering the question by merely recapping your job experiences. In discussing each job, point out what you liked about it, what factors led to your leaving and how the next job added to your continuing professional education. If you *have* been fired, say so. It's very easy to check.

"What are your strengths and weaknesses?"

Or *"What are your hobbies (or outside interests)?"* Both questions can be easily answered using the data you gathered to complete the self-evaluation process. Be wary of being too forthcoming about your glaring faults (nobody expects you to volunteer every weakness and mistake), but do *not* reply, "I don't have any." They won't believe you and, what's worse, *you* won't believe you. After all, you did the evaluation—you know it's a lie!

Good answers to these questions are those in which the interviewer can identify benefits for him- or herself. For example: "I consider myself an excellent planner. I am seldom caught by surprise and I prize myself on being able to anticipate problems and schedule my time to be ahead of the game. I devote a prescribed number of hours each week to this activity. I've noticed that many people just react. If you plan ahead, you should be able to cut off most problems before they arise."

You may consider disarming the interviewer by admitting a weakness, but doing it in such a way as to make it relatively unimportant to the job function. For example: "Higher mathematics has never been my strong suit. Though I am competent enough, I've always envied my friends with a more mathematical bent. In sales, though, I haven't found this a liability. I'm certainly quick enough in figuring out how close I am to monthly quotas and, of course, I keep a running record of commissions earned."

"Do you think your extracurricular activities were worth the time you devoted to them?"

This is a question often asked of entry-level candidates. One possible answer: "Very definitely. As you see from my resume, I have been quite active in the Student Government and French Club. My language fluency allowed me to spend my junior year abroad as an exchange student, and working in a functioning government gave me firsthand knowledge of what can be accomplished with people in the real world. I suspect my marks would have been somewhat higher had I not taken on so many activities outside of school, but I feel the balance they gave me contributed significantly to my overall growth as a person."

"What are your career goals?"

Interviewers are always seeking to probe the motivations of prospective employees. Nowhere is this more apparent than when the area of ambition is discussed. The high key answer to this question might be; "Given hard work, company growth and a few lucky breaks along the way, I'd look forward to being in a top executive position by the time I'm 35. I believe in effort and the risk/reward system—my research on this company has shown me that it operates on the same principles. I would hope it would select its future leaders from those people who displaying such characteristics."

"At some future date would you be willing to relocate?"

Pulling up one's roots is not the easiest thing in the world to do, but it is often a fact of life in the corporate world. If you're serious about your career (and such a move often represents a step up the career ladder), you will probably not mind such a move. Tell the interviewer. If you really *don't* want to move, you may want to say so, too—though I would find out how probable or frequent such relocations would be before closing the door while still in the interview stage.

Keep in mind that as you get older, establish ties in a particular community, marry, have children, etc., you will inevitably feel less jubilation at the thought of moving once a year or even "being out on the road." So take the opportunity to experience new places and experiences while you're young. If you don't, you may never get the chance.

"How did you get along with your last supervisor?"

This question is designed to understand your relationship with (and reaction to) authority. Remember: Companies look for team players, people who will fit in with their hierarchy, their rules, their ways of doing things. An answer might be: "I prefer to work with smart, strong people who know what they want and can express themselves. I learned in the military that in order to accomplish the mission, someone has to be the leader and that person has to be given the authority to lead. Someday I aim to be that leader. I hope then my subordinates will follow me as much and as competently as I'm ready to follow now."

"What are your salary requirements?"

If they are at all interested in you, this question will probably come up. The danger is that you may price yourself too low or, even worse, right out of a job you want. Since you will have a general idea of industry figures for that position (and may even have an idea of what that company tends to pay new people for the position), why not refer to a *range* of salaries, such as $20,000 - $25,000?

If the interviewer doesn't bring up salary at all, it's doubtful you're being seriously considered, so you probably don't need to even bring the subject up. (If you know you aren't getting the job or aren't interested in it if offered, you may try to nail down a salary figure in order to be better prepared for the next interview.)

"Tell me about yourself"

Watch out for this one! It's often one of the first questions asked. If you falter here, the rest of the interview could quickly become a downward slide to nowhere. Be prepared, and consider it an opportunity to combine your answers to many of the previous questions into one concise description of who you are, what you want to be and why that company should take a chance on you. Summarize your resume—briefly—and expand on particular courses or experiences relevant to the firm or position. Do *not* go on about your hobbies or personal life, where you spent your summer vacation, or anything that is not relevant to securing that job. You may explain how that particular job fits in with your long-range career goals and talk specifically about what attracted you to their company in the first place.

The Not-So-Obvious Questions

Every interviewer is different and, unfortunately, there are no rules saying he or she has to use all or any of the "basic" questions covered above. But we think the odds are against his or her avoiding *all* of them. Whichever of these he or she includes, be assured most interviewers do like to come up with questions that are "uniquely theirs." It may be just one or a whole series—questions developed over the years that he or she feels help separate the wheat from the chaff.

You can't exactly prepare yourself for questions like, "What would you do if...(fill in the blank with some obscure occurrence)?" "Tell me about your father," or "What's your favorite ice cream flavor?" Every interviewer we know has his or her favorites and all of these questions seem to come out of left field. Just stay relaxed, grit your teeth (quietly) and take a few seconds to frame a reasonably intelligent reply.

Some questions may be downright inappropriate. Young women, for example, may be asked about their plans for marriage and children. Don't call the interviewer a chauvinist (or worse). And don't point out that the question may be a little outside the law—the nonprofessional interviewer may not realize such questions are illegal, and a huffy response may confuse, even anger, him or her.

Whenever any questions are raised about your personal life—and this question surely qualifies—it is much more effective to respond that you are very interested in the position and have no reason to believe that your personal life will preclude you from doing an excellent job.

"Do *You* Have Any Questions?"

It's the last fatal question on our list, often the last one an interviewer throws at you after an hour or two of grilling. Unless the interview has been very long and unusually thorough, you probably *should* have questions—about the job, the company, even the industry. Unfortunately, by the time this question off-handedly hits the floor, you are already looking forward to leaving and may have absolutely nothing to say.

Preparing yourself for an interview means more than having answers for some of the questions an interviewer may ask. It means having your *own* set of questions—at least five or six—for the interviewer. The interviewer is trying to find the right person for the job. *You're* trying to find the right job. So you should be just as curious about him or her and the company as he or she is about you. Here's a short list of questions you may consider asking on any interview:

1. What will my typical day be like?

2. What happened to the last person who had this job?

3. Given my attitude and qualifications, how would you estimate my chances for career advancement at your company?

4. Why did you come to work here? What keeps you here?

5. If you were I, would you start here again?

6. How would you characterize the management philosophy of your firm?

7. What characteristics do the successful_____ at your company have in common (fill in the blank with an appropriate title)?

8. What's the best (and worst) thing about working here?

9. On a scale of 1 to 10, how would you rate your company—in terms of salaries, benefits and employee satisfaction—in comparison to similar firms?

Testing & Applications

Though not part of the selection interview itself, job applications and psychological testing are often part of the pre-interview process. You should know something about them.

The job application is essentially a record-keeping exercise—simply the transfer of work experience and educational data from your resume to a printed applications form. Though taking the time to recopy data may seem like a waste of time, some companies simply want the information in a particular order on a standard form. One difference: Applications often require the listing of references and salary levels achieved. Be sure to bring your list of references with you to any interview (so you can transfer the pertinent information), and don't lie about salary history; it's easily checked.

Many companies now use a variety of psychological tests as additional mechanisms to screen out undesirable candidates. Although their accuracy is subject to question, the companies that use them obviously believe they are effective at identifying applicants whose personality makeups would preclude their participating positively in a given work situation, especially those at the extreme ends of the behavior spectrum.

Their usefulness in predicting job accomplishment is considered limited. If you are normal (like the rest of us), you'll have no trouble with these tests and may even find them amusing. Just don't try to outsmart them—you'll just wind up outsmarting yourself.

28

The Different Perceptions Of Employers And Students

Ralph M. Gaedeke and Dennis H. Tootelian
California State University, Sacramento

Students often base their job search strategy on their perceptions of the attributes they believe employers are seeking. These perceptions, however, may not coincide with those of employers, resulting in a mismatch of employee attributes sought and those offered. An understanding of employee attributes that are most highly valued by employers is of particular importance to graduates entering the job market. Employers typically have a large pool of graduates from which to make their selections and can use stringent employee attributes in evaluating job candidates.

Recently we surveyed 500 junior and senior business students to determine what they believe employers look for in job candidates for entry-level positions and compared them with applicant skills employers actually seek. Employers surveyed included 347 contacts for college recruiting. They represented national firms in various industries seeking to fill positions in marketing and/or sales. The sample was drawn from contacts listed in the November 1987 issue of *Business Week's CAREERS* describing "1,000 Companies that Hire the Most College Grads for 1988." (Results of the employer survey were reported in the March 27, 1989 issue of *Marketing News*.)

Questionnaires asked both sets of respondents to assess 35 employee attributes that have the potential of serving as hiring criteria. Each item on the survey was evaluated on a seven point, Likert-type scale, where one was "extremely important" and seven was "not at all important." Generally, both students and employers viewed selective attributes pertaining to personal, entrepreneurial, and leadership characteristics and specialized skills to be more important than academic and social characteristics. There were, however, differences of opinion between the two groups about the importance of individual attributes.

Using the mean scores, 19 of the 35 employee attributes are ranked for students and employers in the table which accompanies this article. The top five attributes in the students' ranking were: oral communication skills, enthusiasm/motivation, self-confidence, ambition, and entrepreneurship. On the other hand, employers' top five rankings were: enthusiasm/motivation, interpersonal skills, initiative, oral communication skills, and maturity.

Collectively, for both students and employers, the five attributes perceived to be of greatest importance fall into the categories of leadership, entrepreneurial, and personal characteristics.

Communication and leadership skills also were viewed by both groups to be important employee attributes. This finding corresponds to the description of "The Ideal Job Candidate of the 21st Century," as reported by the CPC Resource Information Center, Bethlehem, Pa. The relative low importance attributed to computer literacy, however, which ranked 20 for students and 24 for employers, is somewhat surprising because it's been reported that the ability to use computers will be the most important job skill for the 1990s.

Only four attributes were considered by both students and employers as unimportant: high school record, military experience, membership in fraternal organizations, and sports participation.

To ascertain what attributes employers prefer in potential employees, respondents also were asked to answer an open-ended question regarding the four most important attributes employers look for when selecting a candidate for an entry-level marketing or sales position. The attributes mentioned most by students were enthusiasm/motivation (24%), oral communication skills (22%), self-confidence (14%), and interpersonal skills (13%). Overall, these responses parallel the mean responses to the individual attributes.

Employers cited oral communication skills (20%), interpersonal skills (17%), enthusiasm/ motivation (12%), written communication skills (12%), and related work experience (10%) most frequently. Only 4% of the students listed written communication skills among the most important attributes preferred by employers, and just 3% cited related work experience.

Ranked Importance of Employee Attributes

Employee Attribute	Student Rank	Employer Rank
Oral communication skills	1	4
Enthusiasm/motivation	2	1
Self-confidence	3	8
Ambition	4	6
Entrepreneurship	4	7
Initiative	6	3
Interpersonal skills	7	2
Ability to articulate goals	8	9
Assertiveness	9	11
Written communication skills	10	14
Maturity	11	5
Problem-solving skills	12	9
Leadership skills	13	12
Related work experience	14	15
Personal appearance	15	16
Major area of concentration	16	13
Creativity	17	17
Quantitative skills	18	18
Acknowledging limitations	19	19

Knowing what attributes students will need to obtain their desired job upon graduation is useful in career planning. The challenge is to make sure their college experience prepares them for a career. Students need to take note of the results of this study early in their academic careers to pursue not only their academic interests, but also the leadership, entrepreneurial, and specialized skills a college education can provide. Furthermore, students need to be aware of the personal characteristics which enhance employers' willingness to hire them.

To minimize the possible mismatch of employee attributes sought and those offered, students have to be acutely aware of what their "customers"—the employers—are seeking. As is true in the marketing of goods and services, *caveat venditor* should be the rule.

Guidance should be provided by educators and career counselors long before students graduate so they can choose the course of study, extracurricular activities, and work experience which will help them acquire the appropriate attributes.

RALPH GAEDEKE and **DENNIS TOOTELIAN** are professors of marketing at California State University, Sacramento. This article originally appeared in the May 22, 1989 issue of *Marketing News* and is reprinted with that magazine's permission.

29

Getting An Advertising Internship

B. Steven Nisberg, Manager, Employment USA
Young & Rubicam Inc.

An internship in advertising can be a most important experience for those of you considering a career in advertising. Why? Because it will give you the opportunity to experience firsthand what it's like to work in the industry, probably the most effective way to determine whether you'd be interested in spending several years, if not your entire career, in advertising.

An internship also puts you ahead of the competition—the hundreds of *other* graduates out there interested in advertising careers—by demonstrating your sincere interest in the agency business to whomever is reviewing your resume. Recruiters at major agencies receive thousands of resumes annually; it is impossible for them to interview every person looking for an entry-level position who sends one in. To manage this deluge, recruiters must pare it down, so they skim cover letters and resumes, keying in on related experience or demonstrated interest. If they are lacking, a rejection letter usually follows. However, if an active association with an advertising club or an internship is listed, an interview is probably in order.

What To Expect In An Internship

There are many types of intern programs available today. Some agencies conduct intern programs during the summer months, others during the winter recesses or throughout the school year. Some agencies pay their interns; some do not. The salaries vary widely, but most tend to be in the range of $250 - $350 dollars per week. You shouldn't worry about the money— how much or even whether you're paid at all—because you will be learning a great deal about the industry, and that is compensation in itself!

Internship programs tend to vary from agency to agency, so it is hard to summarize exactly what to expect. Some agencies go to great lengths to make sure that each internship is a rewarding experience for both the participant and the agency. A good program will usually involve interns being assigned to a supervisor who is interested in working with junior-level people and will take the time to answer questions and delegate meaningful assignments on a day-to-day basis.

Some programs also offer frequent seminars involving a variety of people from different departments within the agency, exposing interns to all major agency functions (i.e., media, creative, account management and market research) within one internship.

Current State Of Intern Programs

All of the merger activity that has occurred in this industry over the past several years has led to a greater emphasis on bottom-line profitability, which has often been achieved by cutting expenses and laying off people. Unfortunately, training programs and internships were often considered expendable items when the budget ax fell.

The good news: Based on my own informal survey of several large agencies in the New York City area, most of the people I spoke with agreed that intern programs are still a very useful method of recruiting, giving the agencies a chance to "look over" the newest crop of soon-to-be college graduates without having to commit to hiring them. They noted that their agencies are now re-assessing the need for intern programs; most are hoping to expand or reestablish them.

How To Get An Internship

The first step is to put together a resume, similar to one that you would use for obtaining full-time employment upon graduation. It should include an objective, your education, work experience, extracurricular activities and hobbies.

The next step is to identify the department in which you would most like to work. Do some research in your college or university library, talk to your professors and, of course, read all of the other articles by top agency pros in this *Career Directory*. After this basic research, you may want to speak to friends, relatives or alumni who are currently in the industry to refine your understanding of the business.

Use the *Job Opportunities Databank* in the back of this *Directory* (and the brand-new edition of another Career Press publication—Internships, Volume 1: Advertising, Sales, Public Relations and Marketing) to uncover all the agencies that currently offer intern programs, who to contact, application procedures and deadlines, and other details about the programs. Then call them, one by one, and try to get an interview.

Interviewing For An Internship

Most agencies require an interview with each prospective intern. Your background, degree or major aren't all-important—most agencies select their interns based on their demonstrated interest in advertising as a career and on the individual's understanding of the various agency functions.

Once you have obtained an interview with a particular agency, familiarize yourself with every aspect of its operation, account list, management, etc. by reading any material available in the trade magazines or even from the agency itself (brochures, annual reports, etc.). Then just be yourself. Remember: The person who's interviewing you was probably in your shoes not so long ago!

If you're serious about getting an internship, plan on interviewing with several agencies, not just one. And consider agencies of all sizes—large, medium and small. Look at ones in major cities and those in not-so-major cities. There are probably even advertising agencies right around your school; don't forget to check them out as well.

In Summary

As I mentioned in the beginning of this article, an internship is invaluable in gaining full-time employment upon graduation. It really does put you steps ahead of the competition and, more important, allows you the opportunity to figure out if advertising is the right career for you!

B. STEVEN NISBERG, a graduate of the School of Management at the University of Buffalo, is currently Manager, Employment USA at Young & Rubicam Inc. He is responsible for the implementation and evaluation of Y&R's many Affirmative Action and EEO activities. He also counsels all of Y&R's domestic offices on general recruitment issues.

Steve made his mark early on at Y&R by being appointed their youngest Manager of Employment in 1986. Following this, he then worked with a small group of Human Resource Executives, given the directive to determine exactly what it takes to be successful in Account Management. This research lead to a new way of selecting, evaluating and developing talent for the New York office—an approach which looks for demonstrated success characteristics based on past performance.

He's also responsible for overseeing all of Y&RNY's intern programs, which occur during and between semesters for college students. In addition, he also finds time to work on special projects in line with "giving a little something back" to the local community. The most recent one being the Mayor of New York's Adopt-A-Class Program in which he and other key Y&R executives taught advertising to a class of seventh graders.

Steve is an active participant with the American Association of Advertising Agencies, an Assistant Treasurer and former Lt. Governor of the American Advertising Federation's District Two and a frequent guest speaker at colleges and universities on the east coast.

Although Steve says he never intended to be in the business of advertising (his father wanted him to be a radiologist), if he had the opportunity to do it all over again, he wouldn't have changed a thing.

Section 5

Job Opportunities Databanks

30

Entry-Level Job Listings: United States

Now that you have read through the articles by top professionals on all the possible careers available to you in advertising, where can you find an agency that will give you your first job in the particular one you've chosen?

While there are numerous corporate directories and other reference works (many of them cited in our job search section) that contain important background information on agencies in which you may be interested, none of them can help you identify those that are actively seeking and hiring entry-level people.

This and the following chapter do exactly that, giving you the detailed information you need on hundreds of top agencies, in both the U. S. and, for the first time, Canada. There are three sections in this chapter:

The first lists those advertising agencies *(both U. S. and Canadian)* that specifically requested *not* to be listed in this *Directory.* This does not necessarily indicate that they have no entry-level job opportunities; it probably *does* mean, however, that they are already inundated with resumes from hopeful students and do not wish to do anything, directly or indirectly, to encourage even more interest. We have simply listed these agencies for you.

In the second section, we have listed those agencies we contacted via both mail and phone but from which we were unable to obtain the detailed information we require for listing in this *Directory.* We can intimate nothing about potential openings at these shops but have listed what information we do have so, if you wish, you can contact them yourself. Again, both U. S. and Canadian agencies that fall in this category are listed in *this* chapter.

Finally, in the third section, we have included those U. S. agencies that *did* respond to our survey regarding entry-level job opportunities. And, in the next chapter, we have listed, for the first time in this *Career Directory,* similar information for all of the Canadian ad agencies who responded to our survey. The detailed data included here is not a compendium of information from other sources. *We have printed only the information we obtained directly from the agencies themselves.* This information was compiled by our staff through direct mail questionnaires and telephone calls and represents data that is completely unavailable anywhere else.

As should be obvious, this is not a *complete* listing of U. S. and Canadian ad agencies. It is not meant to be. It does, however, include virtually all of the major agencies and a very representative sampling of smaller ones. If studied and used properly, it should help you identify those agencies—by type, size, location, etc.—that offer the best entry-level opportunities. With these listings as a guide, you should be able to get a better feel for the possibilities out there. You can then use a reference book like the Agency Red Book to find other agencies that match those listed here in size or location.

Most of the information in both chapters should be self-explanatory.

"Average Entry-level Hiring" is that agency's best estimate of anticipated need for new people each year. *"Total employees"* lists all full-time employees. Part-time employees, if any, are noted in parentheses.

Two important points: 1) A "?" following the "average entry-level hiring" entry means *they tend to hire entry-level people;* **they were just unable to come up with any specific number. 2) If the agency indicates they do not plan to hire any entry-level people, they may still have listed "Opportunities." In this case, these should not be considered actual jobs, merely the positions they consider entry-level...whether or not they currently have openings.**

If the agencies themselves had any specific suggestions, we've included them. These will help you get a head start on other applicants—you'll know what the agencies want you to do!

Whenever we couldn't confirm the accuracy of an entry, we merely entered "NA"—Not Available.

Two final notes: First, despite our every attempt to ensure the accuracy of the information we've included, time marches on...and so do contacts. In other words, there will be mistakes in these listings—the very day they're published—just because things change and, in some agencies, change very quickly. But we think you'll find that the vast majority of this previously-unpublished information will remain credible until it is updated in 1992 in a fifth edition.

Lastly, previous editions of this *Career Directory* have also included information on summer and school-year internships. At the request of the librarians, counselors, professors and students who utilize these Directories, we have now published this internship data (and, in fact, increased three-fold the amount of information included in each internship listing) in a completely separate series of books—our *Internships Series.*

Volume 1 of this series lists internship programs at hundreds of major advertising agencies, PR firms and corporations in the United States and Canada. It is available in a new second edition for 1990.

Agencies Requesting No Listing

Altschiller Reitzfeld Davis/Tracy Locke
Ambrose, Carr DeForest & Linton Ltd. (Canada)
Bruce J. Bloom Advertising & Marketing, Inc.
C. Reimer Advertising Ltd. (Canada)
D'Arcy Masius Benton & Bowles Canada Inc.
D.M.C.A.
Dutton Advertising (Canada)
Enterprise Advertising Associates Ltd. (Canada)
Evans Advertising Agency, Inc. (Canada)
Foster Mead Advertising Ltd. (Canada)

Greiner Harries MacLean Ltd. (Canada)
J. Walter Thompson Company Ltd. (Canada)
LaBuick & Associates Media, Ltd. (Canada)
MacLaren Advertising (Canada)
Master Communications Corp. of Canada Ltd.
Medcom Advertising (Canada)
Medicus Intercon Canada
Nationwide Advertising Service Inc. (Canada)
Publicite Bates, Inc. (Canada)
Rainbow Media Inc.

Science & Medicine (Canada)
Sheehy & Knopf, Inc.
Stone & Adler

Stone, Hand & Dewar Inc. (Canada)
Sudler & Hennesey
Wyse Advertising, Inc

Agencies No Information *Supplying*

ALBERT FRANK-GUENTHER LAW
71 Broadway
NewYork, NY 10006
212-248-5200

ARTS & COMMUNICATIONS COUNSELORS
55 Bloor Street West—Suite 1200
Toronto, ON M4W 1A5
416-966-3421

BACKER SPIELVOGEL BATES
405 Lexington Avenue
New York, NY 10174
212-297-7000

TED BATES ADVERTISING INC.
2 St. Claire West
Toronto, ON M4V 1L5
416-925-8835

DAVIDOFF & PARTNERS INC.
Heritage Square
Fairfield, CT 06430
203-255-3425

DCA ADVERTISING
1114 Avenue of the Americas
32nd Floor
New York, NY 10036
212-869-8350

DONER, SCHUR, PEPPLER
65 St. Claire Avenue East—9th Floor
Toronto, ON M4T 2Y3
416-323-0113

DRAKE ADVERTISING LTD.
150 Bloor Street West—Suite 600
Toronto, ON M5S 2X9
416-967-3812

EARLE PALMER BROWN
(Corporate Headquarters)
6935 Arlington Rd.
Bethesda, MD 20814
301-657-6000

EARLE PALMER BROWN & SPIRO
1 Liberty Place
1650 Market Street
Philadelphia, PA 19103
215-851-9600

FCB—LEBER KATZ PARTNERS
767 Fifth Avenue
New York, NY 10153
212-705-1000

FOOTE, CONE & BELDING
101 East Erie Street
Chicago, IL 60611
312-751-7000

GABEL ADVERTISING
P.O. Box 2588
Colorado Springs, CO 80901
303-636-2361

GOODWIN, DANNENBAUM, LITTMAN, & WINGFIELD
5400 Westheimer Court
Houston, TX 77056
713-622-7676

GREYCOM CANADA
Place du Canada—Suite 1850
Montreal, PQ H3B 2N2
514-861-1621

HILL HOLIDAY ADVERTISING INC.
200 Clarendon Street
Boston, MA 02116
617-437-1600

J.H. LEWIS ADVERTISING AGENCY, INC.
P.O. Drawer 3202
Mobile, AL 36652
206-476-2507

MARDEN-KANE CANADA LTD.
7355 TransCanada Highway
Ville St. Laurent, PQ H4T 1Z9
514-747-1313

MULLER JORDAN WEISS LTD.
2200 Yonge Street—Suite 601
Toronto, ON M4S 1S5
416-487-3466

NATCOMMUNICATION, INC.
1420 Sherbrooke Street West—7th Floor
Montreal, PQ H3G 1K5
514-842-9471

OGILVY & MATHER
100 University Avenue
Toronto, ON M5J 1V5
416-593-7711

PRACO LTD.
511 North Tejon
Colorado Springs, CO 80903
303-473-0704

PRICE/McNABB ADVERTISING
86 Asheland Avenue
Asheville, NC 28801
704-254-7461

QLM ASSOCIATES
470 Wall Street
Princeton, NJ 08540
609-683-1177

ROOT AND ASSOCIATES, INC.
Box 751
Baton Rouge, LA 70821
504-344-3198

ROSENFELD, SIROWITZ, HUMPHREY & STRAUSS
111 Fifth Avenue
New York, NY 10003
212-605-0200

SLATER HANFT MARTIN
111 Fifth Avenue
New York, NY 10003
212-674-3100

YORK ALPERN/DDB NEEDHAM
A division of Diversified Services, Inc.
(Omnicom Group)
5757 Wilshire Blvd.—Suite 723
Los Angeles, CA 90036
213-931-9000

U. S. Agency Entry-Level Job Listings

AC&R ADVERTISING, INC.
A member of Saatchi & Saatchi USA Affiliates
16 East 32nd Street
New York, NY 10016
212-685-2500

Employment Contact: Patricia Shelton, VP/Dir.of Human Resources; Robin Ornstein, Personnel Rep.
Total Employees: 320
Average Entry-Level Hiring: 30
Opportunities: Account Coordinator—College degree required; typing proficiency; word processing skills a plus. Media Planner—College degree required; figure aptitude and communication skills.
Internships: No

ACKERMAN ADVERTISING
31 Glenhead Road
Glenhead, NY 11545
516-759-3000

Employment Contact: Skip Ackerman, President
Total Employees: 35
Average Entry-Level Hiring: 0
Internships: No

ACKERMAN, HOOD & McQUEEN, INC.
1600 Rhode Island Avenue NW
Washington, DC 20036
202-223-8270

Employment Contact: Karen Cottrell, PR Account Manager
Total Employees: 8
Average Entry Level Hiring: 0
Opportunities: College graduates (usually majoring in Public Relations or Journalism) may begin as a secretary and move on to account manager after approximately one year.
Internships: Yes

ACKERMAN, HOOD & McQUEEN, INC.
8023 East 63rd Place
Tulsa, OK 74153
918-250-9511

Employment Contact: Department Heads
Total Employees: 35
Average Entry Level Hiring: 5-10

Opportunities: Traffic—College degree preferred; no other requirements specified.
Internships: Yes

ACKERMAN, HOOD & McQUEEN, INC.
1601 NW Expressway—Suite 1100
Oklahoma City, OK 73118
408-843-7777

Employment Contact: Christy Tebow, Manager of Traffic Operations
Average Entry Level Hiring: ?
Internships: Yes

ACKERMAN, HOOD & McQUEEN, INC.
12790 Merit Drive—Suite 616
Dallas, TX 75251
214-458-0376

Employment Contact: Tom Millweard, Sr. VP/Management Supervisor
Total Employees: 18
Average Entry-Level Hiring: Varies
Opportunities: Receptionist, Secretary, Account Coordinator, Traffic Coordinator—College degree and experience preferred.
Internships: Yes

ACKERMAN, HOOD & McQUEEN, INC.
5101 Old Greenwood Road
Fort Smith, AR 72903
501-648-3700

Employment Contact: Glen Williams, Sr. VP/Management Supervisor
Total Employees: 5
Average Entry-Level Hiring: 1-2
Opportunities: Account Executive, Art Director—College degree required; 1-2 years experience preferred.
Internships: No

AD SYSTEMS INTERNATIONAL, INC.
200 Gate Five Road—Suite 214, Box 2109
Sausalito, CA 94965
415-332-4252

Employment Contact: Personnel
Total Employees: 12
Internships: Yes

ADVERTISING DEVELOPMENT SPECIALISTS
2821 South Remington
Fort Collins, CO 80525
303-223-1743

Employment Contact: Linda Roesener, Personnel Director
Total Employees: 6

Average Entry-Level Hiring: 0
Opportunities: Office/Administrative—College degree (Liberal Arts preferred); typing, Word Star experience. Account Executive—College degree (Business and/or Marketing preferred).
Internships: Yes

A.I.M.,INC.
10I Lincoln Center Drive—Suite 240
Foster City, CA 94404
415-349-5555

Employment Contact: Margaret Fieler, Vice President
Total Employees: 8
Average Entry-Level Hiring: 0-1
Opportunities: Sales—College degree (BA/BS); great with people; ability to present effectively. Office Manager—College degree; great typist, very organized and a good social planner for staff.
Suggestions: "We look for bright, creative, independent people—the best out there."
Internships: Yes

ALLY & GARGANO, INC.
805 Third Avenue
New York, NY 10022
212-688-5300

Employment Contact: Paulette Barlanera, VP-Office Services & Personnel
Total Employees: 260
Average Entry-Level Hiring: 0
Opportunities: Applicants with experience only.
Internships: No

ALOYSIUS, BUTLER & CLARK, INC.
30 Hill Road—Bancroft Mills
Wilmington, DE 19806
302-655-1552

Employment Contact: John Hawkins, President
Total Employees: 30
Average Entry-Level Hiring: 1
Opportunities: Account Service—College degree. No other requirements specified.
Internships: Yes

ANDREW/MAUTNER, INC.
324 East Wisconsin Avenue
Milwaukee, WI 53202
414-272-4482

Employment Contact: Christopher M. Vernon, Executive Vice President
Total Employees: 20
Average Entry-Level Hiring: 1-2

Opportunities: Media Asst., Asst. Account Executive—College degree (BA/BS); 2-3 years experience preferred.
Internships: No

ARAGON CONSULTING GROUP
7711 Carondelet—Suite 807
St. Louis, MO 63105
314-726-0746

Employment Contact: Dave Joest, Vice President
Total Employees: 13
Average Entry-Level Hiring: 0
Opportunities: The last position open was for an assistant to the Project Coordinator—College degree required.
Internships: No

BADER RUTTER & ASSOCIATES
13555 Bishop's Court
Brockfield, WI 53183
414-784-7200

Employment Contact: Personnel
Total Employees: 100
Internships: Yes

BARNHART & COMPANY
455 Sherman—Suite 500
Denver, CO 80203
303-744-3211

Employment Contact: Steve Fay, Chief Financial Officer
Total Employees: 48
Average Entry-Level Hiring: 3
Opportunities: Receptionist—College degree. Word Processor—College degree; word processing training/ computer training. Traffic Runner—H. S. graduate.
Suggestions: "Initial contact made with letter & resume. If positions are open, we set up interview. We average 10 resumes per day, so we aren't able to interview everyone. Resumes are kept on hand for six months and are referred to when positions become available. We have very little turnover!"
Internships: Yes

BECKMAN ASSOCIATES ADVERTISING AGENCY, INC.
382 Broadway
Albany, NY 12207
518-465-4573

Employment Contact: Judy Arnold
Total Employees: 35
Average Entry-Level Hiring: 1-3
Opportunities: Copywriting—College degree. Account Executive—College degree; 2-3 years experience. Administrative Asst.—Typing, other basic office skills. Art—College degree; experience preferred.
Internships: Yes

BHN ADVERTISING & PUBLIC RELATIONS, INC.
910 North 11th Street
St. Louis, MO 63101
314-241-1200

Employment Contact: Kay Going, Media Director
Total Employees: 65
Average Entry-Level Hiring: 1-2
Opportunities: Media buyer—College degree; math and marketing skills. Direct mail assistant—College degree; figure aptitude; detail-oriented; experience preferred.
Internships: Yes

WILLIAM R. BIGGS/GILMORE ASSOCIATES
P.O. Box 6099
Hilton Head, SC 29938
803-785-3989

Employment Contact: Kathy Weathers, Office Manager
Total Employees: 12
Average Entry-Level Hiring: 0
Opportunities: Account Executive—College degree required. Production—No requirements specified.
Internships: Yes

BLAIR/BBDO
96 College Avenue
Rochester, NY 14607
716-473-0440

Employment Contact: Tom Tornatore
Total Employees: 34
Average Entry-Level Hiring: 1-2
Opportunities: Marketing Asst., Advertising Asst.— College degree (BA/BS); experience preferred.
Internships: No

THE BLOOM COMPANIES
3500 Maple
Dallas, TX 75219
214-443-9900

Employment Contact: Diane Bynum, Personnel Dir.
Total Employees: 200
Average Entry-Level Hiring: 1-2
Opportunities: No specific titles or requirements other than 4-year college graduate. Using campus recruiting to look for advertising majors.
Internships: No

BOLT ADVERTISING INC.
3512 Brambleton Avenue SW—Suite 6
Roanoke, VA 24018
703-989-2881

Employment Contact: Pete Ostaseski, President
Total Employees: 10
Average Entry-Level Hiring: 0-1
Comments: Very few openings.
Internships: No

BONSIB INC. MARKETING SERVICES
927 South Harrison Street
Fort Wayne, IN 46802
219-422-4661

Employment Contact: Richard E. Bonsib, Chairman and CEO
Total Employees: 34
Average Entry-Level Hiring: 1
Opportunities: Marketing Asst., Accounting/Finance—College degree (BA/BS); two years experience preferred.
Internships: Yes

DICK BRONSON INC.
31 Central Street
Bangor, ME 04401
207-947-7376

Employment Contact: Richard B. Bronson, President
Total Employees: 10
Average Entry-Level Hiring: 1
Opportunities: Graphic Arts—College degree (BA/BS); some experience preferred; demonstrable graphics ability.
Internships: Yes

BROYLES, ALLEBAUGH & DAVIS, INC.
31 Denver Technological Center
Englewood, CO 80111
303-770-2000

Employment Contact: Department Heads
Total Employees: 35
Average Entry-Level Hiring: 0
Comments: "Due to the size of our organization and the performance skills required, we do not hire entry-level people. When a vacancy occurs, or staff additions are required, we seek out experienced professionals, and each department hires individually. At some point in the future we may be in a position to hire entry-level people, but that course of action is not contemplated at this time."
Internships: No

LEO BURNETT COMPANY, INC.
35 West Wacker Drive
Chicago, IL 60601
312-220-5959

Employment Contact: Wayne Johnson, Creative Recruiting Dept.
Total Employees: 1,961
Average Entry-Level Hiring: 50-70
Opportunities: Media or Research Trainee—BS/BA (Liberal Arts or other degree). Client service trainee—MBA (some undergrads accepted, but this is rare). Art Director, Copywriter—Based on portfolio.
Comments: Interview decisions for all entry-level candidates based on resume. Creative candidates must have portfolio.
Internships: No

THE BURNS GROUP, INC.
1575 Sheland Tower
Minneapolis, MN 55426
612-334-6000

Employment Contact: Susan Kroska, Personnel Administrator
Total Employees: 188
Average Entry-Level Hiring: 2-3
Opportunities: Account Coordinator, Account Executive—College degree (BA/BS); 2 years experience preferred.
Internships: Yes

BUSSE & CUMMINS INC.
690 Fifth Street
San Francisco, CA 94107
415-957-0300

Employment Contact: B. J. Cummins, Jr., Vice President
Total Employees: 37
Average Entry-Level Hiring: 2-3
Opportunities: Account Coordinator, Media Assistant—College degree (BA/BS); 2 years experience preferred.
Internships: No

HAROLD CABOT & COMPANY, INC.
One Constitution Plaza
Boston, MA 02129
617-242-6200

Employment Contact: Edmund C. Fitzmaurice, Sr. VP
Total Employees: 125
Average Entry-Level Hiring: 0-1

Opportunities: Account Management—College degree (BA/BS); some marketing and media background; outgoing, hard worker, strong social skills.

Comments: "As a small agency, our personnel needs change from day to day and cannot be predicted by us far in advance of the date we might hire. We are always looking for bright young people."

Internships: No

CAMPBELL-EWALD WORLDWIDE

See listing for Lintas: Campbell Ewald

CAMPBELL-MITHUN-ESTY ADVERTISING

A subsidiary of Saatchi & Saatchi
222 South Ninth Street
Minneapolis, MN 55402
612-347-1000

Employment Contact: Account Svces: Robert Seper, Director of Human Resources; Media: Sharon Moe, Human Resources Administrator

Total Employees: 430

Average Entry-Level Hiring: 5-10 (varies each yr.)

Opportunities: Entry-level Creative openings rarely occur. Account Assistant (Account Services)—Future openings are unpredictable. Media Analyst (planning), Broadcast Assistant (broadcast buying)—Future openings are unpredictable. Requirements for the previous positions—Bachelor degree, possibly Master degree or equivalent work experience.

Comments: Send cover letter and resume to appropriate contact. No phone calls.

Internships: No

CAMPBELL-MITHUN-ESTY ADVERTISING

A subsidiary of Saatchi & Saatchi
100 East 42nd Street
New York, NY 10017
212-692-6200

Employment Contact: Hal Simpson, Senior VP/Dir. of Human Resources

Total Employees: 185

Average Entry-Level Hiring: 0

Opportunities: Rarely available, entry-level openings tend to be in the areas of accounting and media.

Internships: No

CARGILL, WILSON & ACREE, INC.

A subsidiary of The Omnicom Group
3060 Peachtree Road NW, 1 Buckhead Plaza
Atlanta, GA 30305
404-364-8700

Employment Contact: Denise Steiner, Sr. VP/Director Creative Services

Total Employees: 40

Average Entry-Level Hiring: 5

Opportunities: Accounting Clerks, Traffic Asst., Media Estimators—College degree. No other requirements specified.

Internships: Yes

CARTER COMMUNICATIONS CORP.

800 American Tower
Shreveport, LA 71101
318-227-1920

Employment Contact: Fair Hyams

Total Employees: 20

Average Entry-Level Hiring: 1-2

Opportunities: Asst. Account Executive—College degree (Marketing, Advertising preferred). Copywriter—College degree; strong major work experience, good credentials and references, able to handle large work load.

Suggestions: "Please send writing or artwork samples along with cover letter and resume."

Internships: Yes

COLLE & MCVOY, INC.

7900 International Drive—Suite 700
Minneapolis, MN 55425
612-851-2500

Employment Contact: Bob Hettlinger—VP/Director Human Resources; Creatives—Jon Anderson, Executive Creative Director; Public Relations—Doug Spong, Sr. VP/Director Public Relations

Total Employees: 104

Average Entry-Level Hiring: 2-4

Opportunities: Account Coordinator and Assistant Account Executive positions—Undergraduate or graduate degrees in Journalism, Public Relations, Advertising, or Marketing preferred. Internships are advantageous. Entry-level positions in Creative areas are rarely available.

Comments: "We suggest sending a cover letter and resume to contact. Exploratory interviews are conducted as time permits. When an opening occurs, resume file is the first source used to identify candidates for interviews. Agency conducts monthly informational meetings for public relations and account services entry-level candidates."

Internships: Yes (positions filled locally)

COONS CORKER & ASSOCIATES

West 621 Mallon Avenue
Spokane, WA 99201
509-326-8310

Employment Contact: Bob Coons, President

Total Employees: 11
Average Entry-Level Hiring: ?
Opportunities: Asst. Account Executive—College degree (Marketing, Advertising preferred). Copywriter—College degree; good credentials. Support Personnel—No requirements specified. Experience (1-2 years) preferred for all positions.
Internships: Yes

FRANK J. CORBETT INC.
211 East Chicago Avenue—Suite 1100
Chicago, IL 60611
312-664-5310

Employment Contact: Department heads
Total Employees: 80
Average Entry-Level Hiring: 3
Opportunities: "Any position would require a degree in marketing, advertising or communications."
Internships: No

CRAMER KRASSELT COMPANY
733 North Van Buren Street
Milwaukee, WI 53202
414-227-3500

Employment Contact: Paul Counsell, Executive VP or Department Heads—Account Services: Paul Bentley; Creative: Neil Casey; Media Services: Donald Pom or Donald Clow; Research: James Shampley
Total Employees: 170
Average Entry-Level Hiring: 2-3
Opportunities: Copy—College degree; creative writing ability. Art—College or art school degree; layout and mechanical skills. Research—College degree; organizational and analytical skills. Acct. Services—College degree (BA or MBA); people and organizational skills. Media—Positions available for both college graduates with people/organizational skills and high school graduates (mainly clerical).
Internships: No

CTS ASSOCIATES INC.
1150 Griswold—Suite 2600
Detroit, MI 48226
313-965-0575

Employment Contact: Muriel G. Scholl, Vice President
Total Employees: 8
Average Entry-Level Hiring: 0
Internships: No

CUNNINGHAM & WALSH
Merged with N. W. Ayer

DAILEY & ASSOCIATES
A subsidiary of the Interpublic Group of Companies
3055 Wilshire Blvd.
Los Angeles, CA 90010
213-386-7823

Employment Contact: Mrs. Toby J. Burke, Director of Personnel Administration
Total Employees: 200
Average Entry-Level Hiring: 3
Opportunities: Account Management—College degree (4 year). Writers—writing skills and portfolio. Art Director—Art school graduate; demonstrated ability with portfolio. Media—College degree (4 year).
Internships: No

DAN ADVERTISING & PUBLIC RELATIONS
408 West Bute Street
Norfolk, VA 23510
804-625-2518

Employment Contact: Dean Goldman, President
Total Employees: 13
Average Entry-Level Hiring: 1
Opportunities: Only hire experienced help with a college degree.
Internships: No

D'ARCY MASIUS BENTON & BOWLES, INC.
909 Third Avenue
New York, NY 10022
212-758-6200

Employment Contact: Karen Schiller, Personnel Dir.
Total Employees: 6,200
Average Entry-Level Hiring: 50
Opportunities: Asst. Account Executive—College degree (BA); communication and interpersonal skills. Asst. Media Planner—College degree (BA); facility with numbers; strong communication skills.
Suggestions: "If you are looking for an entry-level job post-graduation, send us your resume the January *before* you graduate."
Internships: Yes

DCA ADVERTISING
A division of Dentsu—Tokyo, Japan
1114 Avenue of the Americas
New York, NY 10036
212-703-1433

Employment Contact: Personnel
Internships: Yes

DDB-NEEDHAM WORLDWIDE, INC.
437 Madison Avenue
New York, NY 10022
212-415-2000

Employment Contact: Ms. Mariam Saytell
Internships: Yes

DELLA FEMINA, MCNAMEE WCRS
WCRS (Holding Company)
500 North Michigan Avenue
Chicago, IL 60611
312-222-1313

Employment Contact: Arlene Hamilton, Office Mgr.
Total Employees: 45
Average Entry-Level Hiring: 6
Opportunities: Account Coordinator—College degree required. Accounting—No experience necessary. Copywriter, Art Director—College degree and at least 2-3 years required. Media—College degree required; experience preferred.
Internships: Yes

DETROW & UNDERWOOD
1126 Cottage Street
Ashland, OH 44805
419-289-0265

Employment Contact: Mike W. Detrow, Executive VP
Total Employees: 17
Average Entry-Level Hiring: 1-2
Opportunities: Graphic Designer—College degree or Art school; marketing and sales skills. Jr Account Executive—College degree; marketing/sales/business skills.
Internships: No

DODSON, CRADDOCK & BORN
4711 Scenic Highway—P.O. Drawer A
Pensacola, FL 32581
904-433-8314

Employment Contact: Mary Nolan
Total Employees: 10
Average Entry-Level Hiring: 1
Opportunities: Artist—College degree (BA); 1 year exp.. Copywriter—College degree; 1 year exp.
Internships: No

W. B. DONER & COMPANY ADVERTISING
25900 Northwestern Highway
Southfield, MI 48075
313-354-9700

Employment Contact: *Creative*—Paula Bettendorf, Recruitment-Creative

All Others—Dianne Lemaux, Asst. Personnel Manager
Total Employees: 575
Average Entry-Level Hiring: 7 (3 in Creative, 4 in other areas)
Opportunities: Jr. Copywriter—College degree; previous internship helpful; portfolio required. Jr. Art Director—College degree; portfolio required. Assistant Account Executive—College degree; internship helpful. Broadcast Traffic Coordinator—College degree. Assistant Media Planners and Buyers—College degree; internship helpful.
Internships: Yes

DOYLE DANE BERNBACH GROUP
Merged with former Needham Harper Worldwide. See listing for DDB-Needham.

DREVES & KOEHLER
215 West Ninth Street
Cincinnati, OH 45202
513-421-4411

Employment Contact: Dianne Reese, Vice President
Total Employees: 5
Average Entry-Level Hiring: 1-2
Opportunities: Copywriter, Advertising Dept., Assistant Account Executive—College degree; good writing, spelling and communcation skills.
Internships: No

DUDRECK, DEPAUL, FICCO AND MORGAN
400 Penn Center Blvd.
Pittsburgh, PA 15235
412-261-2580

Employment Contact: Albert W. Dudreck, Chairman of the Board
Total Employees: 42
Average Entry-Level Hiring: 1-2
Opportunities: Secretary. No specific information available.
Internships: Yes

DUGAN/FARLEY COMMUNICATIONS
600 East Cressant Avenue
Upper Saddle River, NJ 07458
201-934-0720

Employment Contact: Ginny Raimann, Vice Pres.
Total Employees: 65
Average Entry-Level Hiring: 5

Opportunities: Traffic, Jr. Account Executive, Account Coordinators, Bookkeeping, Administrative Assistants—College degree preferred; experience is a must.
Internships: No

EARLE PALMER BROWN
100 Colony Square, Ste. 2400
Atlanta, GA 30361
404-881-8585

Employment Contact: Judy Perdew, Personnel Dir.
Total Employees: 50
Average Entry-Level Hiring: 0
Internships: Yes

EDELMANN SCOTT INC.
629 East Main Street—Suite 200
Richmond, VA 23219
804-643-1931

Employment Contact: Richard J. Scott, CEO
Total Employees: 15
Average Entry-Level Hiring: 1-2
Opportunities: Research—College degree (BA/BS). Public Relations—College degree (Journalism preferred). Bookkeeping—College degree (Accounting preferred).
Internships: Yes

ENGELTER, CROSS & McCLYMONDS, INC.
111 West St. John—Suite 440
San Jose, CA 95113
408-288-2400

Employment Contact: Diane Czerny, Owner
Total Employees: 9
Average Entry-Level Hiring: 1
Opportunities: Front Office—typing, telephone.
Internships: Yes

EPSILON
50 Cambridge Street
Burlington, MA 01803
617-273-0250

Employment Contact: Mary Richards Griffin, Head of Human Resources
Total Employees: 400
Average Entry-Level Hiring: 12
Opportunities: Account Exec., Administrative Asst., Production Control Asst.—College degree. Computer Operator—Technical degree. Accounts Payable, Clerks—Experience.
Internships: No

EVANS COMMUNICATIONS
4 Triad Center, #750
Salt Lake City, UT 84180
801-364-7000

Employment Contact: Regional managers of offices in: Atlanta, Denver, Los Angeles, Phoenix, Pittsburgh, Portland, San Francisco, and Seattle.
Total Employees: 289
Average Entry-Level Hiring: ?
Internships: No

EVERETT, BRANDT & BERNAUER, INC.
1805 Grand Avenue—Suite 200
Kansas City, MO 64108
816-421-0000

Employment Contact: James A. Everett, President
Total Employees: 6 (plus one intern)
Average Entry-Level Hiring: 2
Opportunities: Copy Writing, Keyline Artist, Public Relations—College (2 year minimum).
Internships: Yes

FAHLGREN & SWINK
A division of Lintas: New York
P.O. Box 1628
Parkersburg, WV 26101
304-424-3591

Employment Contact: Director of Human Resources
Total Employees: 320
Average Entry-Level Hiring: 4
Opportunities: Account Services, Media Asst. Buyer—College degree preferred, usually in Advertising, Business, or Marketing.
Internships: Yes

FISHER, BRADY & LA BRUE AD & PR, INC.
2033 Sixth Avenue—Suite 717
Seattle, WA 98121
206-448-3456

Employment Contact: Janice Vincent, President
Total Employees: 10
Average Entry-Level Hiring: 1-2
Opportunities: Copywriting, Media, Art (paste-up)—College degree; appropriate skills.
Internships: Yes

FOOTE, CONE & BELDING
11601 Wilshire Blvd.
Los Angeles, CA 90025
213-312-7000

Employment Contact: Melissa Germaine, Personnel Administrator

Total Employees: 185
Average Entry-Level Hiring: 10-20
Opportunities: Account Group Secretary—College degree preferred; typing 50-60 wpm; word processing knowledge helpful. Assistant Media Planner—College degree required; computer knowledge, skill with numbers.
Internships: Yes

FOOTE, CONE & BELDING
1255 Battery Street
San Francisco, CA 94111
415-398-5200

Employment Contact: Personnel Department
Total Employees: 300
Average Entry-Level Hiring: ?
Opportunities: Assistant Media Planner, Assistant Account Coordinator, Secretarial positions—College degree preferred. No other requirements specified.
Internships: Yes

FRANKLIN ADVERTISING ASSOCIATES INC.
88 Needham Street
Newton, MA 02161
617-244-8368

Employment Contact: Harriet L. Wiggin, VP
Total Employees: 10
Average Entry-Level Hiring: 1
Opportunities: Account Coordinator—College degree preferred. Art Assistant—College degree preferred.
Internships: Yes

GARDINER ADVERTISING AGENCY
56 West 400 South—P.O. Box 30
Salt Lake City, UT 84110
801-364-5600

Employment Contact: Department Heads
Total Employees: 21
Average Entry-Level Hiring: 1-4
Opportunities: Advertising, Public Relations—College degree ((BA/BS); 2-3 years experience preferred.
Internships: Yes

GARDNER ADVERTISING COMPANY, INC.
Branch office of Wells, Rich, Greene, Inc
10 South Broadway
St. Louis, MO 63102
314-444-2000

Employment Contact: Peggy Fessler, Act. Supervisor
Total Employees: 100
Average Entry-Level Hiring: 5+

Opportunities: Staff Asst.—College degree (Marketing/Communications preferred); internships or work study experience helpful. Asst. Buyers—College degree (Marketing/Advertising preferred); internships or work study. Asst. Account Executives—College degree (Communications/Marketing/Journalism preferred); internships or work study.
Comments: "We usually do interviewing only when there is an opening. All resumes are forwarded to pertinent departments and kept on file for 6 months."
Internships: Yes

GARFIELD-LINN AND COMPANY
142 East Ontario Street
Chicago, IL 60611
312-943-1900

Employment Contact: Department Heads
Total Employees: 42
Average Entry-Level Hiring: 1
Internships: No

GIRVIN CONRAD & GIRVIN
12401 Folsom Blvd.
Rancho Cordova, CA 95670
916-985-6600

Employment Contact: R. Girvin, President
Total Employees: 22
Average Ent≈y-Level Hiring: 1-2
Opportunities: Copywriting, Art Dept.—College degree, writing/art skills (samples required). Media—College degree; learn to read rating books; have good negotiating skills.
Internships: No

GOODWIN, DANNEBAUM, LITTMAN & WINGFIELD, INC.
5400 Westheimer Court—Suite 900
Houston, TX 77056
713-622-7676

Employment Contact: Barry Silverman, President
Total Employees: 85
Average Entry-Level Hiring: 2
Opportunities: Traffic—College degree; secretarial skills. Mail Service—College degree. Production Artist—College degree; art instruction.
Internships: No

GREY ADVERTISING INC.
777 Third Avenue
New York, NY 10017
212-546-2000

Employment Contact: James Brink, VP/Associate Director Personnel
Total Employees: 2,000 (in NY)

Average Entry-Level Hiring: 50
Opportunities: Asst. Account Executive—College degree (BA Liberal Arts, Social Science, Communications, Business, Marketing preferred); analytic, interpersonal communication skills. Asst. Media Planner—College degree (BA Liberal Arts, Communications, Social Sciences preferred); analytic, numerical and interpersonal communication skills. Research Trainee—College degree (BA Social Sciences, Liberal Arts, Marketing, Statistics preferred); analytic, statistical and interpersonal communication skills, knowledge of quantitative research methods, familiarity with marketing and research.
Suggestions: "Send resume and cover letter giving specific objective and long-range career goals."
Internships: No

HENDERSON ADVERTISING
P.O. Box 2247
Greenville, SC 29602
803-271-6000

Employment Contact: Department Heads
Total Employees: 100
Average Entry-Level Hiring: 2
Opportunities: Media Trainee, Assistant Planner, Assistant Account Executive—College degree. No other requirements specified.
Internships: Yes

INGALLS, QUINN & JOHNSON
855 Boylston Street
Boston, MA 02116
617-437-7000

Employment Contact: Kate Kelly, Office Manager Personnel
Total Employees: 300
Average Entry-Level Hiring: 15
Opportunities: Coordinator—College or Junior College degree; typing 55 wpm. Receptionist—High school graduate; "people" experience. Word Processing Operator—College, junior college or high school graduate; WP experience.
Internships: Yes

JORDAN ASSOCIATES
1000 West Wilshire—Suite 428
Oklahoma City, OK 73116
405-840-3201

Employment Contact: Jeanette L. Gamba, President
Total Employees: 52
Average Entry-Level Hiring: 3-4
Opportunities: Account Executive—College degree (Journalism preferred); good communication, writing and personal presentation skills; 1-2 years experience preferred. Assistant Media Buyer—College degree (Advertising preferred); good organizational and communication skills; 1-2 years experience preferred.
Internships: Yes

KAPRIELIAN O'LEARY ADVERTISING
99 Madison Avenue
New York, NY 10016
212-696-1300

Employment Contact: Vicki Phair, Traffic & Personnel
Total Employees: 20
Average Entry-Level Hiring: 1
Opportunities: Receptionist—College degree; interpersonal skills, articulate, accurate. Paste-up Artist—College degree; manual dexterity, "pressure capable." Secretarial—College degree; interpersonal skills, accurate, pressure capable.
Internships: Yes

KAUFMAN, GOLDMAN & STRAL, INC.
230 East Ohio Street
Chicago, IL 60611
312-944-0300

Employment Contact: Lee T. Stral, VP—Public Relations & Copy
Total Employees: 15
Average Entry-Level Hiring: 0
Opportunities: "We do not normally hire entry-level people."
Internships: No

KELLER-CRESCENT COMPANY
1100 East Louisiana Street
Evansville, IN 47701
812-464-2461

Employment Contact: Allen R. Mounts, VP-Human Resources
Total Employees: 550
Average Entry-Level Hiring: 7
Opportunities: PR Assistant Account Specialist—College degree (PR, Journalism); strong writing skills. Account Executive—College degree (Marketing, Business Administration or related area); 1-2 years experience. Assistant Art Director—College degree (BFA/BS Advertising). Estimator—College degree (BS Printing Management). Marketing Research—College degree (BS Marketing).
Internships: Yes

KETCHUM ADVERTISING
A division of Ketchum Communications Inc.
6 PPG Place
Pittsburgh, PA 15222
412-456-3500

Employment Contact: Joyce Adler, Personnel Mgr.

Total Employees: 3,500

Average Entry-Level Hiring: 50

Opportunities: Media Asst.—College degree (preferred). Junior Copywriter—College degree. Art Asst.—College degree (or Art Program); design skills. Research Asst.—College degree (Masters degree preferred).

Suggestions: "Send resume first."

Internships: Yes

LAUNEY, HACHMANN & HARRIS, INC.
292 Madison Avenue
New York, NY 10017
212-679-1702

Employment Contact: Robert E. Launey, President

Total Employees: 14

Average Entry-Level Hiring: 1

Opportunities: Secretary, Receptionist, Girl/Guy Friday—College degree (Marketing/Advertising/Communications); typing. Jr. Copywriter—College degree (Marketing/Advertising/Communications, English); creativity; typing; courses in advertising copy-writing; strength in grammar and punctuation a must—bring samples of work. Jr. Media Planner—College degree (Marketing, Advertising, Communications); courses in psychology, statistics, media (where available).

Comments: "We hire aspiring advertising people as we get openings. They become functioning members of our staff. We do not have a separate training program as such; nor do we automatically hire 'x' number of people each year."

Internships: Yes

LAVEN, FULLER & PERKINS ADVERTISING/MARKETING INC
233 East Ontario
Chicago, IL 60611
312-440-1818

Employment Contact: MaryAnne Miller, Exec. VP

Total Employees: 26

Average Entry-Level Hiring: 0

Opportunities: Account Executives—College degree (Advertising, Marketing preferred); history of student employment; proof of grade average; ability to communicate at both verbal and written levels.

Suggestions: "Creative people must bring portfolio of work. Account Executive candidates must provide

pertinent information of part-time performance in work place."

Internships: No

LAWRENCE & SCHILLER
3932 South Willow Avenue
Sioux Falls, SD 57105
605-338-8000

Employment Contact: Craig Lawrence, Partner

Total Employees: 41

Average Entry-Level Hiring: 1-2

Opportunities: Account Executive, Writer/Producer, Graphic Design—College degree (BA/BS); 1-2 years experience preferred.

Internships: Yes

AL PAUL LEFTON COMPANY
Rohm/Haas Building
Independence Mall West
Philadelphia, PA 19106
215-923-9600

Total Employees: 155

Internships: Yes

LEVENSON, LEVENSON & HILL
P.O. Box 619507
DFW Airport, TX 75261
214-556-0944

Employment Contact: Candice Ramsey, Office Manager

Total Employees: 65

Average Entry-Level Hiring: 2

Opportunities: The following positions all require a college student or degree: Asst. in Promotions, Asst. in Account Services, Asst. in Public Relations.

Internships: Yes

LEVINE, HUNTLEY, SCHMIDT & BEAVER, INC.
250 Park Avenue
New York, NY 10177
212-545-3500

Employment Contact: Rose Marie Lyddan, Director of Personnel/Office Manager

Total Employees: 90

Suggestions: Send resume and cover letter.

Internships: Yes

LIEBERMAN APPALUCCI
4601 Crackersport Road
Allentown, PA 18104
215-395-7111

Employment Contact: Michael J. Lieberman, Vice President

Total Employees: 40

Average Entry-Level Hiring: 1-2

Opportunities: The following positions require a college degree and quality summer experience: PR Asst., Research Asst., Account Asst.

Suggestions: "No phone calls please."

Internships: Yes

LINTAS: CAMPBELL EWALD
30400 Van Dyke
Warren, MI 48093
313-574-3400

Employment Contact: Human Resource Department

Total Employees: 900

Average Entry-Level Hiring: 15-25

Opportunities: The following positions require a College degree (BA/BS) plus other skills as noted: Account Coordinator, Asst. Media Analyst (background in statistics), Media Estimator, Research Analyst (background in statistics), Junior Copywriter (major in English a plus, Junior Art Director—College degree (BA or BFA). The following positions require a High school graduate: Mailroom Clerk, Accounting Clerk, Secretary Intern (plus typing and shorthand skills), Driver (license required).

Internships: No

LINTAS: NEW YORK
(formerly SSC&B: Lintas)
1 Dag Hammarskjold Plaza
New York, NY 10017
212-605-8000

Employment Contact: Patricia Ransom, Personnel Manager; Mariann Millar, Creative Management

Total Employees: 600

Average Entry-Level Hiring: 40

Opportunities: Assistant Media Planner, Staff Assistant (Account Management)—College degree; marketing sense; communication and interpersonal skills; strong qualitative and quantitative abilities; management and organizational abilities. Copy Trainee, Asst. Art Director—College degree; marketing sense; imagination; writing and conceptual ability. Art job requires demonstrable art/design skills.

Internships: Yes

LONG, HAYMES & CARR, INC.
140 Charlois Blvd.—P.O. Box 5627
Winston-Salem, NC 27113
919-765-3630

Employment Contact: Department Heads

Total Employees: 140

Average Entry-Level Hiring: 15

Opportunities: Proofreader—College degree (BA/BS English preferred); good grammar, punctuation & proofreading skills. Mechanical Artist—College degree (BFA/BS); mechanical skills. Media Assist.—College degree (BA/BS); writing skills, math aptitude. Research Analyst—College degree (BA/BS); statistical skills. Print Traffic Coordinator—College degree (BA/BS); detail oriented. Broadcast Production Coordinator—College degree (BA/BS); some broadcast production experience. Account Coordinator—College degree (BA/BS). Asst. Account Executive—MBA. Designer—BFA/BA. Junior Copywriter—College degree (BA/BS); samples of published work.

Suggestions: "Please send cover letter and resume to our Personnel dept. for interviewing consideration. Portfolio needed for creative positions."

Internships: Yes

L.G.F.E., INC. (Lord, Geller, Frederico, Einstein)
A subsidiary of WPP Group PLC
655 Madison Avenue
New York, NY 10021
212-421-6050

Employment Contact: Emilie Schaum, VP/Director of Personnel & Administration

Total Employees: 94

Average Entry-Level Hiring: 3-5

Opportunities: Asst. Account Executive, Asst. Media Planner, Asst. Traffic Coordinator—College degree preferred (BA/BS); advertising or similar industry internship or job experience a definite plus. Excellent oral and written skills are a must; coupled with judgement, initiative, an inquiring mind and integrity. Math skills and computer knowledge are important.

Comments: "Applicants most likely to succeed present themselves as mature, high energy and enthusiastic when approaching work."

Internships: Yes

LORD, SULLIVAN & YODER ADVERTISING
250 Old Wilson Bridge Road, P.O. Box 800
Columbus, OH 43085-0800
614-846-8500

Employment Contact: Jo Ella Fosco, Administrative Assistant

Total Employees: 80

Average Entry-Level Hiring: 0

Internships: No

LOWE MARSCHALK
1345 Avenue of the Americas
New York, NY 10105
212-708-8800

Employment Contact: Peter Detels, VP

Total Employees: 365
Average Entry-Level Hiring: 3-4
Opportunities: People with experience only.
Internships: Yes

MARC AND COMPANY, INC.
4 Station Square—Suite 500
Pittsburgh, PA 15219
412-562-2000

Employment Contact: Theodora Ftaklas, Personnel
Director
Total Employees: 94
Average Entry-Level Hiring: 4
Opportunities: Interns (hourly pay)—College junior
or senior; 3.0+ GPA in related major.
Internships: Yes

MARX, KNOLL, DENIGHT AND DODGE
1230 SW First Avenue
Portland, OR 97204
503-226-2867

Employment Contact: Robert Knoll, President
Total Employees: 20
Average Entry-Level Hiring: 1
Opportunities: Account Coordinator—College degree;
3 years work experience. Media Asst.—College
degree; 5 years in-field experience. Administrative
Asst.—College degree; 1-2 years experience
preferred.
Internships: Yes

MEDICUS INTERCON INTERNATIONAL, INC
A subsidiary of D'Arcy Masius Benton & Bowles
909 Third Avenue
New York, NY 10022
212-826-0760

Employment Contact: Personnel Department
Total Employees: 375
Average Entry-Level Hiring: 3-5
Internships: Yes

MILLER, ADDISON, STEELE, INC.
119 West 57th Street
New York, NY 10019
212-247-6060

Employment Contact: Kenneth Miller, President
Total Employees: 12
Average Entry-Level Hiring: 1
Opportunities: Assistant Account Manager—College
degree; background preferred.
Internships: Yes

MILLS HALL WALBORN & ASSOCIATES
29125 Chagrin Blvd.
Cleveland, OH 44122
216-646-9400

Employment Contact: Gloria Zupancit, Office Manager
Total Employees: 40
Average Entry-Level Hiring: 3-5
Opportunities: Front Desk Secretary—High school
graduate; typing and computer skills. Asst. Account
Executive—College degree (BA/BS); no experience
required.
Internships: No

MULLEN ADVERTISING
P.O. Box 2700
Wenham, MA 01982
508-468-1155

Employment Contact: Department Heads
Total Employees: 90
Average Entry-Level Hiring: 0
Internships: Yes

THE NEW ENGLAND GROUP, ADVERTISING
40 Pearl Street
Portland, ME 04101
207-772-6551

Total Employees: 17
Average Entry-Level Hiring: 3-4
Opportunities: Accout Coordinator—College degree (BA preferred) or advertising/marketing
experience. Good organization and communication
(especially writing) skills. Media Assistant—
College degree (BA preferred) or advertising/
marketing experience. Good organization and
communication skills. Statistics oriented. Production Assistant—College degree (BA preferred);
must be extremely organized; comfortable working
with numbers (budgets and estimates).
Internships: No

N. W. AYER INCORPORATED
Worldwide Plaza
825 Eighth Avenue
New York, NY 10019-7498
212-708-5000

Employment Contact: Brenda Rotola, Personnel
Recruiter
Average Entry-Level Hiring: 20
Opportunities: Group Assistant—College degree
preferred but not required. Must type 40 wpm.
Internships: No

OGILVY & MATHER WORLDWIDE
2 East 48th Street
New York, NY 10017
212-237-4000

Employment Contact: Nan Keenan, VP/Manager
Account Management
Total Employees: 8,500
Average Entry-Level Hiring: 10-12
Internships: Yes

PARKER GROUP, INC.
Trinity Centre
4814 Washington Avenue
St. Louis, MO 63108
314-727-4000

Employment Contact: Anne Sauvage, Account
Supervisor
Total Employees: 47
Average Entry-Level Hiring: 1-2
Opportunities: Assistants in Media, Marketing,
Account Management and Data Processing Depts.:
College degree (BA/BS); 2 years experience
preferred.
Internships: Yes

PAUL, JOHN & LEE, INC.
113 Twin Oaks Drive
Syracuse, NY 13206
315-463-1177

Employment Contact: Paul J. Behuniak,
President/Creative Director
Total Employees: 9
Average Entry-Level Hiring: 1-2
Opportunities: Creative Services, Accounting/
Finance, Marketing—College degree (BA/BS);
two years experience preferred.
Internships: No

PERRI DEBES LOONEY & CRANE INC (PDL&C)
46 Prince Street
Rochester, NY 14607
716-442-9030

Employment Contact: Paul Debes, VP/Art Director
Total Employees: 22
Average Entry-Level Hiring: 1
Opportunities: Creative Services, Marketing, Media,
Broadcast Production—College degree (BA/BS); two
years experience preferred. Accounting/Finance—
MBA and 2 years experience (both preferred).
Internships: No

PINNE GARVIN HERBERS & HOCK, INC.
200 Vallejo Street
San Francisco, CA 94111
415-956-4210

Employment Contact: Creative-R. Pinne; Account
Services-Don Herbers
Total Employees: 25
Average Entry-Level Hiring: 0-1
Opportunities: Account Coordinator—College degree;
good communication and presentation skills. Jr. Copywriter—College degree; demonstrable writing skills/
imagination. Jr. Art Director—Graduate art student
(not necessarily college); must be able to draw/indi-
cate and understand production techniques.
Suggestions: "Send resumes first and follow with a
call for an interview."
Internships: Yes

PRINGLE DIXON PRINGLE
245 Peachtree Center—Suite 1500
Marquis 1 Tower
Atlanta, GA 30303
404-688-6720

Employment Contact: Susan Johnson, Jr. Account
Executive
Total Employees: 40
Average Entry-Level Hiring: ?
Internships: Yes

ROMANN & TANNENHOLZ ADVERTISING
100 Fifth Avenue—8th Floor
New York, NY 10011
212-645-0300

Employment Contact: Louise Hollinger
Total Employees: 25
Average Entry-Level Hiring: ?
Internships: No

ROSENTHAL, GREENE AND CAMPBELL
7910 Woodmont Avenue
Bethesda, MD 20815
301-657-3400

Employment Contact: Sheila Campbell, President
Total Employees: 38
Average Entry-Level Hiring: 10
Opportunities: Account Coordinator—College degree
(Advertising, Marketing); maturity, organization,
good speaker and writer. Media Assistant—College
degree (Advertising, Marketing), numbers-oriented,
precise, organized. Some experience preferred for
both positions.
Internships: Yes

ROSS ROY, INC.
100 Bloomfield Hills Parkway
Bloomfield Hills, MI 48013
313-433-6000

Employment Contact: Lori Taylor, VP-Human Resources
Total Employees: 955
Average Entry-Level Hiring: 25
Opportunities: Management Trainee—College degree; advertising major and related activities. Account Administrator—College degree; advertising related experience. Asst. Media Buyer—College degree; media related experience.
Internships: No

SAATCHI & SAATCHI ADVERTISING
375 Hudson Street
New York, NY 10014
212-704-7291

Employment Contact: Linda Seale, Executive VP/Human Resources Director
Total Employees: 1,300
Average Entry-Level Hiring: ?
Opportunities: The following positions require a Bachelor's degree along with good analytical skills and facility with numbers: Assistant Planner, Assistant Account Executive.
Internships: No

SIANO & SPITZ ADVERTISING
530 Oak Street
Syracuse, NY 13202
315-479-5581

Employment Contact: Mike Siano, President
Total Employees: 10
Average Entry-Level Hiring: 1-2
Internships: Yes

SILBERMAN WHITEBROW DOLAN
5 Penn Center
Philadelphia, PA 19103
215-443-9169

Employment Contact: Joy Zwicker, Asst. to President
Total Employees: 50
Average Entry-Level Hiring: 0-1
Internships: No

J. RICHARD SMITH LTD.
175 Sweethollow Road
Old Bethpage, NY 11804
516-293-8700

Employment Contact: Lisa Burton, Employment

Total Employees: 50
Average Entry-Level Hiring: 0 (mostly freelancers)
Opportunities: Artists (freelancers)—Portfolio required; experience preferred.
Internships: No

SMITH, DORIAN & BURMAN, INC.
1100 New Britain Avenue
West Hartford, CT 06110
203-522-3101

Employment Contact: Jean Conte, Personnel Manager
Total Employees: 15
Average Entry-Level Hiring: 2-3
Opportunities: Assistant Account Executive, Assistant in Advertising Dept.—College degree (BA/BS); no experience required.
Internships: No

SMITH/GREENLAND ADVERTISING, INC.
555 West 57th Street
New York, NY 10019
212-757-3200

Employment Contact: Rita Greenland, Personnel Director
Total Employees: 110
Suggestions: "Enclose with your resume and cover letter a stamped, self-addressed postcard with 2 boxes: The first box reads 'We have a position available. Please telephone for an interview appointment.' The second box reads: 'We have no positions open at this time but would like you to telephone for an interview for future opportunities."
Internships: No

SPIRO & ASSOCIATES
100 South Broad Street
Philadelphia, PA 19110
215-851-9600

Employment Contact: Anne Kelley, Office Manager
Total Employees: 150
Average Entry-Level Hiring: 2-4
Opportunities: Media Asst.—Some college (degree preferred); typing, familiar with word & data processing, good with numbers, analytical. Research Asst.—College degree preferred (Marketing, Statistics); typing, familiar with word & data processing. Jr. Account Executive—College degree; some work experience, communications skills, people and business oriented, sales and writing ability.
Suggestions: "Send resume in advance."
Internships: Yes

SSC&B: LINTAS WORLDWIDE
See listing for Lintas: New York

STONE, AUGUST, BAKER COMMUNICATIONS COMPANY
1301 West Long Lake Road—Suite 350
Troy, MI 48098
313-641-0400

Employment Contact: Mr. Stone
Total Employees: 60
Average Entry-Level Hiring: 2-3
Internships: Yes

TAYLOR BROWN, SMITH & PERRAULT
4544 Post Oak Place—Suite 264
Houston, TX 77027
713-877-1220

Employment Contact: Patsy Perrault, Executive VP/ Media Director
Total Employees: 52
Average Entry-Level Hiring: 5
Opportunities: Clerical/Secretarial—College degree; office skills.
Internships: Yes

J. WALTER THOMPSON
A subsidiary of the WPP Group PLC
466 Lexington Avenue
New York, NY 10017
212-210-6993 or 6988

Employment Contact: Mellisa Statmore
Total Employees: 7,380
Average Entry-Level Hiring: Varies
Opportunities: Assistant Account Representatives— MBA or BA (if the latter, prefer work experience); leadership potential, organizational skills. Assistant Media Planner—BA, quantitative skills. Research Assistant—BA (work experience preferred), psychology background helpful. Junior Art Director, Junior Copywriter, Assistant Producer—Must present portfolio with sample campaigns and/or extraordinary writing samples.
Internships: Yes

TRAVIS/WALZ & ASSOCIATES, INC.
8500 West 63rd Street
Shawnee Mission, KS 66202
913-341-5022

Employment Contact: John Walz, President
Total Employees: 18
Average Entry-Level Hiring: 1-2

Opportunities: Marketing, Media, Accounting/Finance—College degree (BA/BS); no experience (will train).
Internships: Yes

ERIC TULIN INC.
236 Hamilton Street
Hartford, CT 06106
203-951-9707

Employment Contact: Susan Winchell, Office Mgr.
Total Employees: 10
Average Entry-Level Hiring: 1
Opportunities: Real Estate, Marketing—College degree; good writing and spelling skills, hard working, good student, good referrals; 1-2 years experience preferred.
Internships: Yes

TYCER FULTZ BELLACK
1731 Embarcadero Road
Palo Alto, CA 94303
415-856-1600

Employment Contact: Department Heads
Total Employees: 45
Average Entry-Level Hiring: 0-1
Internships: Yes

VALENTINE-RADFORD, INC.
911 Main Street—Suite 11
Kansas City, MO 64105
816-842-5021

Employment Contact: Cindy Kitchen, Personnel
Total Employees: 150
Average Entry-Level Hiring: ?
Opportunities: Account Coordinator, Media Asst.— College degree required; experience helpful.
Internships: Yes

VAN BRUNT & CO. ADVERTISING & MARKETING, INC.
300 East 42nd Street
New York, NY 10017
212-949-1300

Employment Contact: Mrs. M. Smith, Personnel Mgr.
Total Employees: 35
Average Entry-Level Hiring: 0
Internships: No

VAN SANT, DUGDALE & COMPANY, INC.
The World Trade Center
Baltimore, MD 21202
301-539-5400

Employment Contact: Kenneth E. Mayhorne, Chairman and CEO

Total Employees: 80
Average Entry-Level Hiring: 0
Opportunities: Service/Traffic—College degree or high school graduate. The following positions require a College degree: Media, Asst. Account Executive, Junior Ad Director, Junior Writer.
Internships: No

WEISS/WATSON
1140 Avenue of the Americas
New York, NY 10036
212-753-9800

Employment Contact: Suzanne Delisle, Office Manager
Total Employees: 35
Average Entry-Level Hiring: 2
Opportunities: Assistant Account Executive, Art Assistant. No requirements specified.
Internships: Yes

WESTIN & ASSOCIATES
150 Airport Road
Lakewood, NJ 08701
201-905-1500

Employment Contact: David A. Hunziker, President
Total Employees: 15
Average Entry-Level Hiring: 2
Opportunities: The following positions require a College degree: Graphic Arts, Copywriting, Account Executive.
Internships: Yes

WETTSTEIN, BOLCHALK, OWENS & COOKE ADVERTISING & PUBLIC RELATIONS
620 North Craycroft
Tucson, AZ 85711
602-745-8221

Employment Contact: Department Heads
Total Employees: 20
Average Entry-Level Hiring: 0-1
Suggestions: "Send resume— call one week later."
Internships: Yes

ROGER WHITE ADVERTISING & PUBLIC RELATIONS
206 State Street
Binghamton, NY 13901
607-724-4356

Employment Contact: Debbie Collett-O'Brien, Marketing Services Manager
Total Employees: 15
Average Entry-Level Hiring: 0-1

Opportunities: Administrative Assistant—College degree (BA/BS); 2 years experience preferred. Art Dept./Design—College degree (BA/BS); 3-4 years experience.
Internships: Yes

YOUNG & RUBICAM INC.
285 Madison Avenue
New York, NY 10017
212-210-3000

Employment Contact: Steven Nisberg, Manager of Employment
Total Employees: 11,000
Average Entry-Level Hiring: 75-100
Opportunities: Traffic Coordinator—College degree; planning & organization, communication/interpersonal skills. Media Trainee—College degree; quantitative skills, computer. Research Trainee—Advanced College degree or MBA; analytic/marketing, quantitative skills. Asst. Account Executive—College degree (MBA—Marketing); marketing skills/background, leadership. Creative Trainee—College degree; portfolio required.
Suggestions: "Send resume and cover letter first, 2-3 week reply by mail, interviews by appointment only."
Internships: Yes

31

Entry-Level Job Listings: Canada

BASE BROWN & PARTNERS LTD.
512 King Street East
Toronto, ON M5E 1M2
416-364-5044

Employment Contact: Harold Bradshaw, Director of Finance
Total Employees: 20
Average Entry-Level Hiring: 5
Opportunities: Account Executive, Secretary, Receptionist, Graphic Artist—No requirements specified.
Internships: No

THE BCP GROUP LIMITED
1000 Sherbrooke Street West—21st Floor
Montreal, PQ H3A 3G9
514-285-1414

Employment Contact: Prefontaine Chrftane, Personnel Agent
Total Employees: 140
Average Entry-Level Hiring: 5
Internships: No

BOZELL, PALMER, BONNER, INC.
399 Church Street
Toronto, Ont. M5B 2I6
416-974-9419

Employment Contact: Jeff Bird, Mike Walker, Garth Garner

Total Employees: 25
Average Entry-Level Hiring: ?
Opportunities: As of January, 1990, this company is the product of a merger—they were not sure of what positions would open up. Call for new company job information.
Internships: No

T. STEWART BROWN & CO., LTD.
207 West Hastings Street—Suite 1111
Vancouver, BC V6B 1H7
604-683-7667

Employment Contact: Mr. Brown, President
Total Employees: 6
Average Entry-Level Hiring: Freelancers only.
Opportunities: Freelance artists—Portfolio required. Freelance copywriters—Samples required.
Internships: No

CASE ASSOCIATES ADVERTISING LTD.
30 Soudan Avenue
Toronto, ON M4F 1V6
416-481-4281

Employment Contact: Bill Kemp, Chairman
Total Employees: 19
Average Entry-Level Hiring: 0
Internships: No

COMMERCIAL ASSOCIATES/ROSS ROY LTD.
1737 Walker Road
Windsor, ON M8Y 4R8
519-258-7584

Employment Contact: Claudette Munger, Human Resource Manager
Total Employees: 80
Average Entry-Level Hiring: ?
Internships: No

CV ADVERTISING
One Eglinton Avenue East—Suite 500
Toronto, ON M4P 3A1
416-486-6695

Employment Contact: Department Heads
Total Employees: 48
Average Entry-Level Hiring: 1-2
Opportunities: Account Executive, Clerical—No requirements specified.
Internships: No

DEACON DAY ADVERTISING
20 Richmond Street East—7th Floor
Toronto, ON M5C 2R9
416-362-8600

Employment Contact: Chris Chow, Office Mgr
Total Employees: 22
Average Entry-Level Hiring: 5
Opportunities: Account Secretary, Jr. Copywriter, Jr. Art Director—College degree required. Receptionist, Account Coordinator—No specific information available.
Internships: No

FCB/RONALDS-REYNOLDS
1500 West Georgia Street—Suite 450
Vancouver, BC V6G 2Z6
604-684-8311

Employment Contact: Ken Bates, VP/Director of Client Services
Total Employees: 30
Average Entry-Level Hiring: Varies
Opportunities: Account Coordinator—College degree preferred; some sales and marketing exp. Media Buyer—2-3 years experience preferred. Product Coordinator—Some experience required.
Internships: Yes

FOOTE, CONE & BELDING DIRECT MARKETING
245 Eglinton East, Suite 300
Toronto, ON M4P 3C2
416-483-3600

Employment Contact: Janice Anderson, Personnel Coordinator

Total Employees: 200
Average Entry-Level Hiring: 3-4
Internships: No

FRANCIS, WILLIAMS & JOHNSON LTD.
635 Sixth Avenue SW—Suite 500
Calgary, AB T2P 0T5
403-266-7061

Employment Contact: Jerry Pasely; department hds
Total Employees: 35
Average Entry-Level Hiring: ?
Internships: No

FRANCIS, WILLIAMS & JOHNSON LTD.
200 Sun Life Place
Edmonton, AB T5J 3H1
403-423-1546

Employment Contact: Derrick Coke-Kerr, President
Total Employees: 15
Average Entry-Level Hiring: ?
Opportunities: Account Managers, Supervisors and Coordinators; Art and Media Directors; Recruitment Coordinators; Accountants—No requirements specified.
Internships: Yes

HARRISON MARKETING COUNSEL LIMITED
512 King Street East
Toronto, ON M5A 1M1
416-947-9167

Employment Contact: Mr. Haferhorn, Vice President
Total Employees: 10
Average Entry-Level Hiring: 2
Opportunities: Primarily commercial artists—No requirements specified.
Internships: No

KELLEY ADVERTISING, INC.
Park Place—3rd Floor
Hamilton, ON L7N 3E4
416-525-3610

Employment Contact: Phyllis Montgomery, Corporate Financial Operator
Total Employees: 35
Average Entry-Level Hiring: 5
Opportunities: Word Processor Operator, Media Assistant, Production Assistant—No requirements specified.
Internships: Yes

KELLY ADVERTISING, INC.
20 Dundas Street West—Suite 1030
Toronto, ON M5G 2C2
416-977-2125

Employment Contact: Denise Marshall, Account Director

Total Employees: 25

Average Entry-Level Hiring: 3-4

Opportunities: Account Secretary, Account Coordinator, Media Secretary, Receptionist—All positions require computer or word processing experience.

Internships: No

LUNAN HOFFMAN ADVERTISING LTD.
1440 St. Catherine West—Suite 716
Montreal, PQ H3G 1R8
514-874-1692

Employment Contact: Sally Davidson, Vice Pres.

Total Employees: 4

Average Entry-Level Hiring: Varies

Opportunities: Coordinator—No requirements specified.

Internships: No

MACLAREN ADVERTISING
Atrium on the Bay
Toronto, ON M5G 2H1
416-977-2244

Employment Contact: Nancy Carroll, Personnel Officer

Total Employees: 318

Average Entry-Level Hiring: Varies.

Internships: No

MARTCOM INC.
1454 Dundas Street East—Suite 116
Mississauga, ON L4X 1L4
416-276-7323

Employment Contact: Corie Clack, Administration

Total Employees: 5

Average Entry-Level Hiring: 0-1

Opportunities: Adminstrative—College degree. Secretarial—Experience preferred.

Internships: No

McCAFFREY McCALL
2 Carlton Street—Suite 801
Toronto, ON M5B 1J3
416-977-2270

Employment Contact: Robert Hobbs, Executive VP/ General Manager

Total Employees: 6

Average Entry-Level Hiring: 0

Opportunities: Account Executives—No requirements specified.

Internships: Yes

McCANN-ERICKSON ADVERTISING OF CANADA, LTD.
Waterpark Place
10 Bay Street—13th Floor
Toronto, ON M5J 2S3
416-594-6000

Employment Contact: Cheryl Fry, Manager of Human Resources

Total Employees: 260

Average Entry-Level Hiring: 6-10

Opportunities: Media Estimators—Post-secondary degree/diploma (preferrably in business or marketing) required; must have strong organizational and communication skills; a commitment to advertising; high energy and enthusiasm, and the ability to work with numbers and people. On-the-job training will be provided, supplemented by in-house seminars.

Internships: No

McKIM ADVERTISING LTD.
600-237 Eighth Avenue SE
Calgary, AB T2G 5C3
403-234-7400

Employment Contact: Chris Bedford, Manager

Total Employees: 28

Average Entry-Level Hiring: Varies

Opportunities: Account Coordinators, Account Executives, Clerks, Artists, Writers—College degree preferred.

Internships: No

McKIM ADVERTISING LTD.
Rene Levesque West—Floor 28
Montreal, PQ H3B 2L2
514-861-8421

Employment Contact: Francine Lepage, Administration Manager

Total Employees: 40+

Average Entry-Level Hiring: ?

Opportunities: Account, Art and Media Directors— College degree and experience preferred.

Internships: No

McKIM ADVERTISING LTD.
2 Bloor Street West
Toronto, ON M4W 3R6
416-960-1722

Employment Contact: JoAnne Porter, Head of Personnel
Total Employees: 200
Average Entry-Level Hiring: ?
Internships: No

NATIONWIDE ADVERTISING SERVICE, INC.
280 Albert Street—Suite 703
Ottawa, ON K1P 5G8
613-236-5839

Employment Contact: Patrick Whalin, Regional Manager
Total Employees: 3
Average Entry-Level Hiring: 0
Opportunities: This is just one of 36 branches. All are similar in size and turnover is not frequent. (See next entry)
Internships: No

NATIONWIDE ADVERTISING SERVICE, INC.
417 Rue St. Pierre—Bureau 700
Montreal, PQ H2Y 2M4
514-845-4153

Employment Contact: Marvin lee, Office Manager
Total Employees: 3
Average Entry-Level Hiring: 0
Opportunities: Office Manager, Client Service Asst.—No specific information available.
Internships: No

OGILVY & MATHER
101 Sixth Avenue SW—Suite 850
Calgary, AB P2P 3P4
403-262-6852

Employment Contact: Mark Pigott, Managing Director
Total Employees: 22
Average Entry-Level Hiring: 0
Internships: No

PIERCELL MERCHANDIZING CO. LTD.
375 Cabana Road East
Windsor, ON N9G 1A1
519-969-4531

Employment Contact: Joseph Piercell, President
Total Employees: 8

Average Entry-Level Hiring: 0
Internships: No

PNMD
1610 St. Catherine Street West
Suite 500
Montreal, PQ H3H 2S2
514-939-4100

Employment Contact: Joy Meyer, Administrative Assistant
Total Employees: 55
Average Entry-Level Hiring: 4
Opportunities: Secretarial positions—Must have experience.
Internships: No

PUBLICITE LEO BURNETT LTD.
175 Bloor Street East
Toronto, ON M4W 3L9
416-925-5997

Employment Contact: Dave Teller; Ruth Jackson, Senior Secretary; Jim McKenzy, President
Total Employees: 165
Average Entry-Level Hiring: 3
Opportunities: Clerical, Account Billing, Budget Controller in Media—No requirements specified.
Internships: No

RECRUITMENT ENHANCEMENT SERVICES
2 Lombard Street—Suite 300
Toronto, ON M5C 1M1
416-362-7999

Employment Contact: Sandra Higgins; Wayne Burnes, Sr. VP
Total Employees: 18
Average Entry-Level Hiring: ?
Opportunities: New Business Director, Account Coordinator, Account Executive, Layout Artists— College degree not required.
Internships: No

IAN ROBERTS INC.
One Brunswick Square
St. John, NF E2L 4V1
506-634-7190

Employment Contact: Brian Eastwood, Director of Client Services
Total Employees: 7
Average Entry-Level Hiring: 1
Opportunities: Account Services, Account Executive, Media Planners, Secretary—College degree required.

Art Director, Mechanical Artist—Formal training required.
Internships: No

SAATCHI & SAATCHI COMPTON HAYHURST LTD.
55 Eglinton Avenue East
Toronto, ON M4T 1G9
416-487-4371

Employment Contact: Department Heads
Total Employees: 142
Average Entry-Level Hiring: 50
Opportunities: Advertising and Media areas.
Internships: No

SAFFER ADVERTISING INC.
180 Lesmill Road
Don Mills, ON M3B 2T5
416-449-7961

Employment Contact: Personnel Department
Total Employees: 165
Average Entry-Level Hiring: ?
Internships: No

TAYLOR-TARPAY DIRECT ADVERTISING, LTD.
1039 McNicoll Avenue
Scarborough, ON M1W 3W6
416-498-5550

Employment Contact: Susie Hulmes, Account Exec.
Total Employees: 30
Average Entry-Level Hiring: 4
Opportunities: Junior Account Executive—College degree (Marketing preferred); experience.
Internships: No

VICKERS & BENSON PROMOTIONAL SVCS.
1133 Yonge Street
Toronto, ON M4T 2Z3
416-926-4380

Employment Contact: Rose Galluzzo, Payroll/Personnel Manager
Total Employees: 220
Average Entry-Level Hiring: 30-40%
Opportunities: Media Dept.—No specifics given.
Internships: No

VRIAK ROBINSON HAYHURST COMMUNICATIONS LTD.
555 West Hastings Street—8th Floor
Vancouver, AB V6B 5G2
604-684-1111

Employment Contact: Jane McQueen
Total Employees: 35
Average Entry-Level Hiring: 6
Opportunities: Administrative—College degree preferred; experience necessary.
Internships: No

WATSON OSTBY DIRECT
468 Queen St. East, Lower Level
Toronto, ON M5A 1T7
416-369-1890

Employment Contact: Gunner Ostby, Production Managing Executive
Total Employees: 12
Average Entry-Level Hiring: 2
Opportunities: Secretarial, Production, Account Services. Experience preferred.
Internships: No

WOLF, RICHARDS, TAYLOR ADVERTISING
35 Prince Arthur Avenue
Toronto, ON M5R 1B2
416-967-9000

Employment Contact: Personnel
Total Employees: 25
Average Entry-Level Hiring: ?
Opportunities: Secretary/Receptionist, Account Coordinator, Traffic Coordinator.
Internships: No

WUNDERMAN INTERNATIONAL INC.
60 Bloor Street West
Toronto, ON M4W 3B8
416-921-9050

Employment Contact: Department Heads
Total Employees: 50
Average Entry-Level Hiring: Depends on what is happening in the industry.
Internships: No

Other Canadian Firms Who Wished Not To Be Listed

Blitz Direct	Interface Direct, Inc.	Ogilvy & Mather Direct
Comcore Direct, Inc.	J. Schmid & Associates, Inc.	Schaffner Direct Marketing, Inc.
Grey DMG Direct	JWT Direct Response	Shulman Communications
Hull Direct Marketing	McLaren Lintas Direct, Inc.	Wunderman Worldwide

Section 6

Appendices & Index

A

U.S. & Canadian
Trade Organizations

THE ADVERTISING CLUB OF NEW YORK
155 East 55th Street—Suite 202
New York, NY 10022
212-935-8080

ADVERTISING AGENCY ASSOCIATION
OF ALBERTA
c/o Baker Lovick Calgary (Roy Elauder)
350 Seventh Avenue SW—22nd Floor
Calgary, AB T2P 3T2
403-262-6161

ADVERTISING AGENCY PRINT PRODUC-
TION ASSOCIATION
c/o Marketing & Promotion Group
92 Jarvis Street
Toronto, ON M5C 2H5
416-862-8300

THE ADVERTISING & SALES CLUB OF
TORONTO
P.O. Box 237, Stn. K
Toronto, ON M4P 2G5
416-483-5599

ADVERTISING AND SALES EXECUTIVES
CLUB OF MONTREAL
#369, 900 Rene Levesque Blvd. West
Montreal, PQ H3B 4A5
514-866-1668

ADVERTISING ASSOCIATION OF BRITISH
COLUMBIA
555 West Hastings Street—P.O. Box 12087
Vancouver, BC V6B 5G2
604-684-1111

THE ADVERTISING EDUCATIONAL
FOUNDATION
666 Third Avenue
New York, NY 10017
212-986-8060

THE ADVERTISING RESEARCH FOUNDATION
3 East 54th Street—15th Floor
New York, NY 10022
212-751-5656

ADVERTISING WOMEN OF NEW YORK
153 East 57th Street
New York, NY 10022
212-593-1950

AMERICAN ADVERTISING FEDERATION
1400 K Street—Suite 1000
Washington, DC 20005
202-898-0089

AMERICAN ASSOCIATION OF ADVERTISING AGENCIES (4A's)
666 Third Avenue
New York, NY 10017
212-682-2500

AMERICAN INSTITUTE OF GRAPHIC ARTS
1059 Third Avenue—3rd Floor
New York, NY 10021
212-752-0813

AMERICAN MARKETING ASSOCIATION
250 South Wacker Drive
Chicago, IL 60606
312-648-0536

ART DIRECTORS CLUB
250 Park Avenue South
New York, NY 10003
212-674-0500

ASSOCIATION OF NATIONAL ADVERTISERS
155 East 44th Street
New York, NY 10017
212-697-5950

BUSINESS/PROFESSIONAL ADVERTISING ASSOCIATION
100 Metroplex Drive
Edison, NJ 08817
201-985-4441

CANADIAN ADVERTISING FOUNDATION
350 Bloor Street East, #402
Toronto, ON K1P 5H9
613-236-6550

CANADIAN ADVERTISING RESEARCH FOUNDATION
180 Bloor Street West, #803
Toronto, ON M5S 2V6
416-964-3832

CANADIAN ASSOCIATION OF PROFESSIONAL ADVERTISING AGENCIES
465 Waterloo Street
London, ON N6B 2P4
519-679-9945

CANADIAN DIRECT MARKETING ASSOCIATION
1 Concorde Gate, #607
Don Mills, ON M3C 3N6
416-391-2362

THE COUNCIL OF SALES PROMOTION AGENCIES
750 Summer Street— 2nd Floor
Stamford, CT 06901
203-325-3911

DIRECT MARKETING ASSOCIATION
6 East 43rd Street
New York, NY 10017
212-689-4977

INSTITUTE OF CANADIAN ADVERTISING
30 Soudan Avenue
Toronto, ON M4S 1V6
416-482-1396

INTERNATIONAL ADVERTISING ASSOCIATION
342 Madison Avenue
New York, NY 10017
212-557-1133

MONTREAL ADVERTISING AGENCY PRINT PRODUCTION MANAGERS ASSOCIATION
P.O. Box 1244, Stn. H
Montreal, PQ H3G 2N2

NATIONAL NETWORK OF WOMEN IN SALES
P.O. Box 59269
Schaumburg, IL 60159
312-673-6697

THE ONE CLUB
3 West 18th Street—3rd Floor
New York, NY 10011
212-255-7070

OUTDOOR ADVERTISING ASSOCIATION OF CANADA
1300 Yonge Street, #302
Toronto, ON M4T 2W4
416-968-3435

THE POINT-OF-PURCHASE ADVERTISING INSTITUTE, INC.
66 North Van Brunt Street
Englewood, NJ 07631
201-894-8899

PROMOTION INDUSTRY CLUB
P.O. Box 2098
Schiller Park, IL 60176
312-991-3285

**PROMOTION MARKETING ASSOCIATION OF
AMERICA**
322 Eighth Avenue—Suite 1201
New York, NY 10001
212-206-1100

RADIO ADVERTISING BUREAU, INC.
304 Park Avenue South
New York, NY 10010
212-254-4800

**SALES AND MARKETING EXECUTIVES
INTERNATIONAL**
446 Statler Office Tower
Cleveland, OH 44115
216-771-6650

**THE SOCIETY OF AMERICAN GRAPHIC
ARTISTS**
32 Union Square—Room 1214
New York, NY 10003
516-725-3990

THE SOCIETY OF ILLUSTRATORS
128 East 63rd Street
New York, NY 10021
212-838-2560

**SPECIALTY ADVERTISING ASSOCIATION
INTERNATIONAL**
1404 Walnut Hill Lane
Irving, TX 75038
214-580-0404

WOMEN IN ADVERTISING AND MARKETING
4200 Wisconsin Avenue NW
Suite 106-238
Washington, DC 20016
301-369-7400

WOMEN IN COMMUNICATIONS, INC.
2101 Wilson Boulevard—Suite 417
Arlington, VA 22201
703-528-4200

WOMEN'S ADVERTISING CLUB OF TORONTO
P.O. Box 1019, Stn. Q
Toronto, ON M4T 2P2
416-481-5595

WOMEN'S DIRECT RESPONSE GROUP
224 Seventh Street
Garden City, NY 11530
212-744-3506

$\mathcal{B}$

U.S. & Canadian
Trade Publications

ADNEWS
#1108, 250 Consumers Road
Willowdale, ON M2J 4V6
416-498-5164

ADVERTISING AGE
Crain Communications, Inc.
740 North Rush Street
Chicago, IL 60611
312-649-5200

ADWEEK
A/S/M Communications
49 East 21 Street—11th Floor
New York, NY 10010
212-529-5500

APPLIED ARTS
20 Holly Street, #208
Toronto, ON M4S 3B1
416-488-1163

ART DIRECTION
10 East 39th Street—6th Floor
New York, NY 10016
212-889-6500

ART PRODUCT NEWS
In-Art Publishing Company
P.O. Box 117
St. Petersburg, FL 33731
813-821-6064

BACK STAGE
Back Stage Publications, Inc.
330 West 42nd Street—16th Floor
New York, NY 10036
212-947-0020

BUSINESS MARKETING
Crain Communications, Inc.
220 East 42nd Street
New York, NY 10017
212-210-0100

**CANADIAN ADVERTISING
RATES & DATA**
777 Bay Street
Toronto, ON M5W 1A7
416-596-5890

COMMUNICATION ARTS
Coyne & Blanchard, Inc.
P.O. Box 10300
Palo Alto, CA 94303
415-326-6040

CREATIVE
Magazines/Creative, Inc.
37 West 39th Street—Suite 604
New York, NY 10018
212-840-0160

DIRECT MARKETING
Hoke Communications, Inc.
224 Seventh Street
Garden City, NY 11530-5726
516-746-6700

DM NEWS: The Newspaper of Direct Marketing
Mill Hollow Corporation
19 West 21st Street—8th Floor
New York, NY 10010
212-741-2095

ELECTRONIC COMPOSITION & IMAGING
200 Yorkland Boulevard
Willowdale, ON M2J 1R5
416-492-5777

G MAGAZINE
C.P. 1122, Place Bonaventure
Montreal, PQ H5A 1G4
514-397-0537

GRAPHIC DESIGN: USA
Kaye Publishing Corporation
120 East 56th Street—Suite 440
New York, NY 10022
212-759-8813

INFO PRESSE CANADA
4316 boul St. Laurent, #400
Montreal, PQ H2W 1Z3
514-842-5873

INTERNATIONAL MEDIA GUIDE
International Media Enterprises Inc.
22 Elizabeth Street
South Norwalk, CT 06854
203-853-7880

MADISON AVENUE
Madison Publishing Assoc.
369 Lexington Avenue
New York, NY 10017
212-425-3466

MARKETING AND MEDIA DECISIONS
Decisions Publications, Inc.
1140 Avenue of the Americas
New York, NY 10036
212-935-9860

MARKETING COMMUNICATIONS
Lakewood Publishers
50 South Ninth Street
Minneapolis, MN 55402
612-333-0471

MARKETING NEWS
American Marketing Association
250 South Wacker Drive—Suite 200
Chicago, IL 60606
312-648-0536 (Association)
312-993-9517 (Editorial)

MEDICAL ADVERTISING NEWS
Engel Communications
Mountainview Corporate Park
820 Bear Tavern Road—Suite 302
West Trenton, NJ 08628
609-530-0044

PRINT & HOW
R.C. Publications, Inc.
355 Lexington Avenue—17th Floor
New York, NY 10017
212-463-0600

PUBLICATION PROFILES
777 Bay Street
Toronto, ON M5W 1A7
416-596-5890

SALES & MARKETING MANAGEMENT IN CANADA
3500 Dufferin Street, #402
Downsview, ON M3K 1N2
416-633-2020

SPORTS MARKETING NEWS
Technical Marketing Corp.
1460 Post Road East
Westport, CT 06880
203-227-4140

STANDARD DIRECTORY OF ADVERTISING AGENCIES/ STANDARD DIRECTORY OF ADVERTISERS
National Register Publishing Co., Inc.
3004 Glenview Road
Wilmette, IL 60091
312-256-6067

STUDIO MAGAZINE
124 Galaxy Boulevard
Toronto, ON M9W 4Y6
416-675-1999

TARGET MARKETING
North American Publishing Company
401 North Broad Street
Philadelphia, PA   19108
215-238-5300

VISUAL COMMUNICATIONS
777 Bay Street
Toronto, ON M5W 1A7
416-596-5909

Index

ADVERTISING Career Directory

The Career Press

America's Premiere Publisher of books on:

- Career & Job Search Advice
- Education
- Business "How-To"
- Financial "How-To"
- Study Skills
- Careers in Advertising, Book Publishing, Magazines, Newspapers, Marketing & Sales, Public Relations, Business & Finance, the Travel Industry and much, much more.
- Internships

If you liked this book, please write and tell us!

And if you'd like a copy of our FREE catalog of nearly 100 of the best career books available, please call us (Toll-Free) or write!

THE CAREER PRESS
62 BEVERLY RD.,
PO BOX 34
HAWTHORNE, NJ 07507
(Toll-Free) 1-800-CAREER-1 (U. S. only)
201-427-0229
FAX: 201-427-2037